Willful Girls

Women and Gender in German Studies

Series Editor:
Elisabeth Krimmer (*University of California, Davis*)

Willful Girls

Gender and Agency in Contemporary Anglo-American and German Fiction

Emily Jeremiah

CAMDEN HOUSE
Rochester, New York

First published 2018
by Camden House

Camden House is an imprint of Boydell & Brewer Inc.
668 Mt. Hope Avenue, Rochester, NY 14620, USA
www.camden-house.com
and of Boydell & Brewer Limited
PO Box 9, Woodbridge, Suffolk IP12 3DF, UK
www.boydell.co.uk

ISBN-13: 978-1-64014-008-0
ISBN-10: 1-64014-008-5

Library of Congress Cataloging-in-Publication Data

Names: Jeremiah, Emily, author.
Title: Willful girls : gender and agency in contemporary Anglo-American and
    German fiction / Emily Jeremiah.
Description: Rochester, New York : Camden House, 2018. | Includes bibliographical
    references and index.
Identifiers: LCCN 2017040200| ISBN 9781640140080 (hardcover : alk. paper) |
    ISBN 1640140085 (hardcover : alk. paper)
Subjects: LCSH: Women in literature. | American fiction—History and criticism. |
    German fiction—History and criticism. | Comparative literature—American and
    German. | Comparative literature—German and American.
Classification: LCC PS374.W6 J37 2018 | DDC 813/.6093522—dc23 LC record
    available at https://lccn.loc.gov/2017040200

This publication is printed on acid-free paper.
Printed in the UK by TJ International Ltd, Padstow, Cornwall

Contents

Acknowledgments   vii

Introduction: Willful Girls   1

1:   Contemporary Anglo-American and German Feminisms   17

2:   Agency and Volition   34

3:   Body and Beauty   65

4:   Sisterhood and Identification   91

5:   Sex and Desire   116

Conclusion: Green Girls, Trainwrecks, and Willful Politics   140

Notes   151

Bibliography   185

Index   195

Acknowledgments

ARLIER VERSIONS OF parts of chapters 2 and 5 appeared in "The Case of Helene Hegemann: Queerness, Failure, and the German Girl," *Seminar: A Journal of Germanic Studies* 49, no. 4 (2013): 400–413. I would like to thank the editor of *Seminar* for her kind permission to reprint these materials here. I would also like to thank my colleagues in the School of Modern Languages, Literatures, and Cultures at Royal Holloway, University of London, for their camaraderie and support. The Centre for the Study of Contemporary Women's Writing at the Institute of Modern Languages Research, School of Advanced Study, University of London, deserves acknowledgment for giving rise to lively and inspiring discussions; warm thanks especially to Gill Rye, director of the Centre until 2016. My fellow women in German studies, among them Helen Finch, Brigid Haines, and Lyn Marven, continue to provide me with much-valued support and encouragement. Jim Walker of Camden House was typically supportive in the early stages of the project. Camden House's Julia Cook has also been most helpful and meticulous, as has series editor Elisabeth Krimmer, to whom very many thanks are due. Thanks, too, go to the anonymous readers whose input has made this book a good deal stronger than it would otherwise have been. Finally, of course, I thank my family. I have especially to acknowledge my own willful girl, Elisa.

Introduction: Willful Girls

THIS BOOK EXPLORES the depiction of girls and young women in contemporary Anglo-American and German literary texts. It focuses on how the novels in question portray the process of "becoming woman," and on the role of will and willfulness in this becoming. "Becoming woman" is an allusion to Simone de Beauvoir's famous 1949 pronouncement "One is not born, but rather becomes, a woman."[1] This assertion, perhaps the defining statement of second-wave and subsequent feminisms, highlights the constructed status of gender. Gender is not a given; rather, it is a cultural construct.[2] I am interested in what kind of becomings are possible in the context of neoliberalism and postfeminism. How do people become what they are? How do they fail to become what they might? What is at stake, politically and ethically, in such becomings or failures to become? I identify four sets of concerns that are integral to the notion of becoming: agency and volition; body and beauty; sisterhood and identification; and sex and desire. These clusters of concerns are all crucial to feminist thought, and urgent for anyone interested in understanding subject formation—especially, but not only, gendered subject formation—in the contemporary context.

The literary texts I examine, all published during the last twenty years in German or English, tease out the complex processes by which female subjects become women in the context of a globalized, neoliberal world.[3] The introduction delineates the theoretical and cultural context for this study and justifies the comparatist approach it adopts. It examines the notion of becoming in gender and feminist theory, putting forward a conception of this process as affective, bodily, and relational. It also argues for negativity, failure, and anger as crucial to conceptualizations of femininity. It then turns to Sara Ahmed's productive notion of willfulness, as developed in *Willful Subjects*.[4] *Willful Girls* tests out Ahmed's concept and expands its implications for understandings of literature and of the contemporary context more broadly. The book demonstrates that femininity is a site of identification and disidentification, of interpellation and resistance, of desire and disgust. It thereby crystallizes and develops ongoing feminist debates concerning agency, embodiment, relationality, and sexuality.

Art and affect are crucial to this project. Art—which, as Elizabeth Grosz suggests, connects us to our animal lineage—involves bodiliness and eroticism.[5] It spans private and public, political and personal, mind and body, in ways that will be become clear throughout this study. It also involves exposures and eruptions of willfulness in Ahmed's sense. I do not suggest that art is the answer to the particular challenges posed by our context. But I do argue that it offers complex and nuanced responses and provocations that challenge instrumentalist and individualizing ways of framing reality. Such responses and provocations are particularly important when it comes to a consideration of young women and their becomings. "Becoming" is itself a generative notion that involves a rejection of rigid and reductive accounts of identity, challenging usefully the obsession of certain feminist theories with that latter category.[6] Literary texts demonstrate and carry out "becoming" as defined by Rosi Braidotti: "the actualization of the immanent encounter between subjects, entities and forces which are apt mutually to affect and exchange parts of each other in a creative and non-invidious manner."[7] They are sites of affect that involve encounters and exchanges with far-reaching implications for the construction and experience of youthful femininity.[8]

Girls and Women: Theoretical and Cultural Contexts

My study focuses on literary depictions of girls and young women, at the same time revealing the elasticity of the categories of age and generation. In this respect, it shares concerns with girls' studies. This field arises from the traditions of feminism and critical youth studies, and involves the acknowledgment of the particularity of youthful femininity.[9] Feminist theory sometimes overlooks this specificity; according to Catherine Driscoll, it is "still dominated by adult models of subjectivity presumed to be the endpoint of a naturalized process of developing individual identity."[10] Inspired by the constructivism long central to feminist thought, scholars in this field are interested in "the social, material and discursive practices defining young femininity."[11] For "girlhood is made up," as Driscoll puts it.[12] And as such, it is subject to change.[13]

Like feminists in general, scholars in girls' studies are concerned with the othering or objectification of female subjects. Valerie Walkerdine, a key figure in the field, notes for example that "girls have been the object of a variety of claims to truth about them and attempts to regulate what girlhood is."[14] Walkerdine examines the ways in which childhood has been produced, suggesting that existing theories of development "start with a norm that already pathologizes girls" (10). This argument bears comparison with Beauvoir's seminal view of woman as "other," as developed in *The Second Sex*; Walkerdine contends that girls are othered in and by dominant theories of education and development, according to whose standards they always fall short (15). Like other scholars in the field, Walkerdine's concern is to stress girls' specificity and their agency in opposition to such othering, pathologizing discourses. For example, she claims that girlhood is a "fictional and fantasy space for actual girls to enter" (14). For Marnina Gonick, similarly, "girls become girls by participating within the available sets of social meanings and practices."[15]

In both these statements, constructivism and voluntarism feature in equal measure. Girlhood is a fiction defined by particular social practices, but girls actively "enter" into it, "becoming" subjects in the process. Agency—or will—emerges as a key issue in girls' studies, and it is crucial for feminist thought more generally. For Driscoll, for example, it is precisely the denial of agency that is at issue when it comes to young female subjects: girls are synonymous with passivity and arrested development, having been "employed to represent conformity and the mainstream," and she adds that "girls also provide a figure for a failure of development."[16] Nonetheless, Driscoll argues, feminist cultural studies must acknowledge subject formation and not see girls merely as objects of power. She notes, interestingly, that the emergence of feminism accompanied the birth of feminine adolescence, and reads the modern girl as "an image of change, crisis, and personal and cultural tensions."[17] In the contemporary Western context, such tensions involve competing ideas around individualism and ethics. Marion de Ras and Mieke Lunenberg point out the contradictory discourses surrounding girlhood in Western societies, which emphasize both "feminine" caring behaviors and economic independence.[18] Bascha Mika has similarly highlighted the nexus of conflicts and crises that characterize youthful femininity:

So wachsen Mädchen und junge Frauen dann auf:
Einerseits werden sie mit dem weiblichen Muster gelockt—andererseits füttert man sie mit Bekenntnissen zur Gleichheit der Geschlechter.
Einerseits werden sie mit weiblichen Klischees vollgestopft—andererseits wird ihnen eingeimpft, Rollenzwänge seien von gestern.
Einerseits werden sie auf Anpassung geeicht—andererseits werden sie beharrlich narzisstisch bestätigt.

[This is how girls and young women grow up, then:
On the one hand they're seduced by the feminine lifestyle; on the other, it's drummed into them the sexes are equal.
On the one hand they're stuffed full of feminine clichés; on the other, people go on about the fact that old roles are outdated.
On the one hand they're trained to conform; on the other, their narcissism is relentlessly confirmed.][19]

Girlhood is a site of contradiction and tension. It is also reflective of the distinct issues haunting specific social contexts at a given time. Young people carry "a great deal of ideological weight."[20] Gonick suggests this is especially true of young women: "When the tensions of race, class, and gender rise dramatically . . . social anxieties converge and tend to be projected onto the bodies of young women."[21] For this reason, an examination of depictions of youthful femininity may prove particularly fruitful and illuminating.

Comparisons

Globalization, global capitalism, and the influence of the media and the Internet, along with the resultant pervasiveness of visual imagery and of pornography, are defining features of both Anglo-American and German contexts, and they help justify a comparatist approach. Girls' studies, like gender studies in general, is comparative in nature, being "transnational" as well as "cross-disciplinary."[22] Comparative studies such as this one allow us, first, to probe how feminism is both transnational and locally or nationally specific, as we will see further in chapter 1. Feminist texts are translated and circulated across national borders. Myra Marx Ferree describes the reception of Judith Butler in Germany, for example, as constituting a "Butler boom."[23] Her book, *Varieties of Feminism*, indeed demonstrates both the linkages between Anglo-American and German feminisms and their specifities.[24] Kathy Davis and Mary Evans comparably note the enormous impact US feminist scholarship has had on the development of women's and gender studies in Europe; indeed, "feminist theory is almost shorthand for theory that has been produced in the USA."[25] Yet, as Christina Scharff reminds us, such transmission is not unproblematic. Her own work on feminism in Germany and the United Kingdom, to which I return shortly, throws up methodological challenges, because of the way theories "travel" between contexts and because of questions of language difference and translation.[26] Such transmission, which has recently been conceived in terms of virality, points to the lively and contagious nature of ideas and phenomena, which are not necessarily "routed through the nation."[27]

Second, a comparative approach grants relativizing insights into the respective cultures, which emerge not as fixed and given, but as manifestations of specific histories and circumstances. The process known as "globalization," which cannot be disentangled from "Americanization," nevertheless shapes these cultures.[28] Comparing texts in a globalized, Americanized world brings home these processes and allows critical insights into their workings and effects. In *Awkward Politics*, Carrie Smith-Prei and Maria Stehle outline their own project in instructive terms: taking Germany as their case in point, they examine how "the transnational circulations and reverberations of contemporary activism gain complexity and texture when examined with a specific historical and

cultural context in mind." A comparative approach allows us to make pronouncements that are broad in scope but not lacking particularism, and
also points up what Smith-Prei and Stehle term "the collision between
transnational flows and national legacies [which] remain murky in their
interaction."[29] It accords, too, with what has been termed the "transnational turn" in literary studies.[30]

Comparatism is in fact arguably inevitable when it comes to literary
studies, and indeed to "theory." Haun Saussy points out that "all literature has always been comparative."[31] Describing comparative literature as "a metadiscipline or even a counterdiscipline," Saussy notes that
it involves an investment in methods rather than subject matter (11).
"Theory" too is of necessity comparative, "because of the undeniably specific and multiple historical origins of the theoretical vocabulary" (18). In
this book, I draw on (mainly) Anglo-American theory to illuminate my
discussion of German- and English-language texts. This method has its
advantages. Saussy argues that being in-between means usefully "owning
up to multiple commitments." "But," Saussy adds, "the big money is in
reifying, as it always is" (20). Indeed, most disciplines are "founded on
successful reifications" (21). The status of comparative literature, on the
other hand, is not certain: its fragility as well as its success spring from its
lack of a permanent defining object, its position within and above disciplines, and its "openness to lateral linkages" (24).

This book manifests such openness, and involves risk. Here I appeal
to Saussy's claim that every comparative project is "in some measure an
experiment" (24). This particular experiment involves bringing German
and Anglo-American literary texts into dialogue with what I identify as
key flashpoints of contemporary feminist theory, and with the idea of
willfulness. The project necessarily involves grappling with the question
of "context," which is itself a fragile and shifting term. Saussy exhorts
usefully: "let us not grant any context the final authority of the real"
(23). He argues: "Comparative literature teaches us to adjust to multiple
frames of reference and to attend to relations rather than givens" (34). I
define the context of this study with the help of the terms "neoliberalism"
and "postfeminism." This definition is of necessity partial and excludes
other possible ways of contextualizing the literary texts under discussion.
As Lauren Berlant notes, the present time is "a mediated affect": subject
to competing, and inevitably political, analyses and interpretations.[32] The
contemporary is also temporary.[33] This particular analysis, while obsoles-
cent even as it comes into being, may yet reverberate.

Neoliberalism and Postfeminism

"Neoliberalism" has been defined as "a mode of political and economic
rationality characterized by privatization, deregulation and a rolling back

and withdrawal of the state from many areas of social provision."[34] It involves the governing of subjects who are constituted as "self-managing, autonomous and enterprising," and it "privileges the individual over the collective."[35] According to George Monbiot, it defines the world order while remaining invisible.[36] The term can usefully be linked to "postfeminism," which Rosalind Gill and Christina Scharff see as "a sensibility that is at least partly constituted through the pervasiveness of neoliberal ideas." In fact, they ask: "Could it be that neoliberalism is *always already gendered*?" Women, they suggest, constitute its ideal—obediently self-regulating—subjects.[37] Neoliberalism and postfeminism "both position women as self-regulating 'empowered' individuals/consumers disembedded from traditional gender roles and relations."[38] The kind of postfeminism that Dawn Foster dubs "corporate feminism," as embodied by Sheryl Sandberg, involves such a view, "tell[ing] a story that is convenient to capitalism."[39]

"Postfeminism has become a key term in the lexicon of feminist cultural critique in recent years," Gill and Scharff observe.[40] Yet its meanings are multiple. The term has been variously used: to signal an epistemological break within feminism, and specifically, a move toward intersectionality; to denote an historical shift after the height of second-wave feminism; to refer to a backlash against feminism; and to define a sensibility.[41] Postfeminism as a sensibility involves an emphasis on self-surveillance; the dominance of the "makeover" paradigm; a resurgence of ideas of natural sexual difference; a marked "resexualization" of women's bodies; an emphasis on consumerism; and the commodification of differences.[42] British writer and activist Laurie Penny—whose work has been translated into German—also stresses the link between femininity and consumerism and commodification. She argues that today, femininity itself has become a brand, and suggests, "Late capitalism quite literally brands the bodies of women." Penny asks rhetorically: "What is girlhood, after all, but shoes, clothes and conspicuous consumption?"[43] Youthful femininity in particular thus merges with consumption, though residual associations of femininity with care and nurture also persist. Sinikka Aapola, Marnina Gonick, and Anita Harris discuss how the "neo-liberal incitement of individualism, rational choice and self-realization bumps up against discourses of femininity creating contradictory and complex positions for girls."[44] Gonick elsewhere describes the "neoliberal girl subject" as caught between a vision of girlhood as powerful and dynamic, and an ideal of femininity as demure and meek.[45] Alison Phipps conceives such debates in terms of neoliberalism and neoconservatism, frameworks that are both "hostile and complementary."[46]

If neoliberalism and postfeminism are mutually reinforcing, neoliberalism and feminism—where this term is fraught with ambivalence, as we will see further in the next chapter—are not natural bedfellows. As

Scharff suggests, the neoliberal, individualist imperative fails to "sit well with perceptions of feminism as involving collective struggle."[47] Scharff's study finds that broadly speaking, young women in Germany and the United Kingdom repudiate feminism, and that neoliberalism facilitates this rejection: "The perceived collectivism of feminism runs counter to the fashioning of neoliberal subjectivities that derive moral self-worth from navigating challenges, and opportunities, individually and self-responsibly."[48] Contemporary feminist writings in Germany, especially, rely on the rhetoric of neoliberal individualism, as chapter 1 explains further, and they are thus flawed. Yet gender persists as a key category governing social and cultural life. As one German feminist notes "heute ist alles frei wählbar" (today, anything goes)—but "beim Geschlecht hört der Individualismus auf" (individualism stops at gender).[49] This insight suggests that gender may be at once coercive and usefully communal. It brings home the continuing need for gendered analysis of the social order, since "gender (thought in an intersectional way) remains a key category in the play for political power."[50]

Feminism is necessary, asserts Sara Ahmed, "because of what has not ended: sexism, sexual exploitation and sexual oppression."[51] I deploy the term "postfeminism" to underscore this necessity. While it is currently being productively supplanted—giving way to urgent discussions concerning, notably, "digital feminisms," "awkward politics," and "living a feminist life"—it remains useful for a reading of texts emerging over the last two decades, because it underscores the simultaneous taken-for-grantedness and dismissal of feminism that characterize recent years, and, in many quarters, the present moment.[52] Hester Baer refers to the "undoing of feminism" in neoliberalism, Scharff, Smith-Prei, and Stehle to "doing feminism in the face of its impossibility."[53] While Ahmed "refuses" postfeminism since it shores up assumptions concerning feminism's pastness, I assert postfeminism here in order precisely to flag up those very assumptions and the consequent urgency involved in the "labor of . . . insistence" in which feminists are engaged.[54] In the context of neoliberalism, such labor is characterized by circularity rather than by goal-directed, teleologically structured endeavors.[55] It involves a redoing and also an undoing of neoliberalism itself.[56] Both neoliberalism and postfeminism are precarious: in the sense that they enforce precarity, but also in the sense that they themselves are unstable.[57] This instability is a source of hope.

"Girls" and "Mädchen"?

But what does it mean to talk of girls in particular? In the English-speaking and the German contexts, the terms "girl" and "Mädchen" have recently undergone redefinition, in some cases being reclaimed: a gesture that involves complex generational dynamics. Aapola, Gonick, and Harris note that in the Anglophone context, the term "girl" has recently been recuperated by young feminists, though for Harris the category has "proved to be slippery and problematic."[58] She posits the age range twelve to twenty years as appropriately covered by the term, but goes on to problematize this categorization by citing the phenomenon of "tweenies," or pre-teens, and noting that one can today observe seven-year-olds baring their midriffs and forty-year-olds sporting "Hello Kitty barrettes."[59] The concepts of age and generation are thus fluid. Walkerdine points to a cultural slippage between the terms "girl" and "woman," suggesting that this arises from a desire to infantilize adult women, who are threatening.[60] This may indeed have been the case in past decades, but more recently—and with the advent, notably, of Lena Dunham's hit US television series, *Girls*, about the lives of young women living in Manhattan—the term has begun to connote young women in more or less positive, emancipatory ways.[61]

In Germany, the authors of *Wir Alpha-Mädchen* (We Alpha-Girls), discussed further in chapter 1, defend their use of this term, explaining: "Alphamädchen sind wir alle . . . alle jungen Frauen, die mitdenken und Ziele haben; die sich für die Welt interessieren und frei und selbstbestimmt leben möchten, jede nach ihrer Art" (We are all alpha-girls . . . all young women who think and who have goals; who are interested in the world and want to live freely and independently, each in her own way).[62] The prefix "Alpha" suggests ambitions and desires, and differentiates their self-definition from mere "Mädchen"; they assert, in fact, "wir sind keine Mädchen mehr" (we aren't girls anymore), and point to the conventional role of the girl as obliging and passive.[63] A key reason the authors of this book choose the term "Mädchen" over "Frau" (woman), as do Jana Hensel and Elisabeth Raether (authors of *Neue deutsche Mädchen*, or New German Girls) is to differentiate themselves from the women's movement (*Frauenbewegung*) of the 1970s "and the negative stereotypes of second-wave feminists which have flourished in postfeminist popular culture," as Emily Spiers explains.[64] Spiers notes that this gesture also "infantilises these thirty-something authors and their readers and aligns their feminism with wider commercial culture which idealises female youth over maturity."[65] The very terms used to designate young women, or girls, are thus, in both linguistic and cultural contexts, to be handled with care.

In academic circles, The Modern Girl around the World Research Group, a group of scholars investigating the figure of the girl in the first half of the twentieth century, assert they are drawn to the "troublesomeness" of the category "girl," which for them "signifies the contested status of young women, no longer children, and their unstable and sometimes subversive relationship to social norms relating to heterosexuality, marriage, and motherhood."[66] This definition is useful to my project, which investigates the state of being prior to "womanhood," as defined by marriage, or coupledom, and motherhood. The subversive instability it implies is potentially productive in academic and political terms. I am less interested in the actual age of the protagonists in the novels I discuss than I am in their "troublesome" or willful status. This concern ties in with Smith-Prei and Stehle's interest in "adolescent aesthetics," a potential component of the "awkward politics" they evoke. Adolescence connotes for them not immaturity, but rather "becomings, processes, and thresholds." Adolescent aesthetics are "closely tied to willfulness, defiance, and impropriety," in line with the arguments of *Willful Girls*.[67]

Identification, "Choice," Agency, Humanity

This book primarily involves the analysis of literature, but in the next chapter I examine feminist nonfiction in English and in German—this as part of my delineation of the "context" in and against which I read the literary works. These nonfiction, mostly polemical texts are, broadly speaking, aimed explicitly at women, and particularly at young women. The novels discussed in chapters 2 through 5, on the other hand, are not aimed at such readers in the same way, being fiction (though of course they may be marketed with particular readerships in mind). It is not my aim to discuss how readers—young, female, or otherwise—may or may not respond to particular texts, in any case. Rather, I read the texts in question alongside feminist theories in order to elucidate their concerns and their implications. That is not to say that questions of identification and identity do not inform my discussion of the literary works. Indeed, they are central. Like Gonick, I am interested precisely in the question: "What are the contradictory and ambivalent (dis)identifications that both interpellate and repel those who might live this category [of girl]?"[68] Like her, I am also concerned with "the complications and ambivalence involved in creating and staking positions within femininity" (7). Drawing on work by Jessica Benjamin and Judith Butler, among others, Gonick suggests that identity is bound up with recognition and relationality, and asks: "What is it to consider femininity as a question of identification?" (13). She notes, in this context, the importance of ambivalence (14). For as Vincent Duindam notes, "there is more to socialization than the internalization of norms."[69] Ambivalent subjects are also agents. As Gonick drawing on Butler suggests, gender practices are "sites of critical agency" (6). There is no easy distinction to be made between agency and passivity, or between power and victimhood. After all, as Walkerdine suggests, there is power in victimhood.[70] And refusing to "become"—failing to do so—can be a powerful gesture, as will emerge in chapter 2.

As we will see in chapter 1, the discourse of "choice" is often invoked as a way to affirm how young women should ideally behave.

But as Natasha Walter argues, such declarations are not always helpful, and: "when it comes to the sexualisation of young girls, the language of choice seems particularly misplaced."[71] Choice is an inadequate notion.[72] So how might we posit beneficial ways of being or becoming female? Inspired by existentialist thought, Beauvoir identified "bad faith" as an impediment so such becomings.[73] To counter bad faith, I suggest turning (back) to ideas of wholeness and holism—not as sentimental methods of celebrating "the feminine," but as a way of affirming ambivalence, disgust, and disgustingness as well as positivity, allure, and appeal. In the contemporary context, in which "happy stories for girls" dominate, such an insistence offers a way of challenging airbrushed images of compliant feminine contentment.[74] Indeed, as we will see, the texts I look at without exception involve at least moments of repulsion and repulsiveness; they thereby assert the complexity of female subjects, and their very humanity. The assertion of women's humanity, or wholeness, was in fact a key part of Beauvoir's aim in *The Second Sex*. Here, Beauvoir considers what it means to be a woman, observing, "Surely woman is, like man, a human being."[75] But femininity as currently defined involves negativity, or otherness: "humanity is male and man defines woman not in herself but as relative to him" (*SS*, 16). To decline to be other involves renouncing the advantages that condition offers (*SS*, 21). Women, then, are not currently fully human: "How can a human being in woman's situation attain fulfilment?" (*SS*, 29). Women, further, have no collective sense of self, being "dispersed among the males" to whom they are attached more firmly than they are to other women (*SS*, 19). I ask here whether women's humanity is now able to emerge more fully than at the time of Beauvoir's writing, and whether, given the development of the women's movement, there is now a collective "we" in existence that is affirmative.

In her 1999 polemic, *The Whole Woman*, Germaine Greer argues that "genuine femaleness remains grotesque to the point of obscenity"—an argument echoed in recent work by Penny and Nina Power, as we will see in the next chapter.[76] Greer argues: "Real women are being phased out" (2). The dominant ideal now is a "hipless, wombless, hard-titted Barbie" (5). Greer's assertion of wholeness is helpful when we consider the sexualization and reduction of young women that emerges as a key contemporary feminist concern in the next chapter. Young women are especially well placed to realize the Barbie-inspired ideal Greer discusses, a fact that makes them both powerful and vulnerable. Women are failures if they are not beautiful, Greer notes (19). Her emphasis on appearance is reiterated by the writers discussed in chapter 1. "Woman . . . knows that when she is looked at she is not considered apart from her appearance," Beauvoir observed comparably. Indeed, because of her socialization, "she wants to be seen, to be attractive" (*SS*, 693).

The novels I examine tell of the shift from girlhood to womanhood. Beauvoir understands this transitional period as involving a revelation of otherness: "it is a strange experience for whoever regards himself as the One to be revealed to himself as otherness, alterity. This is what happens to the little girl" (*SS*, 324).[77] Beauvoir describes a "conflict [within a girl] between her autonomous existence and her objective self, her 'being-the-other'" that comes sharply into view during this transitional phase (*SS*, 308). This conflict grants insights into the formation not only of femininity but also of (adult) humanity. For Beauvoir, being fully human involves "engag[ing] in freely chosen projects" (*SS*, 29). But renouncing the otherness involved in femininity is not easy since "the woman who does not conform devaluates herself sexually and hence socially." Conformity involves laborious effort, given the demands of femininity (*SS*, 692–93). These questions remain pertinent, and they haunt the protagonists of the novels I discuss. What kind of *Bildung* is available to girls and young women today? What form do literary depictions of female figures take? We are a long way from the nineteenth-century choice between dutiful marriage or death, and yet the young women who drift through the novels I examine seem to have no "choices," and nihilism or refusal emerge as dominant tropes.[78] Beauvoir claimed in 1949:

> The free woman is just being born . . . to say in what degree she will remain different, in what degree these differences will retain their importance—this would be to hazard bold predictions indeed. What is certain is that hitherto women's possibilities have been suppressed and lost to humanity, and that it is high time she be permitted to take her chances in her own interest and in the interest of all. (*SS*, 723–24)

What constitutes women's "difference" arguably remains a matter of bold prediction, and women's possibilities are still fully to emerge, as I argue in my conclusion.

Becoming and Willing

As mentioned, and as is now widely acknowledged, gender is not simply a given. Rather, it is a social and cultural construct. Beauvoir's insight that femininity is constructed has led to numerous subsequent discussions of the fabrication of femininity and indeed masculinity. The sex/gender distinction, which differentiates between biological givens and cultural influences, has been important to such discussions. Indeed, it is crucial to feminist thought, opening up numerous lines of enquiry across disciplines. It is attractive because it suggests the possibility of change. If gender is mutable and contingent, then models of gender premised on binarism, and on a logic of hierarchy and domination, are open to revision. It is risky, however, because it can lead to an overlooking of sex and of nature, as materialist feminists have argued.[79] In her 1990 *Gender Trouble*, Butler criticizes the feminist reliance on the sex/gender distinction, since it implies that "sex" is fixed and static and glosses over the ways in which matter is itself constructed. Butler claims that Beauvoir's famous assertion "One is not born . . ." implies a voluntarism that is suspect. The "one" it invokes is imagined as intact, as existing prior to gendering.[80] Trans subjects engage in and prompt discourses that further destabilize the ostensible sex/gender, male/female binaries.[81]

The question of becoming remains urgent in feminist and gender studies, and beyond—this in the context of an image-driven, media-saturated society in which objectification, interpellation, and appearance are ever more fraught with danger and difficulty, especially for girls and young women; Braidotti refers to "the saturation of our social space by media images and representations."[82] In the context of neoliberalism and postfeminism, how can we frame becomings, especially female becomings, in useful ways? Inspired by Deleuze, Braidotti describes "becoming" as involving "neither reproduction nor imitation, but rather empathic proximity and intensive interconnectedness" (*M*, 8). The subject, for her, is "an affective, positive and dynamic structure" (*M*, 7)—"nomadic," as she describes it elsewhere.[83] Grosz also focuses on becoming, favoring this term over an emphasis on identity.[84] And for Jasbir K. Puar, "affirmative becomings" denote the "endless differentiation and multiplicity" that are at work in the emergence of the subject.[85] Going beyond intersectionality, which assumes that factors such as race, class, gender, sexuality, nation, age, and religion are "separable analytics and can thus be disassembled," Puar also deploys the word "assemblage" to describe the subject.[86]

Such theories of becoming involve a rejection of facile voluntarism; choice is an unhelpful, or at least limited term. They thus raise questions about the matter of agency, or will. Sara Ahmed's *Willful Subjects* makes a vital contribution to such discussions. The work of Ahmed is indeed central to current and emergent feminist thought.[87] Throughout this book, I apply Ahmed's notion of willfulness to the process of becoming woman today. Ahmed begins *Willful Subjects* by citing the Grimm story "Das eigensinnige Kind" (The Willful Child). She explains that in the Grimms' text, "the willful child is the one who is disobedient, who will not do as her mother wishes. If authority assumes the right to turn a wish into a command, then willfulness is a diagnosis of the failure to comply with those whose authority is given."[88] Willfulness, then, is a characteristic assigned to the subject, not an inherent property of that subject. Drawing on Augustine, Ahmed notes comparably: "Willfulness [is] an attribution to a subject of a will's error" (*WS*, 4). Usually "a charge made by someone against someone," then, willfulness acts as a rod or straightening device "useful as a technique for making those who are assumed as inassimilable . . . responsible for not being assimilated" (*WS*, 134, 128; cf. *WS*, 148). Ahmed explores the sociality of the will, highlighting the ways in which willfulness is attributed to someone who wills "too much, or too little, or in 'the wrong way'" (*WS*, 3). Willfulness is "that which is striking" (*WS*, 47). Ahmed also points to the association of willfulness and unhappiness (*WS*, 3–4), a linkage to which I will return in chapter 2 especially. Willfulness ties in with ideas of failure, refusal, and rejection that are important here.

But willfulness is not only "an attribution, a way of finding fault"; it is also "the experience of an attribution": what it feels like to fail to fit in or to be found faulty (*WS*, 19). It can also connote "*an experience a subject has of itself,*" when one part of the subject "gets in the way" of a conscious intention (*WS*, 77). Thus, intentionality is a complicated matter. Ahmed acknowledges that will is an unfashionable concern, seeming as it does to connote intentionality, but, she asserts, she is not in fact interested in "rescuing volition" (*WS*, 16). Indeed, she sees herself as "deepen[ing] the critiques of voluntarism by reflecting on the intimacy between freedom and force" (*WS*, 16). She turns here to phenomenology, which for her provides a set of methods for investigating "the voluntary and involuntary aspects of existence" (*WS*, 26). For Ahmed, "even though willfulness is evocative of intentionality, or is even a form of hyper-intentionality, willfulness can bypass intentionality" (*WS*, 175). Ahmed's understanding of willfulness as potentially bypassing intentionality, and her concern with both "freedom and force," will be important to this study.[89]

For willing, as Ahmed makes plain, does not involve the absence of coercion (*WS*, 57). The idea of "willing submission" points up very clearly the fact that "force and freedom can operate in the same register" (*WS*, 93, 97). Willingness can be enforced: "Subjects might become willing if not being willing is made unbearable" (*WS*, 139). It is also possible, as Ahmed puts it, to "obey willfully" (*WS*, 141). As far as the questions of interpellation and resistance are concerned, it is important to note that for Ahmed, willfulness is not the same as "againstness" (*WS*, 150): not necessarily or only oppositional.[90] Willfulness can also take many forms: "To affirm willfulness does *not* mean prescribing a set of behaviors," Ahmed is careful to spell out (*WS*, 133). Neither does willfulness provide us with "a moral ground" (*WS*, 20). Instead, it constitutes a disturbance, and offers a cultural space in which to maneuver: "wiggle room" (*WS*, 204, 192).

How does Ahmed's thinking relate to "neoliberalism" and to "postfeminism"? Ahmed touches on the pertinence of willfulness for a critical analysis of neoliberalism when she observes that in contemporary culture, the will is transformed into "willpower," something that a responsible and moral subject must develop or refine (*WS*, 7). She also suggests that willfulness in our context might constitute a refusal to aspire (*WS*, 184)—that is to say, perhaps, a resolution to "lean out."[91] Her book also addresses the gendering of willfulness. Ahmed argues that willfulness is deposited in certain places, and unevenly distributed in the social field. She states that the young woman or girl is often its container: "No wonder that the figure of the willful subject—often but not always a child, often but not always female, often but not always an individual—has become so familiar. It is the depositing of willfulness in certain places that allows the willful subject to appear as a figure, as someone we recognize, in an instant" (*WS*, 17). In this way, will is gendered. Feminine willfulness can expose and challenge the strictures of neoliberalism and a postfeminist sensibility that requires self-regulation and docility. Indeed, feminism involves a willingness to be willful.[92] In this book, I thus take up and expand Ahmed's "willful" provocations, illustrating her understanding of willfulness as potentially collective, or contagious. Ahmed's goal of creating a "willfulness archive" (*WS*, 17) is akin to my own attempt to bring together contemporary literary texts—as well as their protagonists and their authors—under the sign of willfulness, in order to demonstrate further the importance of such manifestations for the neoliberal, postfeminist present.

Willing Literariness

As part of her investigation into willfulness, Ahmed explores how the will "takes form and is given form" in literary works (*WS*, 15). In particular, she suggests that literary characters "can be given form through will" (*WS*, 85). Exploring George Eliot's *Daniel Deronda*, for example, Ahmed argues: "The novel . . . offers a social diagnosis of will distributions as gendered distributions" (*WS*, 87). Here, I explore characters in contemporary works of fiction, and the texts themselves, as expressions of feminine willfulness, where these are not to be traced back to individual authors' "intentions" but are to be viewed rather in the context of the neoliberal present, and as revealing of the "social unconscious" (see *WS*, 248n3). Gill and Scharff suggest that "a focus on the psychosocial seems to be missing from most work on neoliberalism."[93] I propose to investigate literary texts partly as a way of correcting this bias: namely, German-language novels by Antonia Baum (b. 1984), Sibylle Berg (b. 1962), Kerstin Grether (b. 1975), Helene Hegemann (b. 1992), Zoë Jenny (b. 1974), Elke Naters (b. 1963), Charlotte Roche (b. 1978), and Juli Zeh (b. 1974); and English-language novels by Bella Bathurst (b. 1969), Rachel B. Glaser (b. 1982), Caitlin Moran (b. 1975), Zoe Pilger (b. 1984), Emma Jane Unsworth (1978), Sarai Walker (b. 1972), Helen Walsh (b. 1977), and, in the conclusion, Kate Zambreno (b. 1977).

Literature can flesh out the work Gill and Scharff refer to, involving as it does affective, embodied encounters. Affect is now a key term in contemporary thought. In her 2017 *Living a Feminist Life*, Ahmed suggests its importance for feminist studies, asserting: "feminism begins with sensation."[94] Affect is way of tracking cultural formations and shifts.[95] It also involves thinking beyond the term "identity": Puar pits affective politics against a reductive "identity politics."[96] The fictions examined here have the potential to feed into such discussions and manifestations of affect. Hester Baer comparably suggests that novels' "ability to generate affect . . . make[s] palpable . . . otherwise imperceptible aspects of the neoliberal everyday."[97] The novels examined here deploy a diverse range of narrative strategies, but in different ways, all of them conduct and provoke investigations into the meaning of femininity, and in particular into feminine willfulness. Chapter 2 demonstrates clearly that anger, negativity, and failure feature prominently in these texts, as do disgust and disgustingness; they thus challenge "happy stories for girls" and support Ahmed's insistence on the "complex, ambivalent, and messy feelings that women have."[98] They also call to mind Katie Jones's reference to "the increased prevalence of disgusting themes in contemporary women's writing."[99] In many of the texts, we find deliberate provocations of the kind that might be described as "youthful," where the term connotes unruliness, or willfulness in Ahmed's sense. But even in more commercial or more palatable works, and even in texts where the protagonists appear not so much willful as passive or even lifeless, will—as excessive, misdirected, ambivalent, or lacking—features as a thematic concern, in some cases very explicitly. Willfulness, in my reading, also forms a connecting subtext. This subtext reveals and relates to the cultural unconscious. Read together, the works constitute an eruption of willfulness, so my willful reading goes, disturbing and disrupting neoliberal and postfeminist givens, and especially what Berlant identitifies as the "cruel optimism" inherent to neoliberalism.[100]

This is not to suggest such eruption is in any way pure or unmediated, *pace* Ahmed's understanding of willfulness as not necessarily or only oppositional. In *Spieltrieb* (Play Instinct), a novel discussed in chapters 2 and 3, Juli Zeh parodies contemporary literature, especially women's writing, by means of a imaginary novel, *Fliegende Bauten* (Temporary Structures). She points to the way contemporary fiction is packaged and marketed, and to the celebrification and stylization of authors. In an extract from the novel, Zeh also mocks the flip, weary, disaffected tone of such texts.[101] Zeh's witty take on contemporary German fiction by attractive young women draws attention to the fact that literary production and reception are shaped by fads and fashions, and that—increasingly, perhaps—authors are (compelled to be) celebrities.[102] While reception is not my concern here, it is important to note that "literariness *emerges from* contexts and methods of reading, rather than being a property of literature."[103] Even as I suggest that literariness is a distinctive enactment of willfulness, and that it can denote "an embodied and shared vitality" (*WS*, 140), context shapes how such willfulness takes form, and the interpretation to which it gives rise—this in line with notions of virality and circularity already mentioned here.

Outline

For this reason, I include a chapter on nonfiction writings; chapter 1 is intended to serve as an additional form of contextualization, further delineating my comparative, cross-cultural engagement with feminist concerns, and indeed probing the term feminism itself. I am not suggesting here that such feminist texts have had a direct effect on the literary texts subsequently under discussion: some of the literary texts in any case appeared before certain of the nonfiction ones. I am, instead, setting contemporary feminisms alongside recent fictional treatments of femininity with the aim of showing important shared areas of concern, as well as significant methodological and affective differences, especially as far as the question of will is concerned. The second chapter moves to the questions of agency and volition, which, as I have already suggested, are crucial to feminist thought. Here I draw on Braidotti, Grosz, and Ahmed to explore a range of expressions of willfulness in a number of literary texts. In chapter 3, on body and beauty, I move to the key questions of appearance and weight as a way of addressing the interpellation, pornographization, and segmentation of young female bodies in the culture at large. I trace a number of strategies that emerge in the literary texts as willful responses to this reductiveness. Chapter 4 returns to the questions of identification and intersectionality, and specifically asks how "sisterhood" manifests itself, or fails to manifest itself, in a postfeminist era, and what strategies literary texts adopt in the face of the dividedness among women that has arguably persisted since Beauvoir. In chapter 5, finally, I explore the literary texts' depiction of sex and desire, examining its implications for understandings of will, while also probing the status of sex in the contemporary era. In my conclusion to this study, I discuss Kate Zambreno's novel *Green Girl*, an important recent depiction of neoliberal femininity, focussing on the literary strategies it employs and their affective outcomes. I examine the figure of the green girl, and the related trope of the trainwreck, as I underline the significance of willfulness in the necessarily ongoing assertion of feminine agency and humanity.

1: Contemporary Anglo-American and German Feminisms

"NIEMAND REDET HEUTE MEHR von Sexismus" (No one talks about sexism these days), Bascha Mika claims.[1] In both Anglo-American and German contexts, there is a widespread perception that feminism has "gone too far," and that it is no longer necessary.[2] We are living in a time of "emergent retrosexism," as Alison Phipps puts it.[3] Sociobiological explanations are increasingly proffered in an attempt to naturalize a state of affairs in which issues of power, violence, and money are still very much at play.[4] These observations accord with Rosalind Gill and Christina Scharff's description of a contemporary postfeminist sensibility, which involves an emphasis on self-surveillance and self-transformation, a resurgence of ideas concerning natural sexual difference, and a consumerist, commodifying mentality.[5] In line with work by Angela McRobbie, Scharff explains that in a postfeminist climate, feminism is "both taken into account and, simultaneously, repudiated."[6]

Yet "in spite of it all," there has been in both German and Anglo-American contexts a boom in nonfiction "feminist" writing, where this descriptor is up for discussion.[7] As we will see, the logic underpinning these texts often relies on neoliberalist individualism and leaves out the messiness of embodied, relational experience that fiction can better evoke. But such writing nonetheless helps clarify the status and concerns of feminism today, as well as the mainstream or normative logic that it attempts to counter. It thereby provides further insights into the "willful" workings of the literary texts under discussion in the four chapters that follow. It also flags up the ongoing feminist activity that both emerges from and counters neoliberalism, in the face of its own impossibility.[8] In Sara Ahmed's 2017 formulation, "Feminism needs to be everywhere because feminism is not everywhere."[9]

Contexts

On the matter of contextualizing feminist debates, Scharff notes: "The story of feminism is told differently in Germany than in the UK and, in fact, also encompasses the existence of two German states [East and West Germany] until 1989."[10] As an example of such differing narratives and histories: a significant trigger for the emergence of the "new" feminism in

Germany was the public debate on demographic changes, and especially the low birth rate, which in some cases involved blaming feminism and individual women.[11] In the United States and the United Kingdom, such demographic debates have not been so prominent, and the triggers are more multiple and scattered. Scharff also observes that young women's positioning in relation to gender, class, sexuality, race, and ethnicity may be "lived out differently" in different contexts.[12] Nevertheless, the striking finding of her book *Repudiating Feminism* is that there are in fact few differences in young women's relationship to feminism in Germany and the United Kingdom: as its title suggests, she finds rejection of feminism to be the norm among young women. The variants Scharff observes relate to the individuals associated with feminism and to the sartorial choices feminists are alleged to make.[13] As indicated in the introduction, then, "context" is of course not to be ignored, but as Scharff reminds us, it always "remains to be seen how exactly this context affects the phenomenon under study."[14]

There are common concerns, too, in contemporary, popular publications on feminism in Germany, in the United Kingdom, and in the United States.[15] These texts vary in form, encompassing memoir, journalism, interviews, and sociological analysis, sometimes mixing genres. Many interweave personal material or anecdotes with general or factual data such as statistics. The books vary, too, in the degree of academic analysis they aspire to, and in their intended populism. Most of these texts are concerned with girls and young women, some more overtly than others focussing on issues affecting girls directly (such as body image, the influence of the media and the Internet), rather than on more "adult" issues such as pay and political representation. Here, I explore the term "feminism" and the related question of feminist waves or movements as they appear in such new-feminist texts.[16] I then outline the concerns of these writings under the headings body and beauty, sisterhood and identification, and sex and desire. Finally, and in anticipation of chapter 2, I turn to the implications of these texts as far as the matters of agency and volition are concerned.

"Feminism"?

"Feminism" is an unstable term, and to invoke it is potentially problematic. British philosopher Nina Power asserts: "we are [now] dealing with . . . a fundamental crisis in the meaning of the word ["feminism"]." She suggests that given dubious usages of the term, "we may simply need to abandon the term, or at the very least, restrict its usage to those situations in which we make quite certain we explain what we mean by it."[17] She criticizes US feminist Jessica Valenti's assertion that feminism is "something you define for yourself"—a statement redolent of the neoliberal stress on individual choice that has already been mentioned—asking, "what's to stop it being pure egotism, pure naked greed? Absolutely nothing."[18] I will come back to this question later. However, one feature of feminism appears stable. According to many commentators in both Anglo-American and German contexts, the term provokes discomfort and hostility. Laurie Penny refers to "the popular stereotype of feminists as hairy-legged, loose-breasted, man-hating or man-repelling lesbians who wear . . . dungarees."[19] The authors of *Wir Alpha-Mädchen* note comparably that in Germany, many people deem feminists "hässlich, spaß- und männerfeindlich, ironiefrei und unsexy" (ugly, hostile to fun and men, lacking in irony, and not sexy).[20] Scharff indeed notes how similar are these negative associations and representations. Nonetheless, the terms "feminism" and "Feminismus" are still retained and defended, notably by Caitlin Moran in the British context. She titles a chapter of *How to Be a Woman* "I AM A FEMINIST!" While noting that the term constitutes "a political, lexical and grammatical mess," Moran asserts: "We need the word 'feminism' back real bad."[21] In Germany, the authors of *Wir Alpha-Mädchen* are also keen to retain the term "Feminismus," dismissing the idea of "Postfeminismus," which they associate with an apparently ironic yet actually harmful return to stereotypes of femininity as involving incompetence and decorativeness.[22] Thea Dorn, however, wishes to distance herself from "classic" 1970s feminism, which, according to her, understood men as bad and women as good and lamented "Zwangsheterosexualität" (compulsory heterosexuality). She rejects the term "feminism" for her volume, and instead refers to "die F-Klasse" (the F-class), a group of women she admires and whose views she solicits in interviews.[23]

Generational tensions indeed inform both German and Anglo-American feminist debates, though this is more the case in Germany, where a single figure—Alice Schwarzer—is widely viewed as the figurehead for feminism; in the United Kingdom and the United States, there is no such figure.[24] Schwarzer has unquestionably dominated public debates on feminism in Germany during the past decades; Emily Spiers describes her as an "institution" in her own right.[25] The authors of *Wir Alpha-Mädchen* are keen to distance themselves from Schwarzer, who, they note, has become conflated with feminism per se in Germany, as the go-to woman whenever the media requires comment on a story relating to gender.[26] As Spiers observes, however, the authors themselves also tend to "conflate Schwarzer with the movement as a whole."[27] In *Neue deutsche Mädchen*, Jana Hensel and Elisabeth Raether acknowledge Schwarzer's achievements but argue that her brand of feminism is irrelevant today.[28] The author and media figure Charlotte Roche, whose work will be discussed in chapters 3 and 5, is a prominent antagonist of Schwarzer.[29] She has voiced criticism of Schwarzer's domination of feminist discussions in Germany, suggesting it is time for new voices to emerge.[30] Miriam Gebhard's *Alice in Niemandsland* offers an extensive elaboration of this position, one informed by historical analysis of the German women's movement.[31]

Spiers argues, however, that "the rhetoric of discontinuity employed by the New German Girls appears as a marketing strategy, designed to make feminism palatable to the mainstream, but [it] results in the capitulation of radical feminist politics to the demands of postfeminist mass culture."[32] She suggests the New German Girls' ambivalence toward Schwarzer's generation, combined with the continued reinforcement of negative perceptions of feminism, "paradoxically entail that the new feminism ultimately colludes with the anti-feminist rhetoric saturating the media and the public sphere."[33] Scharff is also critical of the new German feminist texts, whose authors, she notes, are white, heterosexual, and well-educated. She refers to Dorn's book, for example, as "elitist" and "strongly neoliberal."[34] The injunction to "lean out," in the British context, involves a challenge to such tendencies.[35]

Making Waves

In the Anglophone context, there is talk of a "fourth wave" of feminism, as Kira Cochrane discusses in *All the Rebel Women: The Rise of the Fourth Wave of Feminism*.[36] Cochrane highlights the issues of abuse, sexual pressures, body image, and eating disorders as key to this movement, for which the summer of 2013 marked an important turning point in the United Kingdom: this period saw the establishment of the Everyday Sexism project, and the successful campaign, led by Caroline Criado-Perez, to feature a woman on a British banknote. Cochrane also mentions high-profile protests at so-called "lads' mags" and other incidents of resistance to mainstream, masculinist cultural phenomena. As she notes, new campaigns are popping up on a weekly and even daily basis, thanks to the Internet and especially Twitter (7%). Despite her title, though, Cochrane herself is wary of the reference to "waves" of feminist thought and activism, noting that the model does not necessarily take account of global developments, and that it may be reductive. This "wave"—to which technology is key—is, she notes in her conclusion, "nascent." Moran observes humorously, in this connection: "I don't know if we can talk about 'waves' of feminism anymore—by my reckoning, the next wave would be the fifth, and I suspect it's around the fifth wave that you stop referring to individual waves, and start to refer, simply, to an incoming tide."[37] Carrie Smith-Prei and Maria Stehle view contemporary feminism as "categorically beyond the waves."[38]

Talk of a fourth wave has not been widely heard in the German context. Here, the focus has instead been on "Popfeminismus."[39] In her introduction to a collection of essays, *Hot Topic*, Sonja Eismann does not seek to define this term, which she acknowledges is controversial, but suggests rather that her volume gives an overview of current debates. However, she does assert that a feminist popular culture is not simply a matter of making feminism palatable and unthreatening, "sondern . . . sollte Popkultur durch feministische Strategien perforiert und erschüttert werden" (rather . . . pop culture should be pervaded and shaken up by feminist strategies).[40] Spiers sums up popfeminist texts as sharing "a mode of engagement and self-presentation, as well as thematic concerns which potentially fit beneath the umbrella term 'pop'." "Pop," she explains, is short for "popular," but in the German context is associated with a style of writing that arose in the early 1990s that is readable, affectless, and peppered with references to consumer products and brands. In general, Spiers asserts, "new German popfeminist texts actively engage with the global channels of popular culture and wider Western feminist discourse" and they employ "colloquial, often sexualised language peppered with Anglicisms."[41] Carrie Smith-Prei further explains that German pop involves subversive forms of parody and artifice, and associates the pop roots of new German feminism with "unrest and performativity."[42] Such feminism has been influenced by the Riot Grrrls of the 1990s and their legacy, as manifested in the numerous zines and now ezines that have sprung up for "grrls," or rebellious young women.[43]

Indeed, German feminist texts refer frequently to Anglophone thinkers, in particular Judith Butler, as sources of inspiration, illustrating the "Butler boom" referred to in the introduction.[44] They also use English words such as "working class," "Coming Out," and "Community."[45] Recent books by Caitlin Moran, Laurie Penny, Nina Power, and Natasha Walter have been translated into German, further illustrating the transnational nature of contemporary feminism.[46] Eismann, for example, takes such a comparative view when she points to the numerous feminist zines emerging from the United States and the United Kingdom, where Germany simply has Alice Schwarzer and Charlotte Roche—though she does also note manifestations of German feminism such as "Ladyfeste" (feminist art festivals) and drag-king acts.[47] The authors of *Wir Alpha-Mädchen* comparably cite UK and US artistes "[the late] Amy [Winehouse], Lily [Allen], Lindsay [Lohan]" as significant figures. Acknowledging their struggles with drugs and alcohol, the authors nonetheless view these celebrities as representatives of a new generation of young women who are bent on self-actualization.[48]

Hollywood film and global advertising are concerns for both German-speaking and Anglophone feminists. Moran argues: "any modern feminist worth her salt has an interest in the business of A-list gossip; it is the main place where our perception of women is currently being formed."[49] In line with the Americanization of global culture in general, both feminism and popular culture are inflected by US concerns; studies and statistics from the United States are cited in UK authors' works.[50] In Germany, US culture has spawned "local" variants (for example, television programs like *Germany's Next Top Model* and *German Idol*). Numerous US television series are aired on German television and dubbed (for example, *Gilmore Girls, Ugly Betty*). Katja Kullmann even labels a generation of women in their late twenties and thirties "Generation Ally," after Ally McBeal, a character in a US drama series from the 1990s, who in Kullmann's view exemplified the then-current state of femininity, caught between various imperatives.[51] Such linkages further justify the comparatist approach I employ here. And indeed, as already implied, what is striking is the similarity of concerns that feature in German-language and Anglophone feminist texts. The authors deal with the sexualization, silencing, and othering of women as practiced through trivialization and mockery, bullying and intimidation, and sexual violence and rape; or "the continuum that stretches from minor social misery to violent silencing and violent death."[52]

Body and Beauty

There is widespread agreement among feminist commentators that girls and young women are "bombarded" with unrealistic and damaging images, which they internalize and against which they measure themselves.[53] Indeed, the very amount of coverage of this issue is itself a source of comment, and even of suspicion: Melissa Benn observes an "industry of worry" about girls and weight.[54] Such worry is apparently justifiable. Benn cites therapist and writer Susie Orbach's view that girls' relationship to their bodies is deeply problematic and that when women become mothers they transmit these issues to their daughters.[55] Kat Banyard notes that "monitoring and manipulating their appearance remains a daily feature of women's lives."[56] She refers to feminist thinker Sheila Jeffreys, for whom beauty regimes signal women's deference to male norms and ideals. She also cites evidence that the more a girl views herself only in terms of her appearance, the lower her self-esteem and the greater her propensity for suicide.[57] Laura Bates similarly refers to the "obsessive focus on girls' looks."[58] Valenti asserts, "We're on display—everywhere."[59] Objectification is "at an all-time zenith," for Banyard.[60] Indeed, for Power, the language of objectification "may not be useful any longer, as there is no (or virtually no) subjective dimension left to be colonized."[61] Penny views eating disorders as the horribly logical outcome of such appropriation; they represent the "private, violent expression of the cultural trauma whereby the female body is appropriated as a market resource." She locates the roots of this phenomenon in fear of women: "Fear of female flesh and fat is fear of female power."[62] Benn argues comparably that girls' educational achievements have led to a retrograde focus on their appearance as a way of belittling and shaming girls and women.[63] Such a move can be seen as part of a backlash against feminist gains made in previous decades.

Women's bodies are routinely divided up into parts: "It's as if young women are being broken up into bits before our very eyes."[64] Cochrane observes, "women's bodies . . . are more and more divided into their constituent parts" (11%). And Power refers to "the all-pervasive peepshow segmentarity of contemporary culture."[65] Female flesh is rendered docile, according to Penny, who asks: "Why are we so afraid of women's bodies?"[66] The authors of *The Vagenda*, a book derived from a blog, reference Naomi Wolf's 1990 *The Beauty Myth*, suggesting the continuing relevance of that earlier book for contemporary feminists. Wolf argues that myths of female beauty are restrictive and oppressive, referring to "the iron maiden," a torture device, to conjure up the imprisoning and tortuous nature of such ideals.[67] *The Vagenda* itself explores the damaging effect of women's magazines, citing research to suggest that women's self-esteem is negatively affected by exposure to images of idealized female attractiveness, as are found in mass-market publications.[68]

When women appear in public life, if they deviate from the standard ideal of beauty, they are the recipients of abuse, as the case of the classicist Prof. Mary Beard in the United Kingdom demonstrates.[69] Beard has written about how the female voice, since antiquity, has been silenced.[70] Slights upon appearance function as "a Shut-the-Fuck-Up-Tool."[71] Women's concern with their appearance stymies them.[72] Penny argues, in connection with the ideal of thinness: "we have been persuaded . . . to slim down, to take up less space,"[73] a project that can be linked to the broader "silencing of women through shame, normalization, dismissal, disbelief and blame."[74] In this context, such a voice as Moran's is subversive. Her defense of pubic hair—an issue linked to the contemporary normalization of porn, in which pubic hair generally does not appear[75]—is at odds with mainstream representations and ideals, as is her reminder to readers that their bodies are theirs, and private ("What happens in your bra and pants STAYS in your bra and pants"), and her challenge to the widespread obsession with fatness ("fat" has become "a swearword").[76] Moran also writes about women's efforts to conceal their age, arguing for lines and gray hair as positive signs of experience and status. Moreover, cosmetic surgery "makes us look like losers."[77] Noting that "women are supposed to adore heels," she herself refuses them—where Valenti's pronouncement "I'm a fan of makeup and heels" serves as a challenge to stereotypes of feminists as opposed to beautification.[78]

Moran, Penny, Power, and Walter have all been translated into German. In original German-language texts there is a similar concern with "die Reduktion von Frauen auf ihre Körper" (the reduction of women to their bodies), and with coercive ideals.[79] Mika notes, "Frau is Body. Das kriegt sie [the teenage girl] auf jedem Cover, auf jedem Plakat, an jeder

Straßenecke, in jedem Mädchenmagazin mit" (Woman is body. That's what she's given to understand on every cover, every poster, every street corner, in every magazine for girls).[80] The *Alpha-Mädchen* note that the cosmetics industry thrives on people's insecurity, with magazines aiding their cause by continually identifying new bodily "Problemzonen" (problem zones). The authors also point to the power of the media, claiming that today we see more bodies on advertising posters, on television, in films, and in newspapers than we do in real life, and that this affects the general view of what constitutes a normal or ideal body. The pressure this places upon young women (and men) is immense.[81] Body hair and eating disorders also emerge as concerns in German texts.[82] The female body is "defizitär[ ]" (faulty), always in need of correction.[83] As we will see further in chapter 3, the questions of embodiment and appearance have immense implications for the well-being or otherwise of contemporary young, female subjects.

Sisterhood and Identification

Broadly, new feminist texts are concerned to affirm supportive relationships between women. The *Alpha-Mädchen* stress the importance of female networks and of solidarity, for example.[84] In *Bad Feminist*, Roxane Gay also celebrates female connections—this in the face of a dividedness she sees as fostered by the culture. Noting that there is a "cultural myth that all female friendships must be bitchy, toxic, or competitive," she suggests this myth is unhelpful and based on internalized misogyny.[85] The question of "sisterhood"—of identification between women—is complex and contested, however; it raises broader concerns around "difference" that have long been debated within feminist thought. Intersectionality proves a useful term for a number of writers: Cochrane terms it "the defining framework" of contemporary feminist campaigns.[86] Valenti explains: "Some folks call it intersectionality; others call it multiple oppressions; some call it the intersection of oppressions. Whatever you call it, the point is that different kinds of '-isms' (sexism, classism, racism) all intersect in a truly fucked-up way."[87]

In the United Kingdom and the United States, the emphasis on intersectionality has arguably meant a more nuanced understanding of "difference" as multiple, overlapping, and various, than in Germany, where—as Hester Baer notes—the contributions of migrant women, Afro-German women, and Jewish women to feminist debates have often been overlooked and ignored.[88] One current key area of debate in the United Kingdom is FGM (Female Genital Mutilation), for example, as feminist campaigners draw attention to the practice, widespread among immigrant communities, and engage necessarily in complex debates about "other" cultures and "traditional" behaviors.[89] In Germany, where Alice Schwarzer has argued against the veil, and where Thea Dorn writes of Western tolerance of "Muslim" misogyny, and conflates Islam, FGM, and the veil problematically, difference between women is not necessarily subjected to sophisticated treatment.[90] The *Alpha-Mädchen* acknowledge but then quickly dismiss difference in favor of claims about what most, or even all, German women want: "Alle jungen Frauen wollen heute das Gleiche" (All young women want the same thing today).[91] And while acknowledging differences between women, polemicist Mika nonetheless asserts common patterns and trends; her rhetoric indeed frequently relies on claims as to what we (*wir*) women do.[92] It is perhaps this less flexible approach to difference that has led to the overlooking of trans issues until recently in Germany. For feminists in the United States and the United Kingdom, trans issues have emerged as key in recent years, and as integral to feminisms—Ahmed claims, "An antitrans stance is an antifeminist stance."[93] Nonetheless, there are signs of trans identities also gaining attention in Germany.[94] Such issues and identities are highly instructive, prompting vital new debates.

Heterosexual, cisgender women are, generally speaking, the target audience in both German and Anglo-American contexts. Men are affirmed as key both to the success of feminism and to the happiness of individual woman. While Moran, for example, notes an alliance between women and gay men, who are also "other," lesbians get only a brief look-in, and the emphasis is very much on straight desire, here given a refreshing, revisionary treatment. Benn makes cursory allowance for the fact that some of the "daughters" addressed in her book's title (*What Should We Tell Our Daughters?*) will not be straight. Walter acknowledges her focus is heterosexual women in Britain. Valenti alludes to queer desire, and usefully discusses intersectionality, but her own position is that of a heterosexual woman.[95] In *Wir Alpha-Mädchen*, the authors claim: "Die meisten von uns wollen auch Kinder. . . . Viele Männer unseres Alters haben den gleichen Wunsch. Gemeinsam mit ihnen wollen wir unser Leben gleichberechtigt managen—jeder verdient die Hälfte des Geldes, jeder kümmert sich zur Hälfte um die Kinder und um den Haushalt" (Most of us also want children. . . . Many men our age have the same desire. Together with them we want to manage our lives on an equal footing—each earns half the money, each takes a fair share of childcare and housework).[96] Spiers observes the "heteronormative" tendencies of the New German Girls, suggesting, "a group of young, white, middle-class, educated, heterosexual feminists" is perhaps not best placed to speak for those differing from that description.[97] As far as feminists' relationships with men are concerned, Mirja Stöcker notes that men prefer working women—"Aber das nur nebenbei" (But that's just by the by).[98] The implication is that men will still like you if you have a career. Mika is less concerned with placatory moves, asserting, "Männer haben uns Frauen ausgetrickst und abgewatscht" (Men have tricked us women and fobbed us off).[99]

Feminist "sisterhood" involves acknowledging the legacies of past endeavors. Benn argues that "particularly in a world of instant reaction and disposable dissent," it is vital that feminists engage with and understand the struggles of the past.[100] In keeping with this assertion, Moran discusses her admiration of Germaine Greer, and Valenti gives a quick tour of US feminism. The authors of *Wir Alpha-Mädchen* also provide a potted history of feminism. While apparently rejecting some aspects of "1970s feminism," they acknowledge its contemporary necessity and relevance. They list the gains of feminism, including criminalization of marital rape and "die Entdeckung der Klitoris" (the discovery of the clitoris).[101] Yet generational struggles feature in new-feminist texts, as indicated. Sisterhood and identification thus emerge as crucial, if not easy, matters for feminists and women in general. They are bound up with questions of difference, intersectionality, and generationality, as we will see further in chapter 4.

Sex and Desire

The new-feminist texts both assert female desire and critique the widespread sexualization of young women and the pornification of culture. Valenti notes: "Girls aren't supposed to like sex, especially teenage girls."[102] Yet girls are sexualized from a very early age, as Walter's *Living Dolls* argues. In the United Kingdom, various campaigns have sprung up to drive sexist or sexualizing products from stores' shelves; the Let Girls Be Girls campaign is but one example.[103] The ubiquity of the Playboy bunny points to the commodification and sexualization of girls.[104] Penny argues that while the female body appears to be everywhere, it is in fact "marginalised and appropriated by a culture of monetised sexuality that alienates us from our authentic personal and political selves."[105] As suggested before, the discourse of "choice" in this context can be very damaging.[106]

Debates about female pleasure are often inflected by references to a joyless and prohibitive "1970s feminism." In Germany, the key figure of Alice Schwarzer is anti-porn and allegedly anti-sex, and has served as a point of departure for German feminist debates about sexuality and pleasure. The authors of *Wir Alpha-Mädchen* associate "1970s feminism" with a view of heterosexual sex as a matter of male dominance, citing Kate Millett and Alice Schwarzer. They do put the views of these authors in context, noting that marital rape was not illegal when Schwarzer published her early work.[107] Acknowledging the importance of earlier feminist work in shaping the current situation, they assert a different vision, however: "Der neue Feminismus geht mit dem Thema Sex entspannter um. Feministinnen sind heute eher für viel Sex und für guten Sex. Weil sie ihre Körper mögen und deswegen gern spaßige Dinge damit anstellen"

(23; The new feminism is more relaxed about sex. Feminists today are in fact for lots of sex, and for good sex. Because they like their bodies and so enjoy getting up to fun things with them). They offer this as an alternative to what they see as the restriction of young women's sexuality. Girls who do explore their sexuality freely are judged and denied respect (42).

Feminists in the United States and the United Kingdom have long drawn attention to the low conviction rates for rape in those countries, and have highlighted misogynist comments by judges and commentators.[108] They have taken part in and championed activist movements such as SlutWalk, which arose as a response to the victim-blaming tendencies in evidence worldwide. Noting that "a woman is never responsible for a man raping her," Banyard suggests: "Rape myths count in the courtroom."[109] The term "rape culture" is used to denote the persistence of such myths; "we . . . live in a time that necessitates the phrase 'rape culture.'"[110] Banyard also states that sexist violence is pervasive and prevalent, citing statistics indicating that a quarter of women in the United Kingdom will experience violence at the hands of a current or former partner. Banyard points to "the desire to control women's sexuality" as the common driver in incidents of sexual violence and assault. She also cites US statistics that suggest a third of American women will experience sexual assault.[111] Cochrane similarly refers to the "fucking depressing" statistics relating to violence against women (93%).[112]

Pornography is now an urgent concern for feminists, given the wide availability of pornographic images via the Internet and its normalization.[113] Ariel Levy has written about the pornification of popular culture, arguing that the pervasiveness of "raunch" has damaging effects on girls and young women.[114] As far as the consequences of this normalization are concerned, Walter observes that in pornography "there is no before and no after . . . little individuality . . . no communication . . . no emotional resonance."[115] Walter thus points to the dehumanizing effects of porn, and the impact it can have on relationships. The expectations of boys are shaped by the porn they consume. The *Alpha-Mädchen* also note the influence porn has on its viewers' expectations of what is "normal" in bed.[116] The dominance of pornographic ideals leads to hair removal on the part of young women, and even cosmetic surgery.[117] Mika suggests that young women "pornographisieren ihr Äußeres" (pornify their appearance).[118] For Banyard, violence against women is "tragically logical," given the images in widespread circulation. She argues against the idea that a career in the sex industry is a positive "choice," given the backgrounds sex workers come from and the high rates of PTSD among (former) sex workers.[119]

Women's control over their reproductive ability is also a significant concern of contemporary feminist discourses. In the United States, where far-right antiabortion campaigners are prominent and violent, this concern is an urgent one, as Valenti suggests. She sums up the views of such campaigners thus: "Abortion means that you're selfish, that you're a slut, that you're a murderer."[120] Banyard, in relaying the story of a young mother influenced by antiabortion campaigners on the street, suggests that this is an urgent issue in the United Kingdom too. Moran's account of an abortion she underwent should be seen in this context. She points to the shame around abortions, arguing that women, as the bearers of life, should have the choice to sustain or terminate pregnancies.[121] Access to contraception and to good advice are further priorities, in both English- and German-language texts.[122] Sex and desire, as we will see further in chapter 5, are thus complex and urgent topics: female desire and embodiment are at once pornified and curtailed.

Note: Omissions

This summary demonstrates that new-feminist texts evince a number of key clusters of concerns—these inform the structuring of this book. This is not an exhaustive account, however. A major issue it omits is motherhood, and in particular the difficulty of reconciling paid work with mothering, as well as the related issues of women in public and professional life, childcare, and the division of labor in households. I have not focussed on these questions, but they are obviously linked to the observations above. Given that the prospect of motherhood if not (yet) the lived reality affects girls' and young women's self-image and aspirations, they require at least brief acknowledgment.[123] Many feminist commentators indeed flag up the uneven distribution of labor in the home, and the struggle women—primarily women—face in combining parental responsibilities with paid work.[124] Childcare is seen as a matter for women alone. In the United Kingdom, the costs of childcare are prohibitive and the subject of ongoing political debate.[125] Writing in the United States, Valenti urges: "Start fighting for childcare now!"[126] German working mothers today are demonized, with the term *Rabenmutter* (raven mother) still widely in use—the demonization of working mothers represents, according to Mika, "eine deutsche Spezialität" (a German speciality)—and popular texts such as Eva Herman's *Das Eva-Prinzip* (The Eva Principle) reinscribe women's primary goal as being a "good" mother.[127] Indeed, motherhood is "foundational to feminism in Germany," as Smith-Prei and Stehle point out.[128]

In public life, women do not fare well either and are underrepresented. Walter notes the "sexual bullying" of women in public life, citing examples of politicians in the United Kingdom and the United States who have experienced this; Bates claims, "Over and again, female politicians are subjected to ridicule, criticism and dismissal on the basis of their sex."[129] In the British context especially, "banter" is a term often applied to men's abuse of women; insults or sexual innuendo are to be read as jokes, and the woman who fails to laugh is humorless or hormonal.[130] Benn argues that "girls are often subtly discouraged . . . from finding or using a public voice."[131] This observation appears valid when one looks at instances of online bullying and harassment.[132] Such dismissal is internalized and leads many women to feel insecure, or to experience "imposter syndrome," the sense that their expertise is sham.[133] Since sexism is covert—"like Meryl Streep, in a new film," as Moran puts it, alluding to that actor's famously mutable appearance—it is hard to challenge.[134] Successful or powerful women are not likeable.[135] While Angela Merkel's position as chancellor of Germany is often cited as evidence that feminism has had its day and is now redundant, it has in fact given rise to public misogyny there; Merkel's appearance has attracted much negative comment, and she has been accused of being insufficiently feminine—though studies suggest "masculine" women are felt to be more competent.[136] Femininity is not an asset—yet a perceived lack of femininity leads to derision or worse.

Girls do well at school in the United Kingdom and Germany, but this success is not reflected in the workplace, in the form of status and high pay. Feminist commentators address the issue of unequal pay in Anglo-American and German contexts and note the prevalence of women in low-paid, low-status roles such as care work.[137] Banyard contends that there are three main barriers preventing the advancement of women to the higher ranks and better pay grades in the workplace: the lack of flexible working (in the United Kingdom); the unequal division of care work; and discrimination based on gender stereotyping. This division of work into men's and women's realms also occurs in Germany, with "men's work" attracting better pay, status, and prospects.[138] The authors of *Wir Alpha-Mädchen* similarly call for flexible working and argue for a *Frauenquote* (women's quota), an issue that has been controversial in the German context in recent years.[139] This question connects obviously to that of family norms and ideals—and, indeed, to the clusters of concerns I mention above.[140]

Agency and Volition

How do these texts explain or account for the continued objectification of women, and what strategies do they suggest might overcome it? In particular, what resources do they offer a critic seeking new ways of framing agency and volition? Capitalism and consumerism emerge as major concerns in many new-feminist texts, and historical, political, and structural factors feature with varying levels of emphasis and detail, so that agency and volition emerge as necessarily contingent on context. Representation, especially in popular culture, is also widely acknowledged as crucial, as a method both of enforcing dominant discourses and resisting them. Many texts manifest a concern with constructivism and socialization, and suggest ways of challenging these in their current forms. For example, children's clothes and toys serve to shore up ideas concerning the sexes' essential differences. Popular campaigns such as Pinkstinks and Let Toys Be Toys have sprung up to challenge these assumptions.[141] Other methods of reinforcing sexual difference have attracted criticism, such as neuroreductionism—a reduction of human behavior to the effect of neural processes that is common in popular culture and in media discourses and that is often used to support essentializing views of the sexes. Walter discusses the "new determinism" involved in such reductive accounts, as well as the refutations to which it has given rise. She notes that such challenges do not garner the media attention that popular binarist views enjoy. Walter also examines popular myths about the genders, revealing the evidence on which they are based to be scanty or indeed faulty. The *Alpha-Mädchen* similarly underline female socialization and gender binarism, and are equally critical of biologism and neuroreductionism.[142]

Other texts, however, tend toward essentialism or individualism, while others still consist of a tangle of approaches. I have mentioned that contemporary feminist writings in Germany rely often on the rhetoric of neoliberal capitalism; Spiers argues that in such writings, "the subject's ability to behave autonomously remains a given constant, a feature which constitutes an almost wilful disregard of socio-cultural pressures."[143] Indeed, claims such as "es geht um Freiheit" (it's a matter of freedom) and assertions of choice are problematic, or at least limited.[144] Mika's *Die Feigheit der Frauen* offers a particularly interesting case study in terms of conceptions of female agency. The author's central thesis is that women are complicit in their own subjugation. Women are lazy and cowardly, refusing to assume responsibility for their own fates. Instead, they take refuge in stereotypical roles, becoming passive and dependent. Mika's text veers between affirmations of individualism—women should take responsibility for themselves and their choices—and assertions of constructedness and false consciousness. For example, "In ihren Augen hat sie individuelle Entscheidungen getroffen . . . Sie lügt sich in die Tasche" (In her eyes, she has made individual choices . . . She's telling herself barefaced lies). There is a contradiction at the heart of her thesis—women are "individuals" capable of choice, and yet their lives are conditioned by ideological, political, and structural factors. Mika claims: "Psychologie hin, Sozialisation her—Frauen haben die Wahl!" (Never mind psychology, socialization, all that—women have a choice!).[145] Her text is a tangle of constructivism, individualism, and essentialism which neatly illustrates the major dilemmas that have long faced feminist theory.

A similar confusion is to be found in Natasha Walter's *Living Dolls*. At points, the book challenges the idea of choice as free and unconstrained. It highlights the contexts in which such choices are made, observes that when speaking of young girls, choice is not a helpful notion, and asks us to consider the effects of particular decisions.[146] But in her introduction, Walter retains this term as part of her answer to the problems she identifies:

> Of course, it has to be a woman's own choice if she makes a personal decision to buy into any aspect of what might be seen as stereotypically feminine behaviour, from baking to pole-dancing, from high heels to domestic work. I am just as sure as I ever was that we do not need to subscribe to some dour and politically correct version of feminism in order to move towards greater equality. But we should be looking for true choice, in a society characterised by freedom and equality. Instead, right now a rhetoric of choice is masking very real pressures on this generation of women. We are currently living in a world where those aspects of feminine behaviour that could be freely chosen are often turning into a cage for young women. (14)

Walter thus pits "true choice" against the false choices young women are currently making in response to the narrow range of role models on offer to them today; such models are "shrinking and warping" their choices (38). Choice emerges as an unstable term—both desirable and suspect. It is malleable and manipulable. Walter ends her book with a reference to the "full human potential" that she wishes women might achieve, in opposition to what she sees as a dominant plasticity and passivity (238).

We return, then, to the questions of wholeness and humanity. The idea of "being oneself" is popular in new-feminist texts and ties in with these questions. Penny, for example, refers to "our authentic personal and political selves."[147] Valenti often enjoins her readers to be aware of what they are doing and how they are feeling, pleading for a kind of self-awareness: "Do what feels right for you," she urges.[148] And Moran observes comparably: "Simply being honest about who we really are is half the battle."[149] Banyard, who describes how girls come to objectify themselves in the face of widespread pressures, at the end of her book encourages women readers to "look inwards": that is, to ignore the messages from "outside" and discover their own desires and ambitions.[150] The *Alpha-Mädchen* suggest their readers be awkward, challenging, and curious.[151] Such enjoinments aim to foster a critical stance in readers. They also highlight how crucial, and how problematic, the ideal of full or authentic humanity remains.

Conclusions, Anticipations

The new-feminist texts take very different forms, but there is in many cases an emphasis on personal experience. Banyard interweaves accounts of women's experiences with factual analysis; *Everyday Sexism* is based on individuals' contributions to a website, detailing every-day experiences; Moran's book is a memoir as much as (or more than) it is a polemic. Eismann indeed notes in her introduction to *Hot Topic* that "das Private ist . . . nach wie vor politisch" (the private is . . . political, as it always was). "The personal is political" is a slogan the *Alpha-Mädchen* reference, too.[152] Hensel and Raether argue that the following are important topics:

> Wie es sich anfühlt, wenn man eine Affäre beginnt oder beendet. Oder warum Frauen häufig so unsicher sind und sich gern bescheiden geben und man Männern immer noch nicht recht zutraut, dass sie liebenswürdige Wesen und verlässliche Väter sein können. Oder die Frage, ob Männer anders verliebt sind als Frauen.

> [How it feels when you begin or end an affair. Or why women are often so insecure and do themselves down and why one still doesn't really trust men to be nice people or reliable fathers. Or the question as to whether men fall in love differently from women.][153]

They appear to reject the concerns of *Emma*, the magazine Schwarzer founded—namely, prostitution, eating disorders, Islam, the veil, and forced marriage—in favor of such issues.[154] Dorn's book, for its part, takes the form of interviews with women she views as part of "die neue F-klasse" (the new F-class). Benn argues that the turn to memoir—she cites here Moran, as well as the work of Rachel Cusk and Shela Heti—perhaps arises from the paucity of available representations of (rich, messy, variegated, female) experience otherwise.[155]

This speculation lends weight to my own contention that novels—which relate and prompt affective, "personal" experiences—can supplement other public discourses concerning being and becoming woman. They counter an arguably excessive jubilance in popular feminist texts, asserting negativity, failure, and disgust as central to young women's affective states. Penny notes, in this regard: "Contemporary pseudo-feminism is all about the power of yes."[156] And Power criticizes the self-help aspects of Valenti's youthful brand of feminism, observing that "liberating" feminism shares a great deal with "liberating" capitalism; that is, that it is bland and unthreatening. Valenti's feminism "brooks no failure."[157] As mentioned, Power also problematizes Valenti's suggestion that one can define feminism for oneself. Valenti does indeed argue that feminism is a matter of "making your life better," and that feminists themselves are "pretty cool (and attractive!)." Feminism is "fun." There are moments when Valenti herself becomes aware of the unpalatable nature of the facts she is dealing with, noting—"Yeah, I know, all of a sudden I'm not so jokey"—but these are apologetic: "I'm not trying to be a downer."[158] The subtitle of *Wir Alpha-Mädchen*—"Warum Feminismus das Leben schöner macht"—contains a similarly positive message: feminism makes life *schöner* (nicer). The book's authors argue that feminists have more enjoyable sex because they can see dominant ideals of feminine beauty for the artificial constructs they are and and are thus able to take pleasure in their own bodies. Stöcker's subtitle also suggests that "Feminismus is sexy" (feminism is sexy).

In line with Valenti's claim that "liking yourself . . . is a revolutionary act," and Moran's defiant assertion of pleasure in her own body, we might indeed see these affirmations of (erotic) pleasure as useful rebellions against a dominant culture that most often makes women miserable and ill.[159] Smith-Prei and Stehle indeed assert "joy" as a feature of feminist politics.[160] But celebrations of fun, sexiness, and self-love are of limited value if the dominant cultural context does not play ball. Similarly, the idea that one can "choose" what kind of woman to be, that one can play with one's femininity, is problematic.[161] The literary texts I explore in the next chapter eschew such simplifications, in particular by asserting negativity and failure. They thus undermine "the happiness myth" dominant in contemporary neoliberalism, asserting complexity, ambivalence, and messiness.[162] In so doing, they manifest willfulness.

2: Agency and Volition

A GENCY AND VOLITION are crucial concerns for feminist theory, and they underlie all of the chapters that follow. Ahmed's notion of willfulness offers a powerful way of conceiving female agency today. In this chapter, I begin by returning to the question of "becoming" raised in the introduction. I link the idea of becoming to Ahmed's willfulness, as well as to the matters of negativity, failure, and anger—this following J. Halberstam and Elizabeth A. Wilson. I then turn to an exploration of a number of literary texts that depict and manifest a range of "willful" female responses to the postfeminist, neoliberal condition. Literary texts allow for ambiguity and contradictoriness and so complement and extend feminist nonfiction and theory. Literary texts also counter the individualism and rationalism that one finds in much nonfiction, involving as they do affectivity. The encounter between reader and text itself involves a becoming that challenges instrumentalizing and individualizing discourses. The willfulness of the texts is potentially contagious.

Becoming, Willing, Failing, Refusing

I have already described "becoming" as involving a challenge to "identity." In *Metamorphoses: Towards a Materialist Theory of Becoming*, Rosi Braidotti also opposes notions of subjectivity as fixed and unified, and argues, following Deleuze, that the subject is "an affective, positive and dynamic structure."[1] She defines the "becomings" the subject undergoes as involving "empathic proximity and intensive interconnectedness," thereby also critiquing individualism, and by implication neoliberalism (*M*, 8; cf. *M*, 3). I have elsewhere highlighted the importance of Braidotti's "nomadic" conception of subjectivity for an understanding of ethics and suggested that it is particularly pertinent to the contemporary era.[2] Braidotti refers, notably, to "the fictional unity of a grammatical 'I'" (*M*, 22).

In *Becoming Undone*, Grosz similarly investigates the questions of individuation and individuality. She suggests: "The individual is a solution or response to the problem posed by intense yet incompatible forces struggling with each other."[3] This questioning of (individual) "identities" constitutes a challenge to certain feminist theories. Grosz stresses instead becoming, which she links to the question of "difference." Difference, for Grosz, is not only a matter of distinctions between entities; rather, it is the driving force of things themselves.[4] This thinking ties in with Jasbir K. Puar's ideas of affirmative becomings and of assemblages, and it means rethinking the idea of intersectionality. Intersectionality has been an important term in feminist writing, including popular writing, yet it involves an unhelpful understanding of factors such as race, class, and gender as fixed, static, attributes rather than, as Puar puts it, "encounters."[5]

Such a challenge to "identity" undermines conceptions of subjecthood that rest on ideals of individuality—and indeed identity politics more broadly. It also entails a consideration of the matter of agency, or will. Noting that the questions of autonomy, agency, and freedom have been central to feminist politics for over half a century, Grosz problematizes the way these have been conceptualized in feminist thought, especially in light of Henri Bergson's theory of freedom as involving "innovation and invention" (*BU*, 72). She argues that feminist theory needs new concepts, and in particular—recalling critiques of neoliberalism—that the feminist focus on identity and on the subject is constraining:

> To the extent that feminist theory focuses on questions of the subject or identity, it leaves questions about the rest of existence—outside of and beyond or bigger than the subject, or what is beyond the subject's control—untouched. Feminism abdicates the right to speak about the real, about the world, about matter, about nature, and in exchange, cages itself in the reign of the "I": who am I, who recognizes me, what can I become? Ironically, this is a realm that is increasingly globally defined through the right to consumption, what the subject can have and own. (*BU*, 84)

Thus the concern with the individual is limiting and shores up neoliberal discourses that conflate agency with consumerism. Grosz asserts doing over being: "I become according to what I do, not who I am" (*BU*, 85). She also critiques what she sees as the privileging of the epistemological over the ontological in feminism, arguing that this area of feminist concern should be "displaced" (*BU*, 85). Linked with this assertion is her argument that feminism needs to address the nonhuman.[6]

A view of the subject as affectively assembled might seem to involve a challenge to "agency," however. In *Metamorphoses*, Braidotti hints at this potential conflict when, following Deleuze and Irigaray, she refers to an oscillation in the subject "between wilful choice and unconscious drives" (*M*, 76). Willfulness here connotes intentionality, which is thwarted, at least potentially, by "unconscious drives." The term "wilful" is used elsewhere by Braidotti, here to refer to political activity, which is apparently at odds with, or anyway not straightforwardly compatible with, the messiness of subjectivity: Braidotti claims she wishes "to reconnect the wilful agency required of politics with the respect that is due, both theoretically and ethically, to the affective, libidinal and therefore contradictory structures of the subject" (*M*, 39). She thus points up the challenge involved in effecting political agency with only chaotic, fractured individual subjectivities as a resource. But Braidotti takes inspiration here from Deleuze. Explaining her Deleuze-inspired conception of agency, she spells out: "It has nothing to do with voluntarism and all to do with a shift of grounds, a change of rhythms, a different set of conceptual colours" (*M*, 75). That is to say, agency is not in fact a matter of voluntarism, or intentionality, but of subtle shifts, or performative acts, as Judith Butler might put it.[7]

Here Ahmed's notion of willfulness comes usefully into play. Ahmed also asserts agency as ambivalent and contradictory, and yet possible. Willfulness is an attribution to a non-compliant subject, but it is also the experience of this attribution.[8] Drawing on phenomenology, which is concerned among other things with the relationship between the voluntary and the involuntary, Ahmed explores willing as "an energetic relationship to a future possibility," that may yet be anxious (*WS*, 37). Indeed, a willful feminism involves an insistence on negativity.[9] The texts I explore here thematize and manifest willfulness, which proves anxious, angry, even aggressive. In the previous chapter, I addressed what might be seen as an excessive jubilance in popular feminist texts. Roxane Gay's self-designation as a "bad feminist" usefully counters and complicates this tendency:

> I am failing as a woman. I am failing as a feminist. To freely accept the feminist label would not be fair to good feminists. If I am, indeed, a feminist, I am a rather bad one. I am a mess of contradictions. There are many ways in which I am doing feminism wrong, at least according to the way my perceptions of feminism have been warped by being a woman.[10]

Gay points to the contradictoriness of the (feminist) subject, and the "warping" effects of femininity on perceptions and enactments of feminism. I have already suggested that wholeness might serve as a useful term in thinking about female subjectivity, as involving failure, negativity, and refusal, as well as, potentially, "success," confidence, and positivity. In this, I am seeking to reconcile the fruitful work of queer theorists Lee Edelman and J. Halberstam on failure and death, as well as Gay's "bad feminism" and the "gut feminism" of Elizabeth A. Wilson, with ideas of doing, becoming, and willing. The literary texts I explore in most cases evince refusal and bile. But that does not, cannot, place them or their protagonists outside the dominant order, or outside the condition of postfeminist neoliberalism. It nonetheless constitutes a useful provocation, a prodding, an attempt to effect "a shift of grounds, a change of rhythms, a different set of conceptual colours" (*M*, 75): that is to say, a manifestation of willfulness.

Failure and refusal, important tropes in queer theory, are significant features of this willfulness. In *No Future*, Edelman links queer to a refusal of "reproductive futurism," and to the death drive.[11] In *The Queer Art of Failure*, Halberstam argues: "Failing is something queers do and have always done exceptionally well"; indeed, under certain circumstances, failing "may . . . offer more creative, more cooperative, more surprising ways of being in the world [than 'success']."[12] Contemporary neoliberalism operates on the assumption that failure is "one's own fault rather than the result of social inequality and disadvantage."[13] So defiant, demonstrative failure is at the very least worthy of note and may act to undermine ideals relating to normality and success. Such notions of failure and refusal bear comparison with Dawn Foster's exhortation to "lean out" from global capitalism.[14] Wilson also addresses negative states and affects, and enquires into their implications for feminist theory, asking: "What if feminist politics are necessarily more destructive than we are able to bear?"[15] Arguing that biology is more dynamic than feminists have presumed, she focuses on the gut, and makes a case for "the necessary place of aggression (bile) in feminist theory" (*GF*, 5).[16] She links this argument to recent queer work by Leo Bersani and Lee Edelman and notes that such scholarship "isn't antisocial at all." Instead, it wants to construct theories that are able to account for and address "the fundamental involvement of negativity in sociality and subjectivity" (*GF*, 6). As Ahmed argues, in being willing to receive an assignation of negativity, "we are affirming something."[17]

The texts I explore here offer a spectrum of responses, more or less negative and premised on failure, to the postfeminist, neoliberal condition. They thus involve "interpretation of our ongoing, anxious implication in envies, hostilities, and harms" (*GF*, 179), countering the "happiness myths of neoliberalism and global capitalism."[18] The texts in question are Antonia Baum's *vollkommen leblos, bestenfalls tot* (perfectly lifeless, preferably dead, 2011), Juli Zeh's *Spieltrieb* (Play Instinct, 2004), Zoë Jenny's *Das Blütenstaubzimmer* (1997; *The Pollen Room*, 1999), Helene Hegemann's *Axolotl Roadkill* (2010; *Axolotl Roadkill*, 2012), Emma Jane Unsworth's *Animals* (2014), and Caitlin Moran's *How to Build a Girl* (2014). I trace a trajectory from extreme refusal and self-destruction (Baum, Zeh, Jenny, Hegemann) to more positive and vitalist assertions of becoming (Unsworth, Moran) which nonetheless draw attention to a context that is inimical to female agency. In all of these texts, agency and volition emerge as problematic but crucial matters. The female protagonists refuse and resist dominant discourses and expectations in various ways. The texts depict and constitute disruptions and disturbances to the social order, highlighting the fact that "socialization is not secure at all."[19]

Antonia Baum, *vollkommen leblos, bestenfalls tot*

Antonia Baum's *vollkommen leblos, bestenfalls tot* charts the fortunes of
a nameless young woman who has left her family home for the city. Her
namelessness is significant, suggesting a lack of identity and tying in with
the text's depiction of an anxious subject-in-process; the novel takes the
form of a hallucinatory journey, and is composed of impressionistic, surreal snapshots. The protagonist comes from an unhappy home; her parents are divorced and the narrator reflects that they should never have
met.[20] Familial roles involve falsity and entrapment (*vl*, 164–65). Here,
the rejection of family is tied to the protagonist's scorn for social arrange-
ments in general and suggests a queer stance that rejects heteronormative
imperatives. Indeed, the novel early on recalls queer rejections of futurity,
or reproductive futurism, when the narrator questions the obsession with
the future foisted upon pupils at school, and a neoliberal logic that rests
on ideas of individual responsibility and career progression—this in the
shadow of precarity and of what Lauren Berlant calls "cruel optimism":[21]

> In den Klassenzimmern haben sie uns jahrelang terrorisiert mit
> ihren Einschüchterungs-Parolen über die Zukunft und über Berufe
> mit beziehungsweise ohne Zukunft und wenig Zeit, das haben sie
> immer wieder gesagt, dass wir keine Zeit haben und uns beeilen
> müssen . . . und Zukunftsbroschüren haben sie ab der dritten Klasse
> fast täglich verteilt, und den Zukunftsunterricht haben sie erteilt in
> Arbeitsmarkt, Ausdauer, Ausland, Disziplin, Flexibilität, Praktika,
> Wirtschaftskrise, und diese Zukunfts-Besessenheit. (*vl*, 12–13)

> [They've been terrorizing us for years in the classroom with their
> intimidating talk about the future and jobs, jobs with or without
> futures, and the lack of time, they kept on saying that, we have no
> time, we have to get a move on . . . and from the third grade on
> they handed out these brochures about the future, practically every
> day, and they taught the future: job market, perseverance, abroad,
> discipline, flexibility, apprenticeships, economic crisis, and this whole
> obsession with the future.][22]

The narrator's mockery of the teachers' talk involves a parody of discourses concerning employability and appropriate life choices and courses,
or what Berlant terms "the heterofamilial, upwardly mobile good-life
fantasy."[23] It also brings to mind Halberstam's observations regarding
models of maturity in Western culture. Halberstam suggests: "we . . .
pathologize modes of living that show little or no concern for longevity," instead privileging the "middle-class logic of reproductive temporality."[24] Adolescence is viewed as a "dangerous and unruly" period that

culminates in "a desired process of maturation."[25] Baum's narrator rejects this "Zukunfts-Krankheit" (future sickness) (*vl*, 13). Her rejection of the "rod" of education recalls other protagonists this chapter examines— Hegemann's, Moran's, and Zeh's—and further suggests her willfulness, as well as her awkwardly adolescent positioning, to refer to Smith-Prei and Stehle.

At the same time, she asserts her desire to become "something": "Ich weiß noch nicht genau, was, aber ich will" (*vl*, 16; I'm not sure what yet, exactly, but that's what I want). At this point, early on in the novel, she does not reject the idea of becoming outright. However, dominant models of being fail to appeal. Her parents, who seem dead to her, emphatically do not provide role models (*vl*, 11). This is a material-istic society, paranoid about immigration (*vl*, 53). The narrator's father embodies such greed and superficiality, lacking as he does any substance, or even life (*vl*, 65, 53). The association of rigid political views with life-lessness is notable and ties in with assertions of subjectivity as dynamic and in process, and with a feminist vitalism, as well as with Grosz's asser-tion of animality as positive and corrective.[26] However, and significantly for such feminist discussions of subjectivity, the novel insistently links ideas of nothingness to femaleness in particular. The narrator is merely a nameless *Mädchen* (*vl*, 19, 31, 32; girl), adorning social occasions and complementing her boyfriend Patrick—this in line with Beauvoir and with Ahmed's discussion of "girl" as connoting a restricted form of emergent personhood.[27] The narrator's relationship with Patrick, whom she dislikes, rests on a perverse social contract (*vl*, 25). Heterosexuality involves the assertion of male will over passive female subjects, in keep-ing with Ahmed's discussion of the institution of marriage (*WS*, 115). The ideal girl, according to the narrator, would in this contemporary, urban, neoliberal context, be lifeless, preferably dead, a reflection that gives the novel its title and highlights femininity as a key marker of the stagnation and deadness the work evokes (*vl*, 33).

This novel is set in an era marked as postfeminist. The narrator rejects feminist narratives of progress, terming emancipation a failed project (*vl*, 34). For her, this is "eine Gesellschaft enttäuschter Frauen-Wünsche" (*vl*, 55; a society of disappointed female wishes). Women's work is invisible, women are subordinate to men, and a husband and a child are obligatory, or one is punished. The narrator resolves to kill herself—at the age of thirty-five, at the latest—rather than becoming so dumbly compliant (*vl*, 56–57). This is a bleakly critical diagnosis of a postfeminist society. The narrator can be seen at once to embody postfeminism and to critique it, though her critique leads only to utter negativity—unlike the text itself, which practices and perhaps provokes aggressive, willful reflection. It thereby exposes the "cruel optimism" of feminism.[28] Refusing the ready-made female path, the narrator has no foothold in society. She lies to her parents about having a place at university, when in reality she has nothing: she reflects, "Ich brauche ein Leben, aber ich habe keins" (I need a life, but I have none) (*vl*, 48).

The novel's critical depiction of neoliberalism also finds expression in the representation of the narrator's working life. When the narrator does get a job, it is for a highly satirized magazine, which relies on *kitsch* and cliché (*vl*, 78–79, 89–90). Images of confinement suggest the imprisoning nature of the contemporary workplace (*vl*, 90). Corporate speak is the target of ridicule (*vl*, 96–97). As an employee, the narrator becomes "eine ferngesteuerte Ameise" (*vl*, 108; an ant whose movements are determined by remote control): a description that implies the lack of agency of the neoliberal subject and points up precarity. The narrator willfully performs her own form of protest, inserting into one issue of the magazine the words "Hitler" and "Analsex-mit-Kindern-in-SS-Uniform" (*vl*, 75; anal sex with children in SS-uniform), obscenities that hark back to the horror of Germany's National Socialist past. This gesture can be seen as troubling the bland media talk that whitewashes questions of blame and ethics. Her job, then, fails to provide fulfillment, and she leaves. Later, she searches for a future on the Internet (*vl*, 130)—a detail that points to the digital as a potential locus of agency and ambition that does not live up to its promise.[29]

The novel also challenges the cruel optimism fostered by heterosexual romance narratives, and the "happy stories for girls" to which Ahmed refers.[30] Romantic fulfillment is elusive; once she has dispatched Patrick (whom she appears to murder, though he later appears), the narrator pursues a man called Jo. For all her critique of female dependence on men, she is apparently unable to liberate herself from this model. She is full of venom at her rival for Jo's affections, despite telling herself he is to blame for his infidelity and for his casually cruel treatment of her (*vl*, 175). Romantic love is ultimately deconstructed here. The now pregnant narrator muses:

> Verfaultes Kino, verfaulte Liebeslieder, verfaulte Hotel-Zimmer, verfaulte Blumen, verfaulte Zettel, verfaulte Fotos, verfaulte Wörter, die ganze Sprache verfault . . . Verfaultes *Ich*, verfaultes *liebe*, verfaultes *dich*, alles verfault, gelogen, ausgedacht und nachgemacht, denke ich und spüle den Wein runter zu dem Baby, das keins werden soll. (*vl*, 184)

> [Rotten cinema, rotten love songs, rotten hotel rooms, rotten flowers, rotten notes, rotten photos, rotten words, the whole of language rotten . . . Rotten *I*, rotten *love*, rotten *you*, everything rotten, mendacious, dreamed up, mimicked, I think as I pour down wine to the baby that isn't going to be.]

She has an abortion on the advice of her mother, and later feels she has aborted herself (*vl*, 231). Abortion, then, is not the answer for this female protagonist, though there is no suggestion that motherhood would have been either. Having abandoned university—an intimidating, fearful place where the obsession with the future is again to be found (*vl*, 221–22), and where she studies briefly—she is entrapped and depressed, and, at the end, contemplating suicide. The novel thus depicts contemporary neoliberal, postfeminist society as uninhabitable. The narrator's bile-filled pronouncements act at once as illustrations and critiques of this society. The narrator—and the text—are killjoys, in Ahmed's sense: "to be judged willful is to become a killjoy of the future: the one who . . . gets in the way of a happiness assumed as on the way" (*WS*, 47).

Juli Zeh, *Spieltrieb*

Willfulness characterizes someone who wills "too much, or too little, or 'in the wrong way'" (*WS*, 3). Baum's protagonist wills both too little and wrongly. Juli Zeh's novel *Spieltrieb*, on the other hand, depicts a female will that is both excessive and perverse. Unlike Baum's surreal, bile-filled stream-of-consciousness, Zeh's text takes the form of a controlled thought experiment, and the third-person narration is arch, detached, and self-conscious. *Spieltrieb* tells of Ada, a preternaturally clever teenage girl, and her relationship with fellow pupil Alev. Together they ensnare a teacher, Smutek, whom Ada seduces and whom the pair then blackmail. The novel has already been discussed in terms of its Nietzschean echoes.[31] Stephen Brockmann has also analyzed Zeh's interest in nihilism: like other German writers of her generation, Zeh evinces "a concern with the perceived meaninglessness of contemporary life."[32] Ada and Alev's is a generation "with no criteria or hierarchy for declaring certain ideas or concepts more or less valid than others."[33]

This satirical work underlines the mediated quality of experience in postmodernism, the influence of television and the Internet, and the deadening and ethically harmful effects of such mediation and representation: this is an age of citations ("[ein] Zeitalter der Zitate") (*S*, 136). Ada is thus explicitly embedded in the contemporary context, and she serves a representative function.[34] Her teacher Smutek further diagnoses German young people as lacking an appropriate form of will, critically observing their lack of ambitions and ideals. In his view, these young people have no desires or convictions, let alone ideals. They fail to aspire to any particular job, and wish neither for political influence nor a happy family. The young have no interest in heroes, enemies, or even identities, since these are mass produced and unappealing: "Sie war einfach da, die Sippschaft eines interimistischen Zeitalters" (*S*, 348; They were simply there, the tribe of an interim age). Ada echoes her teacher's diagnosis during her comically long and formal speech in the courtroom where her case is being heard. While problematizing her own use of the pronoun "we" (*wir*), she claims:

> Wir sind nicht einmal in der Lage, eine Familie zu gründen, geschweige denn, uns mit einer Partei zu identifizieren! Wissen Sie, was wir wollen? Wir wollen keine Gemeinschaft. Wir wollen unsere Ruhe . . . Wir passen nicht mehr zu diesem Staat, wir sind dem System vorausgeeilt. (*S*, 551)

> [We are not even in the position to start a family, let alone to identify with a political party! Do you know what we want? We don't want community. We want to be left in peace . . . We don't belong in this state, we've run ahead of the system.]

This rejection of identity and of sociality recalls queer ideas of failure and refusal. Yet one drive does persist: "Spieltrieb" (*S*, 349; play instinct), or a misdirected form of will with ethically disturbing consequences. The novel problematizes this drive, at the same time mining its potential for disturbance and trouble, especially through the figure of Ada.

While Ada may be representative of a contemporary lack of values, of relativism, she is a distinctive character, as well as an outsider: "amoralisch, anormal und asozial" (*S*, 421; amoral, abnormal, and anti-social), as Smutek reflects. "Er mochte sie gern" (*S*, 421; He liked her a lot), the narrator follows up archly, exemplifying the teasing and willful quality of the novel itself, which disrupts generational and gendered norms. Both Ada's age and her gender are unsettled and hard to read (see *S*, 273, 430–31). In the course of the narrative, she ages two years. Her bedroom features children's furniture, but this is swathed in textiles, an image that suggests her instructive position between childhood and adulthood, and recalls Smith-Prei and Stehle's understanding of adolescence as awkward (*S*, 102). Ada's becoming is nonstandard, even oppositional. The narrator contrasts her with other girls whose development follows an apparently destined feminine path:

> In allen Klassen ab der siebenten gab es samt- und seidenweiche Mädchen, deren Geburt durch langsam anschwellende Musik begleitet worden war wie das hochfahrende Windowsbetriebssystem von seiner Begrüßungsouvertüre. Sie kamen als Miniaturprinzessinnen zur Welt, erreichten bereits in der Unterstufe das erste, fohlenhafte Stadium der Vollendung und wuchsen gleichmäßig in die Frau hinein, die sie einmal werden sollten. Ihre Entwicklung vollzog sich routiniert und fehlerlos, als hätten sie die Aufgabe des Älterwerdens schon etliche Male zuvor bewältigt. Jene Pubertätsprofis unterschieden sich auf den ersten Blick von den Dilettanten. Sie hatten

das gepflegte, schulterlange Haar erwachsener Frauen, trugen ihre Hüfthosen, breiten Gürtel und knappen Hemdchen mit wohl-temperierter Lässigkeit und ließen glatte Kinderhaut und aufge-worfene Kindermünder zu Mädchenhaut und Mädchenmündern werden, ohne dass Pickel, Schweißausbrüche oder Wachstumslaunen zu irgendeinem Zeitpunkt die Harmonie ihrer Erscheinungen gestört hätten. (*S*, 11–12)

[There were, in every class from the seventh on, girls as soft as vel-vet and silk, whose births had been accompanied by music, slowly swelling, like Windows starting up, greeting one with its overture. They came to earth in the form of miniature princesses, achieved the first, foal-like stage of completion already in the lower sixth and grew steadily into the women they were destined to become. Their development occurred in a routine, error-free manner, as if they had already mastered the task of growing older a number of times. You could differentiate between these puberty pros and the amateurs immediately. They had the well-cared-for, shoulder-length hair of grown women, wore hipsters, wide belts and tight tops with well-tempered casualness and let smooth child's skin and turned-up child's mouths become girl's skin and girls' mouths, without spots, outbreaks of sweat, or mood-swings disrupting the harmony of their appearances for a single moment.]

The sardonic narration informs us further that such "Prinzessinnen" (princesses) possess an aura of cleanliness and are only ever decorative. They have no ambition, undertaking only light sport and reading only light literature. They are mediocre students whose life goes downhill after leaving school. Ada, the narrative spells out, is "das Gegenteil einer Prinzessin, sofern Prinzessinnen ein Gegenteil besitzen" (*S*, 12; the oppo-site of a princess, insofar as princesses have an opposite). The reference to "Prinzessinnen" points to a dominant form of femininity as demure and decorative, an image Ada—with her physical strength, her cleverness, and her refusal to take part in "der Kaffeefahrt namens 'glückliche Kindheit'" (*S*, 13; the outing named "happy childhood")—challenges. She is consid-ered "hochbegabt und schwer erziehbar" (*S*, 12; highly gifted and hard to educate).

Ada is thus an oppositional and awkward figure, resistant to the straightening device of education and so willful in Ahmed's terms. The role of education as socializing influence is clear here. The school that Ada attends specializes in difficult pupils, combining discipline and kindness, "Zuckerbrot" and "Peitsche" (*S*, 41; carrot, stick). The school produces students able to take their *Abitur* "in einem Zustand gemäßigter Revolte, gemischt mit sporadischer Anpassung" (*S*, 41–42;

in a condition of tempered revolt, mixed with sporadic conformity). The headmaster takes a paternalistic view of his pupils as prodigal sons, leading Smutek to wonder if Ada, whom he sees regularly smoking in the yard, is one such son (*S*, 42). The novel also satirizes heteronormative and nostalgic views of young people. Ada and Alev, whose relationship is not at all conventionally romantic, are the objects of idealization and romanticization on the part of mothers watching them from their kitchen windows on their way to school: "[Sie] dachten jeden Morgen, was für eine wunderschöne Szene das sei und wie die beiden Kinder da draußen eines Tages heiraten würden, um selbst Kinder zu zeugen und an Küchenfenstern zu stehen, schwach von einer Sehnsucht, die sich so entschieden in die Vergangenheit richtete, als gäbe es dort etwas zu holen" (*S*, 375–76; Every morning, they thought about what a lovely scene it was and how the children out there would one day get married, themselves to have children and to stand at kitchen windows, weak with a longing that was so determinedly directed toward the past, as if there were something to be got from it). This caustic observation involves a challenge to reproductive futurism and also suggests the cruel optimism involved in "the heterofamilial, upwardly mobile good-life fantasy"—to refer again to Berlant—which is geared toward the future but paradoxically rests on nostalgia.[35]

In reality, Ada and Alev are unlikely to reproduce, given Alev's non-standard sexuality (he is impotent). They also bring about Sputek's ruin for the sake of a game (*S*, 284). The seduction of a man by a girl turns conventional power relations on their head. Zeh's book is a game itself, and so, as Brockmann suggests, it would be a mistake to read these characters as realistic.[36] But Zeh's is at the least a striking tale. The seduction of Smutek underlines Ada's control; Smutek appears to lose agency and be subjected to the purely corporeal. His desire only becomes apparent after the act is realized: "Als er in sie eingedrungen war, wusste er, dass er genau das gewollt hatte" (*S*, 327; Having penetrated her, he knew that he had wished for just this). Carrie Smith-Prei and Lars Richter discuss the link between sex, power, and ethics in the text, suggesting: "the variegated desires depicted in the game between Ada, Alev, and Smutek . . . as well as their disturbances are rooted in physical, identity-political, and emotional otherness, which causes a rift in a presumably clear-cut dichotomy of good and evil. Desire appears as structure."[37] While Ada could be seen as a conduit connecting the two main male characters, who arguably engage in homosocial bonding, the authors suggest that she is, more significantly, "an irritant or disruptive factor."[38] Ada herself challenges the idea that she is a victim, a thesis the text as a whole does not support, denying that she has been traumatized by her parents' divorce and is the victim of male abuse. She refuses, in fact, to make any statement that would feed into such a narrative.[39]

This text, in its self-consciousness, in fact problematizes the very idea of narrative—and, indeed, the idea of individuality.[40] In this way, the becoming it presents constitutes a challenge to individualist, neoliberal accounts of the self. What emerges here are complex, interlinked subjectivities and discourses. Owing in particular to its arch, self-conscious narration and its multiperspectival quality, the novel presents social realities as constructed and shifting. This curious text additionally overturns assumptions about femininity as decorative and stupid, asserting female strength and intelligence, or will. Ada is not laudable or "likeable." But such a reflection is misplaced, since the novel does not deal in (conventional literary) "characters," and since "likeability" is an unhelpfully gendered category which serves to bolster norms relating to femininity as agreeable and unthreatening.[41] Its archness, its formality, its self-consciousness, and its frequent and deliberate references to the characters' historical, social, and political contexts invite us to read it as a kind of treatise on will, ethics, and individuality, where all of these terms are subjected to analysis and redefinition. In particular, the novel's challenge to the categories of identity and individuality suggest, in line with Ahmed, that "willful subjects are not necessarily individual persons" (*WS*, 175). It invites us to see disruptions of the sort Ada practices in broader social and cultural terms, as troublesome challenges to (understandings of) the social order.

Zoë Jenny, *Das Blütenstaubzimmer*

In Zeh, female will is forceful and perverse. In Zoë Jenny's *Das Blütenstaubzimmer*, it appears muted and inadequate.[42] The eighteen-year-old first-person narrator Jo seems to lack agency, drifting into situations over which she has no control: that is to say, she wills too little (cf. *WS*, 3). Yet Jo's lack of a fixed base or home is also in line with Ahmed's understanding of willfulness as involving a failure to fit in. The text itself, in its irresolution, is also wayward, refusing to commit to a solution for its protagonist. In the novel, Jo travels to an unnamed southern European country that shares smiliarities with Italy. Her mother Lucy now lives here, having left the family home when Jo was a child. However, "die Reise als Mittel zur Ich-Findung ist in vielerlei Hinsicht gescheitert" (travel as a means of self-discovery was in many respects a failure).[43] Jo fails to establish a connection with Lucy, who is traumatized as a result of the recent death of her partner, Alois.[44] Jo's father, meanwhile, is moving to the country with his partner and stepdaughter, with whom Jo does not get on. Later, he reveals he and his partner are expecting a child. Jo remains detached from society, even sociality.

In this text too, the older generation appears uncaring, even negligent. The novel has indeed been seen as constituting "eine [*sic*] der ersten und radikalsten Romane der Technogeneration, adressiert in aller Härte an die 68er Eltern" (one of the first and most radical novels by the techno-generation, addressed to the 68ers and packing no punches).[45] Ingrid Löwer conducts a detailed analysis of the novel in these terms, reading Jo's father, who runs a non-profit-making small press, as an idealistic, anti-materialistic "68er."[46] She suggests that the novel ultimately demonstrates the failure of "alle neuen Formen familialen Zusammenlebens, die mit dem 'sozialen Wandel' nach der 68er-Bewegung aufkamen" (73; all new forms of familial togetherness that arose alongside 'social change' post-68). Löwer interprets Jo's mother as representing a vulgar form of feminism, used here as a justification for immaturity and egotism.[47] The novel reads as an extended critique of parental selfishness and lack of responsibility. The small pair of shoes that Lucy failed to post to her daughter when she was a child stands now as a symbol of this neglect (*B*, 40; *PR*, 46). Lucy passes Jo off as her younger sister, not wishing to reveal her status as a mother to a male friend (*B*, 45; *PR*, 53). Jo calls her "Lucy," not "Mom." The poignancy of this situation emerges when Jo listens to her mother in the kitchen, and indulges in regressive fantasies of being a cared-for child:

> Lucy ist in der Küche und bereitet das Abendessen für Vito vor. Wie festgefroren warte ich im Garten darauf, daß sie nach mir ruft, damit ich ihr beim Kochen helfe. Ich warte auf ihre Stimme, aber sie ruft mich nicht, ich vernehme nur ihre Schritte auf dem Steinboden und das Klappern von Pfannen. Mit offenen Augen versinke ich in einen Traum, in dem ich mir vorstelle, daß ich viel jünger bin und meine Mutter in der Küche steht und das Abendessen für uns zubereitet, während ich die Schulaufgaben mache. (*B*, 47)

> [Lucy's in the kitchen making dinner for Vito. I wait in the garden, frozen in place, hoping that she'll ask me to come in and help her cook. I wait to hear her voice, but she doesn't call. I listen to her footsteps going back and forth. I hear the clattering pans. With my eyes still open, I slip into a waking dream in which I imagine myself much younger. My mother stands in the kitchen preparing our supper while I do my homework at the table. (*PR*, 55)]

Jo has never experienced the threatening, corrective rod of parental or educational discipline, yet the result of her upbringing is nonetheless a breaking of her will. Ahmed defines will as "an experience a subject has of itself as bringing something about" (*WS*, 24). In Jo's case there is no such agency in evidence. Contemporary feminine willfulness might not be the result of overt coercion or discipline, but rather of a lack of credible ideals, meaningful social or familial bonds, or role models—this in line with

Baum and with Zeh. I will return to this argument in the conclusion to this chapter.

The narrative is in general flat and affectless. As Löwer notes, there is little reflection or commentary (74). Löwer explores Jenny's narrative technique extensively, arguing that the many flashbacks in the novel demonstrate how caught up the protagonist is in her memories: "Dadurch stellt sich beim Lesen das Gefühl ein, die Protagonistin komme nicht wirklich 'vom Fleck,' habe Vergangenes nicht aufarbeiten oder bewältigen können" (67; So one gets the feeling as a reader that the protagonist can't really move on, and has not been able to process or master her past). This device also suggests how the subject is getting "in the way" of her own development (cf. WS, 77). Imagery is another important device in signaling the narrator's awkward failure to progress. The narrator lacks a secure place in the world, a state the following passage reflects:

> Ich lege mich auf den von der Sonne erwärmten Stein. Hier sollte ich liegenbleiben, denke ich, und werden wie dieser Stein. Anfangs würden vielleicht lärmende Spaziergänger kommen und sich in die Wanne legen, aber irgendwann würde es vollkommen still sein, Moos über mich wachsen . . . und sogar das Wasser würde versiegen. (B, 35)

> [I lie back on the warm stone. I should just stay here, I think, until I become part of this stone. At first, perhaps, noisy people would come to take a dip in the pool, but eventually the path would seal itself off and it would be quiet here. Moss would grow over me . . . and even the water would subside. (PR, 41)]

Shortly after, she notices butterflies in the water, and begins to retrieve them using a stalk of grass, but they take flight and head back for the water, "in den Tod" (B, 36; back into the fatal water, PR, 41).[48] This air of fatality is redolent of queer challenges to futurism. Jo's desire to merge with nature brings to mind both Ahmed and Grosz in its challenge to anthropocentric accounts of agency (WS, 193–94). Imagery woven throughout the narrative means that death appears omnipresent, Löwer notes (82). The death of Alois, more concretely, evokes mortality. The narrator also imagines herself dead in a morgue in a vivid and detailed fashion.[49] She pictures a man in green scrubs and his colleague making a dirty joke about her corpse, and laughing: an image that remains with her, seeming to stick to her brain. Her body is figured in terms of objectification. Jo also recalls a sexual encounter in which she is passive; it leads to an abortion (B, 88; PR, 103). Like Baum's novel, this work suggests feminine passivity, even lifelessness.

Torpor and isolation are the hallmarks of this text. The narrator lacks drive, or will: she feels hunger but has no desire to feed herself, or, for that matter, to eat alone (*B*, 44; *PR*, 52). She remains muted and marginal. For example, she watches two girls reading: "Das aufgeschlagene Heft auf ihren Knien wirkt wie das Verbindungsstück einer einzigen gegossenen Figur. Sie sind versunken . . . und heben den Kopf auch nicht, als ich absichtlich laut hustend an ihnen vorübergehe" (*B*, 69; The book between them is a bridge, like a structure that connects the figures in a large cast-iron sculpture. They are completely engrossed . . . and don't even raise their heads as I pass by, though I make a point of breathing loudly, *PR*, 80). In opposition to these girls, who are firmly and solidly connected— by literature, significantly—Jo is isolated. She does meet a girl, Rea, and a kind of intimacy establishes itself, but it is founded on lies. The girls' plan to go to America is unrealistic and never transpires. Löwer comments that the women in this text "treiben . . . ziellos durchs Leben und überlegen sich romantische Fluchtvarianten, ohne sie konkret zu füllen oder aus-zuführen" (84; drift . . . aimlessly through life and indulge in romantic dreams of escape, without being able to fulfill or carry them out). Female intimacy, a matter chapter 4 discusses further, appears unrealizable here, a key factor in the narrator's condition.

Jo fails to express herself, remaining largely silent; paradoxically, this first-person narrative is a study in repression. The narrator's disturbed dreams hint at her trauma, but at least, she reflects, she no longer wakes screaming from nightmares: "Ich hasse meine Träume. Aber ich schreie nicht mehr" (*B*, 68; I hate my dreams. But at least I no longer wake screaming, *PR*, 79). Rather than suggesting progress, this detail implies instead that Jo has become better at repressing her feelings: another method of getting in the way of her own will. Images of darkness and confinement further imply a troubled psyche, as does the closing image of the snow (*B*, 112–13, 122; *PR*, 132, 143). At the end of the narrative, Jo is still lacking a supportive family or any meaningful connection to others or the world. She appears to have no interests or ambitions and so can be seen to bear out Zeh's evocation of isolated, disengaged youthful subjects. In Jo's case, however, will itself appears to be lacking, and there is a distinct lack of the vitalism we see in Moran, say, as discussed later. But willfulness—where this involves a failure to fit in and adopt the norms and expectations of a society—does manifest itself here, though it is anxious and decidedly lacking in optimism (cf. *WS*, 174).

Helene Hegemann, *Axolotl Roadkill*

Axolotl Roadkill is both a nightmarish and surreal trip that recalls Baum and an arch, self-conscious text that at points brings to mind Zeh. Its sixteen-year-old protagonist, Mifti, who lives in Prenzlauer Berg with her half-siblings, Annika and Edmond, also in some respects recalls Jenny's isolated, parentified protagonist. As a young girl, Mifti appears to have taken responsibility for her "soziopathisches Elternteil" (sociopath parent), her alcoholic mother, who died when her daughter was thirteen.[50] Mifti moved from Düsseldorf to Berlin to live with her father, a remote figure of whom she sees little. The novel consists of loosely connected scenes, as Mifti, described by one reviewer as "ein Nervenzusammenbruch auf zwei Beinen" (a nervous breakdown on two legs), staggers around Berlin in a state of intoxication.[51] Mifti manifests a queer willfulness. The novel's thematization of failure, and its own failure to be clearly legible or obviously useful, are also queer, recalling Edelman and Halberstam.[52]

In formal terms, the novel's dissonance and disconnectedness pose a challenge to what literary critic Iris Radisch describes as "unsere alte Literatur der bürgerlichen Subjektivität mit ihren subtilen Noten" (our old literature of bourgeois subjectivity with its subtle notes); Hegemann's vision is "echt-unecht . . . herrschaftsfrei . . . gesetzlos . . . jargonverschmiert . . . polysexuell und undurchschaubar" (genuine-fake . . . free of mastery . . . anarchic . . . smeared with jargon . . . polysexual and impenetrable).[53] The narrative offers little in the way of guidance. The preface begins only on page twenty-one; this is not a linear narrative, then, but a self-consciously ruptured one. Drug-induced lacunae mean that there are gaps in the narrative. The occasional use of lists, as well as text messages and emails, serves further to disrupt the idea of a single, all-knowing narrator. The novel explicitly reflects on the role of language in the construction of the subject, in line with Radisch's view of the work as challenging the taken-for-grantedness of bourgeois subjectivity: Mifti considers, for example, "Mir wurde eine Sprache einverleibt, die nicht meine eigene ist" (*AR*, 47; They've imbued me with a language that is not my own, 42). The novel's self-declared intertextual quality accords with Mifti's understanding of language as having its own life, and of the subject as dependent upon it (*AR*, 208). The novel quotes frequently.[54] Smith-Prei and Stehle usefully describe the novel's fragmentary and intertextual aesthetic as "awkward."[55]

The novel presents a decentered subject in a process of becoming marked by trauma, failure, and refusal. The narrator reports that she wakes up screaming "weil so viele Gedanken da sind, dass man seine eigenen Gedanken gar nicht mehr von den fremden unterscheiden kann" (*AR*, 7–8; because there are so many thoughts that you can't distinguish your own from other people's, 1). Mifti struggles to define herself. As she puts it, "Es ist megahart, ein Individuum zu sein" (*AR*, 159–160; It's mega-tough being an individual, 157). Trauma is possibly behind Mifti's state: Mifti refers to people who are "(im weitesten Sinne) traumatisiert" (*AR*, 72; traumatized [in the broadest sense], 68), apparently classifying herself as such. "Psychosis" offers another possible label, with Mifti providing the textbook-style observation: "Auffällige Symptome für eine Psychose sind Halluzinationen" (*AR*, 79; Hallucinations are clear symptoms of psychosis, 75). Elsewhere, she speculates that she has borderline personality disorder, a diagnosis another character dismisses as vague (*AR*, 73).[56] Mifti is in addition found to be incurable and "therapieresistent" (*AR*, 147, 171; therapy-resistant, 144, 169). Her own view is that believing "Psychologiescheiß" (psychology crap) can cure ills is mere superstition (*AR*, 175; 173). Thus she rejects psychoanalysis, insisting on her own perversity. Hegemann views Mifti as courageous in this respect:

> Miftis Situation hat mich literarisch interessiert: komplett befreit zu sein von Konventionen, was aber nicht möglich ist, ohne sich komplett zu zerstören. Sie hat nichts mehr mit der regulären Auffassung eines Teenagers zu tun. Und die, die sie liebt, den abwesenden Vater, die ältere Modelfreundin, sind gleichzeitig ihre Anti-Vorbilder. Mifti ist mehr als nur irgendeine Drogenabhängige vom Kotti, sie hat eine Biografie. Und sie entscheidet sich bewusst für eine negative Entwicklung, indem sie Heroin probiert. Das zeugt auch von Mut.[57]

> [Mifti's situation interested me as a writer: being completely liberated from conventions, which isn't possible without destroying yourself totally. She has nothing to do with the regular idea of a teenager. And those she loves, her absent father, the older model-friend, are at the same time anti-role-models to her. Mifti isn't just some druggie at the U-bahn station, she has a biography. And she consciously decides on a negative development in trying heroin. That shows courage.]

Mifti's "negative Entwicklung" (negative development) is thus a positive choice, and involves both destruction and liberation. It also bears comparison with Hegemann's own self-diagnosed "failure" to conform to dominant stereotypes of young people, a failure I have read as queer. In particular, I suggest that Mifti's and Hegemann's refusal or inability to fit in, to look to positive role models, exemplifies what Halberstam terms "the queer art of failure."[58]

It also involves willfulness. Despite the dangerous consquences, Mifti rules out the idea of doing anything but what she wants: "Es ist gefährlich, das zu tun, was ich will, weil mich das wirklich verletzbar macht. Es zu lassen ist vollkommen unmöglich" (*AR*, 21; Doing what I want is dangerous because it really makes me vulnerable. Not doing it is not an option, 15). Mifti's prioritizing of desire recalls Ahmed, for whom willfulness describes subjects "whose will is in accordance with their own desire" (*WS*, 85). Mifti's refusal to go to school—to undergo *Bildung*—is explained by her as an act of desperation, for example, since she finds the process rigid and imprisoning (*AR*, 99). She resists the straightening rod of education, and asserts her own will. In this sense her refusal is vitalist: she claims to favor "das unseriöse Element am Leben . . . das Vorläufige, das Luxuriöse und das Spielerische" (*AR*, 99; the unserious side of life . . . the provisional, the luxurious and the playful elements, 96). At this point, Mifti's willfulness appears optimistic (cf. *WS*, 174). In a passage in which she introduces herself to the reader, she explains comparably that despite the cost, she is compelled to reject society, and in particular what it means for her—namely, school and depression: "Ich bin sechzehn Jahre alt und momentan zu nichts anderem mehr in der Lage, als mich trotz kolossaler Erschöpfung in Zusammenhängen etablieren zu wollen, die nichts mit der Gesellschaft zu tun haben, in der ich zur Schule gehe und depressiv bin" (*AR*, 22; I'm sixteen years old and presently capable of nothing but wanting to establish myself—despite colossal exhaustion—in contexts that have nothing to do with the society in which I go to school and suffer from depression, 16). Discussing Hegemann's film, *Torpedo*, Smith-Prei and Stehle note "the defiant *no* of the adolescent who refuses systemic control and disrupts power structures," a description that applies to Mifti's comparable gestures of refusal in the novel.[59]

This refusal ties in with the text's challenge to conventional generational categories. One character tells Mifti that when he was her age, he was not smoking but instead learning how to tie balloons. There is here an ironic exposure of idealizations of childhood and youth, such as we find in Zeh. Mifti rejects such sentimentalization, responding with a mocking repetition of his words—a kind of critical mimicry—and reflecting explicitly: "Wie mich das alles ankotzt, diese Erwachsenenschwadroniererei" (*AR*, 20; It makes me want to puke, all that adult blustering and filibustering, 14). Mifti's position as a teenager grants her a vantage point from which to view critically the constructs adulthood and childhood.[60] The figure of the axolotl, a kind of salamander that remains in a state of suspended youthfulness, acts as an image for this in-between state. The narrator's identity as a teenager is hardly fixed, however, but subject to repeated, playful redefinition. Mifti evokes a performative view of her own youthful persona: "Ich . . . erfreue mich an der von mir perfekt dargestellten Attitüde des arroganten, misshandelten Arschkindes, das mit seiner versnobten Kaputtheit kokettiert und die Kaputtheit seines Umfeldes gleich mit entlarvt" (*AR*, 47; I . . . am pretty pleased at my perfectly displayed attitude of arrogant, abused arsehole of a kid that flirts with its snobbish fucked-up status, unmasking the whole fucked-up status of its entire surroundings in one fell swoop, 42). This declaration is irritating in its simultaneous suggestion and refutation of a symbolic or revelatory function to Mifti's persona. Willfully perverse, it ties in with journalistic reactions to Hegemann herself, as exposing kidulthood and general dysfunction, but also coquettishly performing for an audience, in a self-aggrandizing and narcisstic fashion.

Generation and age are thus uncertain terms in the novel. When in the company of her schoolmates, Mifti is a silent, integrated member of a group of young people. However, Mifti's precocity still marks her out (*AR*, 94). Mifti therefore fails to take her proper place in society. As Ahmed notes, "A queer girl stretches the meaning of *girl*."[61] What are the broader implications of Mifti's, and Hegemann's, refusal to toe the line in this respect? As we have seen, Hegemann's novel casts doubt upon the possibility of individuality. But it does not attempt to establish a historical context or a lineage for its decentred protagonist, who instead remains unanchored. Mifti's resistance to social groupings that rely on age suggest that generationality, for her, is not an "answer" to the question of identity. This novel is thus both post-individual and post-generational, occupying instead a queer space that privileges failed, fractured modes of being/becoming. The novel is queer not only in its challenges to heterosexism and its assertion of nonnormative desires, but also in its rejection of normality. The novel criticizes and satirizes dominant, mainstream ideals. Early on in the novel, Mifti asserts:

> Ich will ein Kinderheim in Afghanistan bauen und viele Anziehsachen haben. Ich brauche nicht nur Essen und ein Dach über dem Kopf, sondern drei titanweiß ausgestattete Villen, jeden Tag bis zu elf Prostituierte und ein mich in plüschigen, güldenen Zwanziger-Jahre-Chic hüllendes Sowjet-Uniform-Kostüm von Chanel. (*AR*, 8–9)

> [I want to build a children's home in Afghanistan and own loads of clothes. I don't just need food and a roof over my head; I need three villas with titanium white fixtures and fittings, up to eleven prostitutes every day and a Soviet-style Chanel suit swathing me in plush golden twenties chic. (2–3)]

This comically excessive vision points to the grotesque materialism of the age, evoking a rapacious consumerism that is apparently tempered by showy acts of charity. Hegemann's work thus evokes an individualistic, materialistic society whose norms Mifti both mocks and internalizes. The novel offers an invitation to embrace failure and abnormality, and critically to examine what passes for success and acceptability today: to lean out. Hegemann's vision of a decentred subject, neither an individual nor a member of a generation, queer and postnational, offers no usable answers. Its negativity and perversity force us to rethink how we might conceive the postfeminist female subject. As Smith-Prei and Stehle argue, "The text . . . presents readers with their own cruelly optimistic stance towards the societal expectations for girls, a stance that also counters lifestyle feminism's positive coding of empowerment."[62] And Hester Baer observes Mifti's critique of "globally ascendant hegemonic femininity."[63] But although the novel, like Baum's, seems to mock the feminist project and view it as a failure (see *AR*, 19), Mifti does evince a kind of gut feminism, as the early reference to her "Magen-Darm-Exzesse[ ]" (*AR*, 8; gastric excesses, 8) suggests. When Mifti's body appears to scream, we witness the bodily assertion of willfulness (*AR*, 188). Her queer desires supplement this assertion, as I argue further in chapter 5.

Emma Jane Unsworth, *Animals*

The young female protagonists I have discussed so far are all clearly oppositional or outsider figures. Emma Jane Unsworth's novel *Animals*, however, features an older character standing before the threshold to normality and adulthood.[64] At thirty-two, Laura Joyce is the oldest of the protagonists addressed here, but given that her current condition involves a staving-off of adult norms and lifestyles, and a consideration of what such norms entail, it is instructive. Laura is struggling with making the transition from her current existence, which involves frequent drunkenness, to a more sober form of life. Her dilemma is represented by two characters who embody her opposing desires: her hard-drinking American friend, Tyler, who owns the flat they share in Manchester, and her teetotal concert-pianist fiancé, Jim. This triangular relationship is a source of conflict and acts as a means of crystallizing the protagonist's dilemma: whether or how to move on from her current life, and what course to choose, where choice emerges in the narrative as a problematic notion. The self here is at odds with itself as well as with social norms: the text explicitly reflects on the matters of will and willpower.

The novel starts with a hungover awakening and with an impressionistic evocation of the night before that is reminiscent of Hegemann: "A montage of images spooled through the brainfug. Fizzy wine, flat wine, city streets, cubicles, highly experimental burlesque moves on bar stools" (*A*, 1).[65] Such episodes are habitual, constituting "a chain of events that amounted to the same headache, the same ransacked purse, same wasted day-after" (*A*, 5). This existence involves denial and self-deception (*A*, 2, 5). In this sense, it is not an authentic life—but the alternatives, especially mothering and domesticity—do not seem promising. In this way, the narrator represents the cultural contradictions of youthful femininity as outlined in my introduction. The young women's relationship to domesticity—shopping, cooking, cleaning—is oppositional and involves a rejection of norms relating to adult feminine behaviors.[66] Laura and Tyler are, in this sense, "definitely still girls."[67] Their attitude toward motherhood likewise suggests resistance to dominant or ideal forms of femininity. Tyler's sister gives birth at the age of twenty-eight, and the response of Tyler and the narrator is one of mournfulness and disappointment;

pregnancy amounts to a "betrayal" (*A*, 8). Tyler's friend, Agnes, has also "'gone over to the dark side' (childrearing)" (*A*, 81). Tyler equates becoming a parent with "suddenly losing all your privacy, all your hope of self-development" (*A*, 17): that is to say, with a lack of sovereignty and agency. Laura, for her part, observes fatigued new parents, "bloodshot, sleep-starved, unsexed," desperate to preserve their legacy: "*And yet you're still going to die—that's the punchline!*" (*A*, 12). Such a perspective on parenting, legacy, and futurity is redolent of queer challenges to reproductive futurism and to dominant views as exemplified in the novel by Jacqueline, a mother Laura visits who appears to think that "a childless woman was The Most Tragic Thing she could think of" (*A*, 146).

Laura's own ambivalence when it comes to mothering is clear (*A*, 17). It finds expression in the fact of her having unprotected sex with Jim, which leads her to muse on the possibility of her being pregnant. Jim points out that conception would be more likely if Laura did not smoke (*A*, 119).[68] The question of maternity causes tensions between Tyler and Laura. When Tyler learns that Laura and Jim are not using contraception, she feels betrayed (*A*, 127). The questions of will, choice, and agency, are complex here: Laura tells Tyler that parenting is something best begun unwittingly, given the rigors it brings with it (*A*, 127). Laura also questions whether maternity, and particularly conception and pregnancy, is truly an act of voluntarism: "did you feel it as a desire that was totally yours?" she asks Jacqueline:

> "Or was it a case of feeling like some sort of failure if you didn't?
> . . . it's just a physical state, isn't it, so why is there a value attached?
> Or did you love her, Daisy [her daughter] I mean, when she was
> *in there*, did you feel that? Because that changes things, I'm sure.
> I suppose I'm just scared of not knowing why I'm doing what I'm
> doing." (*A*, 147)

When Jacqueline responds that she did not want to miss out on anything, Laura wonders if that is not the impulse of a spoilt child. Maternity, then, does not necessarily represent an ethical ideal, or a positive and empowering choice. Laura's question as to Jacqueline's possible fear of failure hints at the neoliberal imperative to self-regulate and "succeed" in conventional terms, and at her critical awareness of this injunction.

Tyler also resists dominant expectations and assumptions as far as parenting is concerned, explaining to Laura that if she does decide to become a parent, "it'll be something I just do and not something I try and sell as an exclusive event" (*A*, 124). She resists the marketing and packaging of parenthood as a "club," asserting on her own "developing theories" and her "longing" as constants. By her own account, then, she is a subject-in-process: nomadic, in Braidotti's terms. She and her sister argue about the matter, with Jean accusing Tyler of immaturity and suggesting she needs to "grow up" (*A*, 125), a conversation that calls to mind Halberstam's discussion of models of temporality and maturity in Western culture. For Jean, becoming a parent is an adventure. For Tyler, it represents stasis and entrapment; moreover, it is more ethical *not* to reproduce, given overpopulation (*A*, 126–27). As elsewhere in the novel, such discussions bring together personal tensions with broader sociopolitical and cultural debates. Later, Jean is reported as having gone back into rehab (*A*, 155), so that the links between parenthood and sobriety, maturity and coupledom, emerge as less than clear-cut.

Marriage, comparably, represents a daunting prospect to Laura: while it had previously seemed irrelevant, even abstract, now, "it was white and huge and heavy and expensive, like a Fifties American fridge" (*A*, 11). The future appears oppressive and limiting: Laura experiences "panic, the feeling that we were somehow closing down, reducing possibilities" (*A*, 49). The wedding industry is also subjected to satire: Laura looks at a bridal magazine whose cover shows "an actor-bride . . . with . . . stony whited eyes and rictus grin" (*A*, 62–63). Tyler refers to the traditional wedding in dismissive terms, as "a barely evolved pagan ceremony for needy morons" (*A*, 80). The principle of monogamy is also suspect. Laura has in fact always wondered about its practicability, especially given present-day longevity (*A*, 185). But she nonetheless acknowledges the binding nature of individual contracts between partners.[69] In conversation with Tyler, she introduces the question of sexual ethics, reflecting: "To not dismiss possibilities is immoral" (*A*, 185).

Being "before" marriage and motherhood, Laura is currently free to drink and take drugs, but this freedom is problematic. Laura makes a feminist case for concerns about women drinking resting on patriarchal principles. She avers that women's bodies are not seen as their own, but rather as birthing machines (*A*, 136). Seen in this light, Tyler and she occupy defiant positions, Laura with increasing ambivalence. But her view is challenged by an academic called Marty, who points out that the alcohol and tobacco companies are owned by "the capitalists responsible for sustaining the very system you want to crack." When Laura protests that drinking and drug-taking are matters of "choice," he challenges her: "Wanna bet?" (*A*, 136). Notably, when Laura later decides not to take drugs, she appeals to the idea of "free will" (*A*, 161). Her earlier appeal to choice appears even more problematic, for it was apparently at odds with "free will." A discussion about the "internalisation" of norms introduces greater complexity, implying that individual psyches and broader cultural formations cannot be disentangled (*A*, 204). References to physics involve a further refinement of the questions of choice and agency:

> In the quantum multiverse all eventualities are possible. Which means, paradoxically, that all eventualities are inevitable. They have also quite possibly already happened. Make of that what you will, not that your will has much to do with it. Because here's the thing. . . . There is no x and y, no cause and effect. Nothing is inevitable because it doesn't have *time* to be inevitable. You just are, all at once. Living for the moment isn't even a choice. (*A*, 203)

This reflection gains support later on, when Laura considers further the question of "willpower" and "saying no" (to drink and drugs): "Somewhere in a parallel universe, a Laura Joyce was constantly saying no. This thought was spiritually comforting for two reasons: a) that a version of me with perpetual willpower could exist, and b) that I didn't have to be her" (*A*, 213). This humorous reflection asserts willpower as at once desirable and undesirable. It recalls Ahmed's discussion of Augustine: "willing . . . is *not* or *not yet* to carry out what is willed." Willing in fact rests on the dividedness, or self-variance, of the subject: "on a subject that is out of time with itself" (*WS*, 29).

Unsworth's novel reflects on causality and motivation: Laura attributes to "The Night" her susceptibility to the lure of alcohol and drugs, figuring it as a tempting force that is outside of, yet complicit, with herself (*A*, 29). The question of will recurs in this context. Laura is induced to go out by Tyler (and The Night), and to take cocaine. But it was her own desire that compelled her; she herself wanted to: "*Wanted*. Therein lies the crux . . . *This is my will*" (*A*, 33). As far as her relationship to drugs is concerned, she claims not to be addicted. Yet "ironically," this fuels her desire to continue taking drugs (*A*, 33)—a further challenge to ideas of will and willpower, desire and need, as straightforward matters. We might see Laura as perverse: she has no real need or excuse for her self-destructive behavior, unlike Tyler. While Laura was an "anxious" child who felt "pressured," as she reported to the psychiatrist she saw at age twelve, Tyler appears to have clearer cause to be dysfunctional, and part of Laura envies her friend's "dark causality" (*A*, 89–90, 183). Tyler harnesses her own destructiveness: "The Night didn't beckon Tyler— she summoned it, saddled it and rode it down the street" (*A*, 229). Tyler's willfulness—the coincidence of her desire and her will—recalls that of Mifti. Jean indeed says of her sister: "She's always been more wilful than me" (*A*, 125).

As in other works I discuss, health and well-being—self-care—are thus low down the list of the protagonist's priorities ("I drank water like it was a job to do" [*A*, 5]). Laura has had gout (*A*, 22). The recommended weekly allowance of alcohol for women is in her view laughably small (*A*, 22). The narrator in fact reflects on alcohol at some length. She drinks "to settle the battles within, or at least freeze-frame them" (*A*, 27).

Intoxication involves a welcome escape from reality—"I *tire* of reality" (*A*, 195)—in particular the reality of the divided, messy self. Jim, who does not drink, apparently has no need of such escape. He is attractive to the narrator precisely because he knows who he is, in contrast to her, "a fucking shambles" (*A*, 11). The narrator's is periodically a "broken" self (*A*, 113). Yet at the same time, mythologies of the self are questionable (*A*, 43–44). The novel thus asserts selfhood as an untidy and trouble-some matter. It also explores the role of others in willing, of relationality: Ahmed describes willing as "a way we experience inhabiting a world with others" (*WS*, 26). As we have seen, Tyler and Jim embody, and affect, Laura's will. Laura is aware of her own susceptibility to others: she spurns the Internet, for example, and does not trust social networking because she gets too "*involved*" (*A*, 21; cf. *A*, 107). The novel situates its protag-onist in class terms: she is "first-generation middle-class with an unstable core of entitlement and parents poised at home for results" (*A*, 24; cf. *A*, 13, 27). This is one factor, perhaps, in Laura's lack of a foothold in society, and in her unstable self. Her current job in a call center typifies contemporary widespread precarity (*A*, 230). She is writing an absurd-sounding novel that sounds unpublishable (*A*, 19). In terms of her rela-tionship to educational institutions: like other protagonists here, Laura's attitude toward education is ambivalent. Her literary studies have inspired her, but she has now left education, and academia does not appear attrac-tive (see *A*, 129).

For all her problematization of dominant norms and ideals, and for all her unstable, precarious self and existence, the narrator of this novel does not "say no" to everything, unlike Baum's, Zeh's, and Hegemann's protagonists. Crucially, "family" is not jettisoned, as it is in the other texts, in which parent figures are distant and unsympathetic. As Ahmed notes, some bonds, including familial ones, are sustaining.[70] Laura's par-ents are depicted with affection. Her father is a vivid and moving pres-ence, and his lung cancer forms an affecting strand of the narrative (*A*, 59–60; *A*, 23). Moreover, it prompts Laura to think "of care and lack of care" (*A*, 210): that is, of the importance of nurture and support. Laura is aware of her rootedness in place and genealogy (*A*, 27–28). Her relation-ship to the family home is complex: it both is and is not home, and this feeling is complicated by the factors of politics and class (*A*, 53–54). Tyler and Laura's visit to Jean prompts Laura to reflect positively on domestic-ity and family.[71] Even though her relationship with Jim breaks down, the end of the novel does see an affirmation of being and of belonging: "I was here and here and here, everything in its place, everything something like belonging" (*A*, 245). The novel ends with a commitment to being "here and here and here," to a dispersed yet harmonious belonging, and with the implication that the narrator's will may now have found appro-priate direction.

Caitlin Moran, *How to Build a Girl*

Of Unsworth's novel, Caitlin Moran has written: "I wish I had written this book."[72] Moran is herself the author of the commercially successful nonfiction book *How to Be a Woman* (see chapter 1). Her novel's title suggests a conscious tie-in with that earlier title, and also implies a focus on construction. *How to Build a Girl* is a *Bildungsroman*, as its title makes clear. Set in the 1990s, it charts the "becoming woman" of Johanna, who lives in Wolverhampton, England, on a council estate. The novel is not strictly speaking autobiographical, as the author's note at the start of the book clarifies, but Moran did grow up in Wolverhampton as part of a large family, like her protagonist, who is one of five children.[73] At the beginning of the novel, Johanna's mother has just given birth to twins and is experiencing postnatal depression (*HBG*, 17). Her father is registered disabled, following an accident while on duty as a fireman (*HBG*, 25, 97). The family has money worries and lives in cramped conditions (*HBG*, 161). Class is important to Johanna's self-definition; she asserts a specifically working-class identity and culture. Her politics is derived from her father, in large part (*HBG*, 88–89). She is acutely aware of the role of class in determining experience; were she to have lived at another time, she would have been "in a factory, or a field . . . one of a million sad cattle" (*HBG*, 214). As in Unsworth's novel, the working-class father is a supportive presence, poignantly evoked (see, for example, *HBG*, 137). As a depiction of family life, the novel eschews romanticization, however, and the book's humor coexists with an acknowledgment of poverty, the complexity of relationships, and the difficulties of establishing and living out one's sexuality. Johanna, who is fat, is at the start of the novel desperate to lose her virginity: as I discuss in more detail in chapter 5, sexuality is a key theme of the book (*HBG*, 28).

Female willfulness and hedonism also emerge as important concerns, and they are explicitly at odds with what the narrator sees as a traditional female tendency toward martyrdom and self-sacrifice. Johanna wants on the one hand to be "noble," and committed to a cause or idea that she has not yet identified. The lack of such a clear cause accords with other characters under investigation here, who are similarly adrift. But Johanna possesses a commitment to vitalism and pleasure that makes her stand out:

> I don't want to be noble and committed like most women in history were—which invariably seems to involve being burned at the stake, dying of sadness or being bricked up in a tower by an earl. I don't want to *sacrifice* myself for something. I don't want to *die* for something. I don't even want to walk in the rain up a hill in a skirt that's sticking to my thighs for something. I want to *live* for something,

instead—as men do. I want to have fun . . . I want a rapturous quest.
I want to sacrifice myself to glee. I want to make the world better, in
some way. (*HBG*, 30)

Johanna asserts that she wants to live "as men do," in a spirit of commitment, not denial. She is aware, then, of the gendering of will (cf. *WS*, 90).
Her vitalism coexists with her confusion about her self-identity and her
aspirations. Even though she feels her current identity is inadequate, she
does not want to die:

> I am thrilled by the idea of killing myself. It seems like such a gratify-
> ingly noble thing to do . . . I'm not *actually* going to kill myself, of
> course. For starters, I suspect I might put up a struggle, and fight
> dirty . . . and, secondly, I don't actually want to *die*. . . . I don't want
> to *not live*. I just . . . want not to be *me* anymore. Everything I am
> now is not working. (*HBG*, 65)

Considering the phrase "self-made man," Johanna reflects that she wishes
to be a "self-made woman," born of herself (*HBG*, 66). While such individualism is obviously youthfully naive, its willfulness is notable. Johanna
can be seen as challenging the passivity and precarity of neoliberal femininity. Ahmed notes "how easily willfulness is confused with, and reduced
to, individualism" (*WS*, 150; cf. *WS*, 242n24), suggesting that such self-
assertions as Johanna's are in any case not only "individual" matters.

Johanna's becoming is framed in terms of both constructedness
and voluntarism. As a strategy, Johanna gives herself a new name, Dolly
Wilde, and cultivates this new self (*HBG*, 68). She assembles a collection
of icons and love objects from scraps of high and low culture, in an episode that shows both how the self constructs itself through processes of
appropriation, interpellation, and identification, and how that construction is contingent upon particular cultural contexts and resources. "I am
collaging myself," Johanna asserts, referring to this act of self-bricolage,
and "I am branding me" (*HBG*, 70, 72). She styles her body through
clothing, makeup, and hair dye (*HBG*, 70–71). Being a teenager, according to Johanna, means being a rocket, fueled by music and guided by
information in books (*HBG*, 103). The young person, then, is very much
a subject-in-process, unlike the older people Johanna observes, who all
"know their roles and tropes" (*HBG*, 114). Maturity appears to involve
dissimulation. Johanna learns: "Growing up is about keeping secrets, and
pretending everything is fine" (*HBG*, 44). Youthfulness grants a vantage
point from which to view such performances of maturity, in line with the
idea of adolescence as usefully awkward.

Dolly Wilde is a protective device, allowing Johanna briefly to feel
relaxed and confident in London (*HBG*, 102). She can be seen as an

assertion of will, where will is directed toward the future (cf. *WS*, 39). As Dolly, Johanna pretends to know how to interact with the journalists she encounters ("Fake it 'til you make it" [*HBG*, 111]). But while she looks like Dolly, she is still acting like her old self, Johanna: she needs to make the two identities align in order to fit into the future she wishes for (*HBG*, 117). As Ahmed notes, will is an expression of the present failure of the subject to achieve its aims (*WS*, 39). In Johanna's case, this failure is manifested in bravado as well as anxiety. She conceals the fact that she is on an airplane for the first time: "I don't want anyone watching me *change*. I will do all my changing in private. In public, I am, always, the finished thing" (*HBG*, 138). While on the one hand, Johanna's intentionality is forceful, on the other, she is timidly conformist. Summoned to a meeting, Johanna resurrects Dolly in a willful way: "I prepare Dolly for London like I am her lady's maid" (*HBG*, 183). Yet her performance as Dolly involves a kind of willing submission to the prevailing norms of her milieu. She makes notes on "how to build a girl":

> Everyone drinks. Everyone smokes. . . . You come into a room, and say things, like you're in a play. You fake it 'til you make it. You discuss sex like it's a game. You have adventures. You don't quote musicals. Whatever anyone else is doing, you do that. You say things to be heard, rather than to be right. (*HBG*, 183–84)

She furnishes herself with cigarettes and alcohol, which she carries into her meeting (*HBG*, 184–85). Drinking and smoking become habitual, and she finds drugs "pleasantly communal, and bonding" (*HBG*, 275).

As in Kerstin Grether's novel *Zuckerbabys*, discussed in the next chapter, music is an important site at which the main character's identity is worked out (*HBG*, 74). Yet record shops are male-dominated spaces (*HBG*, 75). The office of the magazine Johanna writes for, a thinly disguised *NME* (*New Musical Express*), is "built out of trousers, confidence and testicles" (*HBG*, 110). Like Grether's novel, this text is replete with allusions to songs and bands (for example, *HBG*, 87, 103–6); the protagonist is rooted in, and constructed by, popular culture. Johanna identifies with the makers of music, who, "in the furious, messy, white-light act of self-creation, try[ ] to invent a future they can be in" (*HBG*, 106).[74] Riot Grrrls feature, recalling pop feminist texts in German; Bikini Kill and Courtney Love are namechecked (*HBG*, 104–5). Popular culture is important in enabling new self-definitions and identifications.[75] The influence of American culture is clear: "they're making new kinds of girls in America. Girls who don't give a fuck. Girls who dare" (*HBG*, 105). Johanna thus finds role models who help her define and assert herself.

Like other protagonists examined here, Johanna is not keen on school, resisting the straightening device of education. Indeed, she "resigns" from it, to her parents' dismay (*HBG*, 134–36).[76] Johanna is a writer, despite her background—as she observes, "Poor people can write" (*HBG*, 31)—and her writing grants her agency and mobility. In particular, music journalism will be her "way out," she realizes (*HBG*, 79). Her family's reaction to her ambition is supportive; comically, Johanna's anticipation that she will feel "rejected and outsiderish" is not fulfilled (*HBG*, 93). Willfulness here does not only connote againstness—though it does involve self-affirmation in the face of norms relating to class and gender. Writing means Johanna is recognized and acknowledged as existing (*HBG*, 205). It also constitutes a form of revenge: Johanna enjoys writing negative pieces on "the kind of people who would usually look down on a fat teenage girl from a council estate" (*HBG*, 260). But later she states her ambition to go beyond such negativity and do better: to do "something great, like men do" (*HBG*, 305), again claiming for herself a privilege and an expertise that are traditionally deemed masculine.

Indeed, Johanna in fact learns *not* to be negative in the course of her *Bildung*. Her cynicism proves to be suspect. She realizes that "the world is difficult, and we are all breakable" and we should "just be kind" (*HBG*, 261). Cynicism, she comes to see, is destructive and negative, a cover for fear that leads only to stasis (*HBG*, 262). Reflecting on the cynicism of the young, the narrator muses:

> the deepest irony about the young being cynical is that they are the ones that need to move, and dance, and trust the most . . . When young people are cynical, and snarky, they shoot down their own future. When you keep saying "No" all that's left is what other people said "Yes" to, before you were born. Really, "No" is no choice at all. (*HBG*, 262).

In this way, Moran's narrator eschews the negativity of other protagonists examined here. Her focus on kindness—on ethical imperatives—marks this text out as an attempt to salvage from neoliberalism and postfeminism a moral injuncture ("be kind"). Yet it is notable that this turning point seems not to be one at all. Johanna's cynicism persists. She continues to antagonize people with her negativity and to produce hateful reviews, adopting a "bile-filled persona" (*HBG*, 309, 311). She has, "bafflingly, pretended to be a massive arsehole" (*HBG*, 311). She concludes, however, that the experiment has been a failure and resolves to go back to the way she used to write and thereby "prove that [she is] a halfway decent human being" (*HBG*, 311–12). Her remorse drives her to self-harm, disturbingly (*HBG*, 313–14). Eventually, though, she becomes an enthusiast again, a position that is "more fun" than being against things all the time (*HBG*, 323–24).

A further possible transitional moment in the novel occurs when Johanna walks out of her boyfriend's house, having been humiliated there, and experiences a sense of agency, or will. Having previously been resigned to any fate, and worried about "making a fuss," she realizes: "I am in charge of me" (*HBG*, 301). Her process of self-discovery is enhanced by this discovery. Johanna addresses herself, asking herself what she wants (*HBG*, 302). The answer is John Kite, a musician she interviews and falls in love with. Having been forced to reassess herself, she asks what one does when one has built oneself "with the wrong things":

> You rip it up and start again. That is the work of your teenage years— to build up and tear down and build up again, over and over, end- lessly, like speeded-up film of cities during boom times, and wars. To be fearless, and endless, in your reinventions—to keep twisting on nineteen, going bust and dealing in again, and again. Invent, invent, invent. (*HBG*, 320)

She reflects here on the limitations of parents' understanding of their chil- dren, who are born into a different world, raising the question of genera- tionality (*HBG*, 320). There is a programmatic address to the reader that is in keeping with Moran's popularity with young women and girls, and with her status as a kind of role model:

> you go out into your world, and try and find the things that will be useful to you . . . You find a record, or a poem, or a picture of a girl that you pin to the wall, and go, "Her. I'll try and be her . . . but *here*." What will be useful? What will be, eventually, *you*? . . .
> And you will be quite on your own when you do all this. There is no academy where you can learn to be yourself; there is no line man- ager, slowly urging you towards the correct answer. You are midwife to yourself, and will give birth to yourself, over and over, in dark rooms, alone.
> And some versions of you will end in dismal failure . . . Others will achieve temporary success. . . .
> But one day, you'll find a version of you that will get you kissed, or befriended, or inspired . . .
> Until—slowly, slowly—you make a viable version of you. (*HBG*, 320–21)

The self here is multiple and shifting, undergoing a precarious, falter- ing emergence. Notably, romantic fulfillment is just one option when it comes to being acknowledged—friendship and creativity are others.

Johanna herself ditches aspects of her persona that are pernicious, and retains others (such as alcohol and her fondness for the poetry of Philip Larkin) (*HBG* 325). The end of the novel asserts a kind of positivity, though the "warning scars"—a reference to the self-harm that is briefly depicted earlier—imply that this *Bildung* is not necessarily easy or effortless: "I believe in music and gin and joy and talking too much, and human kindness. I have warning scars on my arms, a new blank wall to fill with faces and words" (*HBG* 340). Reflecting on her activities, she concludes that as with all the best quests, she "did it for a girl: me" (*HBG* 340). The girl herself is the agent as well as the motivating force behind this quest narrative: both subject and object. Her will as well as her willfulness motivate this story.

Conclusion

Moran's novel is vitalist in its affirmation of female becoming, and the text explicitly challenges cynicism and nihilism. In contrast, the novels by Baum, Zeh, Jenny, and Hegemann all in different ways assert failure and trauma. Yet Moran's novel, too, stresses the wounds incurred by its protagonist, and as we will see in chapter 5, Johanna's discovery of her own sexuality is thwarted by her internalization of the male gaze and by the lack of representations of female pleasure in her culture. Unsworth's novel ends with an assertion of self, too, but this self, it is clear, is shifting and in process, and the subject here is caught in complex and harmful relationships with others, as we will see further in chapter 4. Thus, all of the texts show agency and voluntarism as problematic: either because these are ill-directed or because they are lacking.[77]

To different extents, the novels identify diagnoses for their protagonists' refusals and failures: parental dysfunction and neglect; psychic trauma; societal malaise in the form of materialism, selfishness, and ignorance; pressures imposed by class. As noted, it is not a matter here of coercive, overtly disciplinarian individuals or institutions exerting their influences on the characters, but rather of a political and ethical vacuum. There is a lack of adequate role models or ideals, and a dearth of sustaining relationships, except in Moran and Unsworth, where familial and other bonds are supportive, if complex. There is no clear, single antagonistic factor in the texts. This accords with an understanding of neoliberalism as all-encompassing and as thriving on its own crises and contestations, and with a view of the subject as anxiously implicated in the order of things.[78] In terms of literary form and technique, the texts' willfulness manifests itself, notably, in satirical, grotesque, or humorous forms—this in all texts bar Jenny's. These modes involve both engagement with and critique of dominant norms and assumptions. Jenny's subdued narrative, characterized by its use of imagery, in particular, to express mental states, performs a more muted form of protest.

Gender is a concern of all the novels, and it underpins their differing diagnoses. We find here a collective critique of femininity as involving expectations of demureness and dutifulness. In Baum, feminine passivity is the harmful norm. In Zeh, the "princesses" embody feminine decorativeness and emptiness. Jenny, too, evokes a lack of agency and purpose. Hegemann critiques and queers sentimentalizations of girls. In Unsworth, domesticity and maternity are ideals with which the main character has to negotiate, and Moran's protagonist has to work to claim "masculine" agency and challenge preconceptions relating to fat, working-class girls. This critical insight into femininity gains support and acquires texture as we turn to the topics of body and beauty, sisterhood and identification, and sex and desire, subjects of the following chapters and sites at which femininity is lived out and contested, framed and reframed. In the neoliberal, postfeminist context, female bodies, crucially, are both docile and potentially willful.

3: Body and Beauty

APPEARANCE AND BEAUTY are key concerns of new-feminist texts. Writers of such texts are concerned with the objectification and sexualization of young female bodies. This question is linked to the availability of pornography via the Internet and to the continued growth of the sex industry. The issue of appearance has implications for women's professional and public status: slights on women's looks function as a "Shut-the-Fuck-Up-Tool," as Jessica Valenti puts it. Female corporeality involves shame: "to be made of female flesh is to be well-schooled in the abjections and humiliations of embodiment."[1] Eating disorders constitute an extreme, if common, manifestation of such humiliation, as Laurie Penny contends. The questions of diet and weight raise the matter of agency: Ahmed notes that in the contemporary context, fatness is viewed as the result of a failure of will.[2] This assumption accords with the neoliberal imperative to "succeed" at conformity with mainstream ideals. As Alison Phipps argues, in the context of neoliberalism, "success is measured by individuals' capacity for self-care via the market, and those who do not achieve their potential are viewed as failures."[3]

While contemporary feminists have on the one hand challenged dominant standards of beauty, which—as Naomi Wolf has argued—serve as an imprisoning construct, there has at the same time been a defense of self-adornment and enjoyment of one's appearance—this as a reaction to the perceived ugliness and joylessness of "1970s feminists." According to Thea Dorn, the women she interviews in her book wear lipstick without fearing that they are thereby succumbing to the patriarchy.[4] And the authors of *Wir Alpha-Mädchen* assert, "Wir können Freude an Lippenstift und enthaarten Beinen haben, ohne uns deswegen als hilflose Opfer männlicher Fantasien oder einer riesigen Industrie fühlen zu müssen" (We can take pleasure in lipstick and hairless legs without having to feel that we're helpless victims of male fantasies or of a massive industry). Yet they also point to the issues of sexism and objectification, and to profit-motivated representations of bodies. They use the term "Schönheitslüge" (beauty lie) to describe dominant ideals of attractiveness.[5] This is a matter that once again raises the questions of individualism versus collectivism, interpellation versus resistance—that is to say, the issue of will. Emily Spiers notes of the authors of *Wir Alpha-Mädchen* that, while they criticize ever more demanding beauty standards, they "tend ultimately to undermine their own critique" by "making the individualist claim that every woman should ultimately do what she pleases with her body."[6]

Spiers's critique ties in with observations about the "body project" in postfeminist neoliberalism as a manifestation of interpellation and individualization.[7] As Michelle M. Lazar notes, "the beauty project is signified as an extension of women's right to freedom and liberation."[8] Individual female consumers are obliged to perform the work of beautification on themselves, and this endeavor purportedly involves empowerment and "choice."[9] Claire Charles sums up what the "hypersexualized" ideal entails: skimpy clothes, artificial tan and nails, surgically enhanced breasts, long hair, heavy make-up, and sexually suggestive behavior.[10] Through the pursuit of an "ever-changing, homogenizing, elusive ideal of femininity," female bodies become docile.[11] Hester Baer consequently refers to the "precarity" of the female body in neoliberalism, arguing that women's bodies, much more then men's, are "subject to constant regulation."[12]

Reacting to such docility and precarity, new-feminist texts propose resistance and refusal. Penny enjoins: "We need to take responsibility for our part in the cruel machine of enforced feminine starvation psychosis." She advocates a collective rejection of dominant norms: "we refuse to be beautiful and good."[13] Critical awareness emerges in other writings too as an ideal to which young women should aspire. The *Alpha-Mädchen* suggest that women use their "kritisches Urteilsvermögen" (critical faculties) when faced with distortional media imagery of women's bodies.[14] Elke Buhr coins the term "kritische Sexyness" (critical sexiness) to denote simultaneous enjoyment of one's body and the adoption of a critical stance.[15] Emma Jane Unsworth's novel *Animals* hints at such a simultaneity of impulses when the narrator reflects:

> I shaved my armpits. The hair on my legs was downy, mostly invisible; worse when meddled with. I shaved it occasionally in summer when my own treacherous aesthetics meant I couldn't go tightless otherwise. Tyler [her friend]—coarser, darker—kept hers in honour of feminist historian Janet Fraser: *All that time I save in body hair removal I devote to revolution.*[16]

"Treacherous aesthetics" implies complicity with a dominant norm that is distracting and time-consuming. Unsworth's heroine at once submits to and resists such norms, also taking on board the views of a feminist scholar. She thus illustrates the enmeshment of subjectivity, embodiment, and culture.

A Surface of Intensities

This enmeshment also emerges in the work of Rosi Braidotti, who describes the body as a "play of forces, a surface of intensities," that is to say, as subject to social and cultural influences and to affect. Asking how we should theorize the body, she acknowledges the difficulty of this task, for the body is "a bundle of contradictions."[17] Braidotti takes the concept of the body "as referring to the multifunctional and complex structure of subjectivity," putting forward a view of embodied subjectivity as dynamic and in process (*M*, 21). Braidotti and other materialist feminist thinkers thus acknowledge subjectivity as embodied. Agency is an inevitably corporeal matter: Elizabeth Grosz refers to "the creativity and inventiveness of consciousness that correlates quite precisely with the range of possible actions posed by a living body."[18] There is a "quite precise" correlation between physical and other capacities.

Such thinking sees the body as implicated in social and cultural forces and in power relations. Braidotti's conception of embodiment is bound up closely with her understanding of power as both prohibitive and enabling, which recalls Foucault (*M*, 21). Linking questions of power, narrativity, and materiality, she asserts:

> the subject [is] a term in a process, which is co-extensive with both power and the resistance to it. Narrativity is a crucial binding force here, but I interpret it as a collective, politically-invested process of sharing in and contributing to the making of myths, operational fictions, significant figurations of the kind of subjects we are in the process of becoming. This notion of narrativity cannot be adequately contained within the semiological paradigm but needs to be embedded and embodied in a form of neo-materialism. (*M*, 21–22)

Braidotti thus suggests a collective, corporeal agency, "co-extensive with both power and the resistance to it." The popular neoliberal stress on individual choice and autonomy, which insists that one can choose how or whether to style one's body, by means of lipstick and high heels, say, appears crude in this light. It recalls misunderstandings of Butler's theory of performativity as involving a whimsical adoption of gender identities on the part of a stable subject.[19] Embodied subjects are not (only) agents practising voluntarism; their performances, which may be willful, are always contextual and subject to competing interpretations. In contemporary Western cultures, notably, the fat body is reviled in mainstream culture, as a number of the literary texts I examine here attest.

In this chapter, I discuss Charlotte Roche's *Feuchtgebiete* (2008; *Wetlands*, 2009), Juli Zeh's *Spieltrieb* (Play Instinct, 2004), Kerstin Grether's *Zuckerbabys* (Sugar Babies, 2004), Sibylle Berg's *Ein paar Leute suchen das Glück und lachen sich tot* (A Few People Seek Happiness and Laugh Themselves to Death, 1997), and Sarai Walker's *Dietland* (2015). If the female body is labeled as deficient, always wrong and in need of correction and improvement, then these literary responses to this labeling—marked often by hyperbole, the grotesque, or dark humor—constitute defiant eruptions of willfulness. We find here a range of reactions to a culture perceived as plasticizing and pornifying, and a diverse set of more or less vigorous and explicit attempts to engage readers in a provocative dialogue. In Roche and Zeh, there is a refusal of mainstream assumptions concerning female decorativeness and decorum, and in Grether, Berg, and Walker we find both acknowledgment of and resistance to mainstream injunctions, especially in the matter of weight. The texts not only depict and affirm bodily reality—its revolting as well as its pleasurable aspects—and its pathologized status in postfeminism, they also hail the body of the reader in an affective, sensual process.[20]

Charlotte Roche, *Feuchtgebiete*

Perhaps the most striking text of recent times to do this is Charlotte Roche's 2008 bestseller *Feuchtgebiete*, published in 2009 in English translation as *Wetlands*.[21] Its eighteen-year-old protagonist, Helen, is for much of the novel confined to a hospital bed following an unfortunate shaving incident. This gross-out novel—"an exploration of corporeality in all its basal glory"—features graphic descriptions of bodily functions and sexual acts.[22] Helen is unapologetically embodied and shamelessly desirous, and so usefully counters the plasticity and one-dimensionality of mainstream representations of femaleness that Power, Penny, Walter, and others note (see chapter 1): Carrie Smith-Prei observes that the novel "undermines expectations of femininity."[23] And Heike Bartel identifies Roche's "oppositional stance towards cultural dictates concerning female . . . hygiene" as a key impulse behind the writing of the text.[24] The opening of the novel, for example, focuses on the narrator's hemorrhoids, which she herself finds "unmädchenhaft" (*F*, 8; unladylike, *W*, 1); the word recurs shortly after. From the outset, then, the novel highlights the discrepancy between cultural imaginings of female corporeality and the reality as Helen lives it: "Ich habe schon bei vielen Dingen, die mir beigebracht wurden, festgestellt, dass die gar nicht stimmen" (*F*, 20; I've figured out that a lot of the things I was taught aren't true, *W*, 14).

Smith-Prei argues, however, that "the force of the book . . . is disturbed by the framing story."[25] Helen's willfulness is perhaps curtailed by her regressive fantasies of familial togetherness: the heroine mourns her parents' divorce and prolongs her stay in hospital in the hope that it will bring them back together. But family life appears traumatic. Helen's response to an episode from her past—her mother attempted to kill herself and her son—involves no neat resolution. Her recreation of the scene using various props toward the end of the novel may briefly grant a kind of catharsis, but her final scream hints at a trauma that still persists. Smith-Prei indeed states that the novel "embraces the unruly self-expression of the body by providing Helen a loud voice of refusal."[26] Thus while heterosexual romance may offer some kind of closure—Helen leaves the hospital with a male nurse—unruliness and embodiment assert themselves. And while the narrative voice is most often humorous and sprightly, and Helen's pride in her body affirmative, ultimately, the novel stresses trauma and failure, in line with the texts discussed in chapter 2.

In this way, Helen willfully refrains from taking part in sociality as currently defined: as Carrie Smith-Prei and Maria Stehle suggest, "Helen refuses to participate."[27] Helen, in hospital, is away from everyday life, apart from mainstream society. Her musings mark her as willful too. She is explicitly and critically aware of dominant discourses of femininity, to which she does not conform, and in opposition she asserts her own bodily or erotic truths. Helen invents her own terms for parts of her body, recalling 1970s feminist attempts to reclaim language from patriarchy (*F*, 22; *W*, 16).[28] Margaret McCarthy notes, in this connection: "Helen combines a seventies-style, second-wave-mandated natural body with a contemporary stylized selfhood."[29] In terms of the "natural body," Helen reflects, for example: "Uns wird immer erzählt, dass man durch Parfüm erotisch auf andere wirkt. Aber warum benutzen wir nicht unser viel wirksameres eigenes Parfüm?" (*F*, 18–19; We're always told that perfume has an erotic effect on those around us. But why not use our own much more powerful perfume? *W*, 13).[30] Helen criticizes the widespread (German) obsession with hygiene, which in her view is gendered.[31] She also challenges her mother's view that female sex organs are somehow more vulnerable to infection than male ones, asserting, then, the robustness of the female body (*F*, 20). Her decision to undergo sterilization involves a challenge to idealizations of maternity and involves her breaking the cycle of female unhappiness in her family: a gesture that can be read as queer and linked to Hegemann's and Baum's protagonists' scorn for reproductive futurism (*F*, 40–41).

Willfulness coexists with confusion and inconsistency, in both protagonist and text. When Helen wakes, following an operation:

> Ich werde von meinem eigenen Gebrabbel wach. Was hab ich gesagt? Weiß nicht. Ich zittere am ganzen Körper. . . . Was mache ich hier? Ist mir was passiert? Ich will lächeln, um meine Hilflosigkeit zu überspielen, obwohl keiner sonst im Raum ist. (*F*, 28)

> [I'm awoken by my own babbling. What was I saying? Don't know. My whole body is shaking. . . . What am I doing here? Did something happen to me? I want to smile to try to hide my sense of helplessness even though there's nobody else in the room. (*W*, 22)]

Helen's vulnerability is clear, as is her bravado. This assertion of instability and embodiment challenges the fantasy of the coherent, masterful
subject. It also suggests willfulness is not a matter of intention (cf. *WS*,
175). The novel itself has been charged with inconsistency. Bartel argues
that the text "fails to take a clear stance regarding its own genre" (114):
it neither addresses the problematic assumptions of mainstream porn
nor actively challenges the genre by way of parody. Analyzing a passage
describing masturbatory practices, Bartel argues that the overwhelming
effect is not one of female or feminist transgression, but "the overstep-
ping of the boundaries of the disgusting" (115). The novel is not con-
sistent, then, in its subversion of female sexuality (116). Bartel ultimately
deems the novel a failure, at least in terms of Roche's "stated intent to
steer women's writing beyond a male and towards a female gaze" (117).
Yanbing Er also finds the novel inconsistent, drawing attention to the
protagonist's "simultaneous critique of and complicity with many of the
ideals of patriarchy."[32] And Smith-Prei and Stehle argue that the novel
"does not offer a clear position from which to evaluate the text and its
voice; on the contrary, the novel and its narrator create an insecure position for readers."[33]

The disgusting quality of the novel, as analyzed by Katie Jones,
accords well with a view that excessive jubilance is unhelpful, and with a
notion of willfulness as embodied and contagious, as well as potentially
contradictory (*WS*, 120–21, 143). Helen Hester argues that this aspect of
the novel, rather than its perceived eroticism, is indeed the most striking
and subversive, suggesting that "sex [in the contemporary imagination] is
beginning, perhaps, to lose its status as a particularly privileged and iconic
site of transgression."[34] Jones herself describes the text as an "anti-disgust
manifesto" that nonetheless provokes disgust.[35] Jones's assessment of
the novel's disgusting qualities suggests that Roche may have overdone
things a little: while Roche may have wished to challenge sanitized versions of femininity, she "arguably devotes rather more space to the disgusting than a balanced depiction of 'the whole package' might warrant"
(245). Jones discusses, for example, Helen's pleasure in eating her own
bodily emissions, and the reversal of the socialization process that this
entails (252–53).[36] Jones also rightly notes the contradictory and vexing
quality of this novel, and its cultural significance:

> By using a narrator who refuses to recognize disgust, Roche is . . .
> able to suggest logical arguments against disgust, and also to render
> disgust ridiculous, while at the same time inducing feelings of dis-
> gust in her readers. Such a project might seem contradictory—after
> all, it invites us to confirm rather than deny the disgusting status of
> various body parts and emissions—but it also helps to bring out con-
> tradictions in contemporary attitudes to the (female) body. (259)

Roche's disgusting novel accords with the ideas of failure, bile, and refusal discussed in chapter 2. Seen in these terms, it forms a potentially provocative challenge to mainstream norms and assumptions. Er, who refers to the book's "dysfunctional feminism," ultimately stresses its promise, given its illumination of "the hyprocisy surrounding feminine norms that have been institutionalized as obligatory."[37] I will come back to this novel in chapter 5, when I explore its depiction of sex and sexuality.

Juli Zeh, *Spieltrieb*

In a very different way from Roche's, Zeh's *Spieltrieb* challenges normative assumptions and ideals about female appearance and desirability. As mentioned in the last chapter, Ada, the teenage girl at the centre of the narrative, is an oppositional figure. Ada is introduced as follows:

> Ada war ein junges Mädchen und nicht schön . . . [sie war] vierzehn Jahre alt, blond und kräftig gebaut. Ihr Mund war breit, die Handgelenke stark. Über der Nase lag ein löchriger Teppich aus Sommersprossen und wusste bei passender Beleuchtung ein paar Notlügen von gepflückten Wildblumen und Kinderspielen im hohen Gras an den Mann zu bringen. In Wahrheit sah Ada älter aus, als sie war. Ihre Brust war stark entwickelt.[38]

> [Ada was a young girl and not beautiful . . . [she was] fourteen years old, blonde, and powerfully built. Her mouth was wide, her wrists strong. Above her nose was a holey rug formed of freckles, which in the right light evoked illusions of picked wildflowers and childish games in the tall grass. In reality, Ada looked older than she was. Her breasts were very developed.]

It is notable that Ada's lack of beauty is established first off, in light of the contemporary feminist concern with appearance—and in view of Ada's mother's view that female beauty constitutes "eine Verpflichtung" (*S*, 37; an obligation). The reference to wild flowers and child's play serves a mocking function, undermining conceptions of youth and femininity as involving an idyllic form of innocence. Yet "in reality" Ada looks older than she is: an oddly slippery assertion that asserts both truthfulness and deceptiveness. The final sentence emphasizes the size of Ada's bust, and therefore her sexual maturity. Later on, Smutek establishes that she has the voice of a grown woman (*S*, 51). As mentioned, both Ada's gender and her age are the subject of discussion and suspicion in the novel. Appearance, here, is not a guarantor of one's nature or being; when Ada notes that she is blonde, Alev retorts: "Bei dir ist es Tarnung" (*S*, 462;

With you, it's camouflage). That is to say, the cultural associations and assumptions attaching to blondeness do not accord with the reality of Ada's inner life.

The question of appearance and body image recurs when, in a flashback, the narrative relates a trip Ada's mother made into town following her divorce from Ada's father. The purpose of this excursion was to secure new clothing for Ada, or: "eine neue Außenhülle . . . die, frei nach der Regel, dass das Sein das Bewusstsein bestimme, ein attraktives, leichtherziges junges Ding aus ihr machen sollte, das ohne weiteres mit der schwierigen Familiensituation zurechtkommen würde" (S, 77; a new exterior cover that, loosely going by the rule that being determines consciousness, was to make an attractive, frivolous young thing out of her, one that would get on and cope with the difficult family situation right away). This satirical description of clothing pokes fun at discourses of femininity. These are also countered by Ada's refusal to accept the items. She cites her physical characteristics (runner's legs, large head, and so on) as rendering them unsuitable. Her mother's constant exhortations to the effect that her daughter should prettify herself lead Ada to make the claim that she despises her own body and would be anorexic if she were not too lazy. This outburst leads her mother to book her daughter sessions with a psychologist (S, 77). Comically, Ada is thus pathologized for reacting with a defiant, tongue-in-cheek perversity to her mother's campaign to beautify and feminize her. She is diagnosed as in need of corrective treatment for her failure to comply—this in line with Ahmed's contention that "Not to fit, or to fail to inhabit a norm, can often mean being charged with willfulness, whatever you say or do" (WS, 148). Ada's mother's campaign is elsewhere termed a "jahrelanger Kampf um den Körper der Tochter" (S, 184; years-long struggle over her daughter's body). The body, here, is a "surface of intensities," as Braidotti puts it: a battleground on which cultural, social, and familial forces play out (M, 21).

Questions of representation and interpellation also feature here. Media images of women are the subject of mockery when Ada stares at "das Mädchen der Woche" (the girl of the week) in a newspaper supplement: "wie es, anständig bekleidet und mit bürgerlichem Lächeln, das Zitat der Woche präsentierte. Man muss ins Gelingen verliebt sein, nicht ins Scheitern" (S, 184; how, decently clothed and with a bourgeois smile, she presented the quote of week. You had to be in love with success, not failure). The girl is "hübsch" and "mager" (pretty, thin)—in both body and reason, according to Ada (S, 184). Here, Ada's skeptical perspective involves a challenge to neoliberal discourses of success, optimism, and unthreatening femininity—which the image of the girl of the week neatly brings together—and recalls assertions of failure and refusal as appropriate and advisable, given these inane imperatives. Ada's attempt to enter into the image, to merge with it, fails: she is unable, then—or, rather, unwilling—to assimilate herself into such an imaginary, a failure or refusal that underlines her awkwardness.

However, there are also suggestions of a poignant self-doubt, even self-hatred, on Ada's part. When Ada looks at herself in the mirror, she rarely finds herself pleasing to look at.[39] Ada does not use cosmetics out of "geistiger Eitelkeit" (spiritual/mental vanity), though; the constant failure of her efforts at beautification would be unbearable. Ada is in this respect neither an artist nor a fighter, but a "Dulderin," someone who merely tolerates (S, 360). This is an interesting moment. Ada is here "typical" in her self-loathing, but her refusal to buy into the seductions of the cosmetics industry suggests willfulness. Her own ideals are not shaped by this industry, but are instead animal-inspired. She finds cats and horses beautiful—a suggestive detail in light of material feminisms and especially Grosz's Darwninist reflections, which stress the importance of animality in rethinking notions of agency and becoming. It also brings to mind Ahmed's suggestion that will unites humans with other entities (WS, 192). The narrator notes at this point: "Die Tatsache, dass wahre Schönheit mit Selbstvergessenheit zu tun hatte, passte zum seltsamen Humor des Schöpfers" (S, 360; The fact that true beauty had to do with self-forgetfulness fitted with the strange humor of the Creator). Ada herself has lost her childish self-consciousness; "becoming adult" involves relinquishing it, and so relinquishing "beauty" as the narrator understands it. The narrator claims that self-forgetfulness (Selbstvergessenheit) is indeed best given up "am Ausgang der Kindheit" (at the exit of childhood), since it will in any case be taken away from one "irgendwo auf der Schwelle zum angeblich echten Leben" (at some point on the threshold to apparently real life) (S, 360).

This typically dense and playful reflection links growing up with the acquisition of self-consciousness, even as it challenges the notion of "real life" as it should be led. Thus for Zeh, the questions of beauty and appearance merge with ideas of normativity and appropriateness, and involve also philosophical reflections on the nature of being and seeming, belonging and otherness, agency and identification, or will. Carrie Smith-Prei and Lars Richter note the physical otherness of all three main characters in the novel, Ada, Alev, and Smutek, and suggest: "the corporeal otherness of each of the main figures in the novel is key to the social non-normativity that brings them together."[40] The very seriousness of Zeh's treatment of female embodiment is challenging, undermining ideas of femininity as frivolous and highlighting the philosophically problematic status of the body and appearance. Her "nicht schön" protagonist mocks, questions, and internalizes dominant unhelpful norms and ideals. These also find form in the "princesses," Ada's fellow female students, who are decorative and unthreatening, as we saw in the last chapter—unlike Ada herself.

Kerstin Grether, *Zuckerbabys*

Helen and Ada are perversely defiant figures, and their bodies manifest their willfulness. Other female protagonists are more passive, even at risk of disappearance: the neoliberal, postfeminist stress on celebrity, appearance, makeovers, and the body project proves destabilizing and destructive. "Wir [Frauen] sind die Musen des Neoliberalismus—an uns sieht man, was man Menschen alles antun kann" (We [women] are the muses of neoliberalism; you can see in us all the things you can do to people).[41] This reflection, in Kerstin Grether's *Zuckerbabys*, points up the passivity of neoliberal femininity. The novel is an example of *Popliteratur* (pop literature; see chapter 1), most obviously in that it is set in the pop world, in Hamburg. It charts the fortunes of twenty-three-year-old Sonja, a "Medien-Designerin" (*Z*, 41; media designer) and would-be pop singer who also draws comics, and her struggle to assert herself. Sonja develops anorexia, and her increasing obsession with food and with her appearance—exacerbated by her break-up with a short-term boyfriend, Johnny, who tells her he is leaving her for another woman—leads to depression. However, she is invited on tour with her friends, who form the all-female band Museabuse, and sings on stage with them. She gradually begins to overcome her eating disorder. At the end of the novel, she is poised to join a new band, with the sympathetic Tim, and to perform her own songs: pop music thus holds "an ambiguous key to her salvation."[42] The novel is written largely in the first person, from Sonja's point of view, and the effect is one of extreme subjectivity. As Sonja retreats into her own world, this effect intensifies. Yet there are frequent references to pop music and pop culture, and to the music industry and popular press: the novel highlights both the individual's obsessive, private musings and the culture that prompts, sustains, and exacerbates them. It also explores will, willpower, and willfulness as these relate to the questions of appearance and diet.

The social will here is forceful and harmful, in feminist terms. In Sonja's milieu, passivity and compliance are the norms for women: there is explicit and critical reflection on the workings of pop culture, in line with the aims and methods of "popfeminism." Male artistes attract female groupies, who are interested in dieting and appearance and who evince no talent or ambition of their own (*Z*, 74). They live only for their "Künstler-Freunde" (artist-boyfriends), though they seem detached from everything, possibly because of their eating disorders (*Z*, 76). Despite her efforts to cultivate individuality, Sonja realizes that she is no different from the other women around her (*Z*, 216). Fitting in—something Sonja paradoxically found difficult, growing up (*Z*, 59)—is still an issue for her: self-definition and self-assertion are problematic matters. Sonja's struggle with her confidence forms a major theme of the book. Agency and control are also recurrent themes of the narrative: Sonja reflects, "Hey: Ich habe mein Leben gut im Griff—oder hat es mich im Griff?" (Z, 42; Hey: I've got my life well under control—or does it have me under control?). Sonja is thus explicitly aware of the matters of agency and volition, and of gender: the novel references Judith Butler and Naomi Wolf (Z, 100, 132).

These factors come together in the questions of weight and appearance. Sonja's dream of being a singer is hampered by her belief—apparently founded—that she needs to be thin (Z, 16): Sonja refers to "das Wetthungern mit meinen Idolen" (Z, 178; starving in competition with my idols). Female pop singers are marketed on the basis of their bodies and desirability (Z, 68). Sonja watches Christina Aguilera's video for *Beautiful*, a song that ostensibly argues for a more inclusive notion of beauty. But the singer herself participates in the beauty myth. Sonja aligns her with women of her acquaintance who urge her to put on makeup:

> Dieses Haar aus Meer und Weizen. Und ein Milch-und-Honig-Teint . . . Und trotzdem hat sie noch ein knödelndes Maß an Mitgefühl für die Hässlichen und Schwächlichen dieser Welt übrig . . . Danke Christina, dass du uns erzählst, wir wären all gleich schön . . .
> Ist ja wahrscheinlich auch nur eine dieser modischen Grinsebacken, die einen früher in der Wirtschaftsschule immer mit Schminktipps belästigt haben: "Wie kann man nur mit so einer ungesunden Gesichtsfarbe herumlaufen? Wenn ich so blass wäre wie die, würde ich doch wenigstens Make-up benutzen. Hier, probier mal!"
> Genau genommen hat es mit Make-up auch wirklich immer besser ausgesehen. (17–18)

> [That hair of sea and wheat. And a milk-and-honey tone . . . And still she has a good dollop of sympathy for the ugly and the weak of this world left over . . . Thank you, Christina, for telling us we're all equally beautiful . . .
> She's probably just one of those trendy, smiley people who bothered you with makeup tips at business school: "How can you go around with your face such an unhealthy color? If I were as pale as you, I'd at least use makeup. Here, try this!"
> In fact, it always did look better with makeup.]

The pressure to beautify oneself is ubiquitous. The final sentence seems to suggest that acquiescence is unavoidable, even beneficial. Despite herself, Sonja is compelled to watch the video, and refers to her "verdammte Bildersucht" (Z, 18; damned addiction to images). This compulsion is a reflection on an image-driven society and on the interpellation of young women in particular, who internalize such images. The female body is increasingly visible, and so vulnerable, in such a context.[43] Eating disorders are rife among celebrities, according to Sonja's friend Allita, who reads about the case of a pop singer and muses: "Man sollte überhaupt das Ereignis daraus machen, dass jemand *nicht* magersüchtig ist" (*Z*, 53; You should really make a thing out of someone *not* being anorexic)—a blackly humorous reflection. Sonja notes that girls make up "neunzig Prozent aller Hungernden in der ersten Welt" (*Z*, 182; ninety percent of all the starving people in the First World). She also cites the fact that twenty women a year die of anorexia in Germany (*Z*, 183).

Sonja's job, which involves "Bildbearbeitung" (the manipulation of images) ties in with the widespread obsession with image and appearance that the novel highlights. When she tells others about her job, Sonja receives gendered reactions: girls always ask about models, boys about manga porn (*Z*, 45). Discussing the question of digital manipulation, Museabuse members Kicky and Micky raise the questions of role models and of agency:

> "Und die Models sehen in echt gar nicht so aus wie auf den Bildern?" Aus Kicky spricht die pure Empörung.
>
> "Was heißt in echt . . .? [Ellipsis in original.] Wie die in echt aussehen, ist noch mal eine andere Frage. . . . Filmstars gibt es nur im Film," sage ich arrogant. . . .
>
> "Mann, man kann immer alles noch verbessern . . . weißere Zähne, den Bauch dünner, die Haare voller, den Busen größer und so weiter."
>
> . . .
>
> "Was für ein Dreck." In Kickys Stimme schwingt ein extrem verächtlicher Unterton mit: "Und daran sollen wir uns orientieren!"
>
> "Musst du ja nicht." Micky wirft Kicky einen etwas beunruhigten Blick zu.
>
> "Ja, ich weiß, ich muss das nicht. Ich habe so was natürlich nicht nötig. Ich bin die Zukunft!" (45–46)

> ["And the models don't really look like they do in the pictures?" Sheer indignation pours out of Kicky.
>
> "What do you mean, really . . .? How they really look is another matter. . . . Film stars only exist on film," I say arrogantly. . . .
>
> "Man, you can always improve things . . . whiter teeth, smaller stomach, fuller hair, bigger bust, and so on."
>
> . . .
>
> "What a load of crap." Kicky's voice takes on an extremely contemptuous undertone. "And we're supposed to use them as role models!"
>
> "You don't have to." Micky looks at Kicky, rather worried.
>
> "Yes, I know I don't have to. I don't need that, of course. I am the future!"]

This exchange highlights both complicity and resistance in the face of dominant imagery. Kicky is apparently aggrieved at the manipulation of images of women, and she points to the perception of female celebrities as role models. Micky, however, challenges the idea that one must react to such figures by seeking to emulate them. The humor and bravado contained in Kicky's final statement suggest the possibility of resistance, too. The question of imagery, and the consumer's relationship to it, is also a concern of Allita's, who plans to write a series of articles about appearance in pop culture and who points to the ubiquity and pervasiveness of pictures, underlining a specifically feminine response to them:

> "Es ist nämlich so, dass ich das immer wieder vorgebrachte Argument mit den Bilderfluten nicht mehr hören kann. Also dass den Leuten gesagt wird, in der Therapie und so, man muss die Bilder von den superperfekten Körpern einfach an sich abprallen lassen, man darf die gar nicht so ernst nehmen. Aber das geht doch nicht, oder? Da wird man ja blöd im Kopf, wenn man sich zum Beispiel als Frau andauernd von den Bildern der Frauen distanzieren soll. Weil die Bilder doch überall sind." (Z, 68)

> ["It's like this: I can't hear the argument about the influx of images—the one that's repeatedly raised—again. I mean, that people are being told by their therapist and everyone to just let the images of super-perfect bodies bounce off them, you're not supposed to take them that seriously. But that's not possible, is it? You'd go funny in the head, if as a woman, say, you were supposed constantly to distance yourself from images of women. Because the pictures are everywhere, after all."]

To her editor Allita explains her plan to write something on this topic, and perhaps also show other images to counter the dominant, idealizing ones (Z, 68), thus pointing to another method of resistance: the creation of counter-discourses.

Along with the media and the music business, the dieting industry features as a straightening device, or rod, in Grether's study of obsession and control, as it does in Walker's novel, which I discuss shortly. Sonja opts for the SlimFast diet, a regime that involves drinking two shakes a day and eating one meal. The neoliberal logic of the plan, which purports to offer consumers an empowering choice, is clear when Sonja reflects satirically: "die [Mahlzeit] darf man sich, in voller Eigenverantwortung, selbst aussuchen. Bei Slim Fast herrscht nämlich Gewalteinteilung" (Z, 40; you can choose [the meal] yourself, taking on sole personal responsibility. With Slim Fast, you see, there's a division of force). Sonja imposes such regimes on herself, however, practicing willing submission. She resolves to take up jogging, and her obsession with exercise becomes extreme (Z, 40, 133). According to Sonja, such obsession with weight and appearance is widespread among women.[44] Boys, in this culture, have it easier. Musician Kicky compares the feminine obsession with appearance with boys' culture: "die Kultur von den Jungs weiß einfach, dass es gar nicht so schwer ist, ein Mensch zu sein—trotz allem Imagebewusstsein" (Z, 86; boys' culture simply knows that it's not really hard to be a person—despite all that image consciousness). Humanity is more achievable for boys, as Beauvoir suggests (see introduction). Like Power, Penny, and others, Grether evokes the fear of female flesh widespread in the culture, and the resultant disappearance of women. This diminution is explicit when Sonja observes: "Je schlanker ich werde, desto kleiner und mickriger sehe ich aus. Ich bin so komisch unvorhanden" (Z, 63; The slimmer I get, the smaller and more pathetic I look. I'm so strangely absent). She even imagines her own death (Z, 186–88).

Fashion and consumerism also feed into Sonja's development, or rather, her failure to develop. Her relationship to shopping and clothing has been negatively formed by her mother (Z, 31). She begins to be obsessed with clothing shops, imagining buying everything in them, "als wäre ich schon so gestört wie Mama früher" (Z, 43; as if I were as unhinged as Mum used to be). The mother figure here represents and seeks to enforce conventional femininity, like Ada's mother in Zeh, while also sabotaging her daughter's efforts to achieve this successfully by fattening her up (Z, 175).[45] Sonja eyes up clothes wondering when they will fit her and when her SlimFast diet will manifest itself physically (Z, 43). There is thus a clear link here between consumerism, fashion, and the diet industry, all of which exert their influence on Sonja's embodied psyche. In an embarrassing scene in a shop, as Sonja is attended to by a man she has a crush on and a model of her acquaintance, she does not fit into the first dress she is handed to try on; on the second, the button pops off. Anxieties about size and appearance—this in the context of commodification, consumerism, and "lookism," as embodied by Melissa, the model—become painfully clear. Sonja attempts bravado, or "[die] verlogene[ ] Selbstsicherheit eines pummeligen Mädchens, das die besten Jahre seines Lebens in einer Boutique verbracht hat" (Z, 33; the put-on self-confidence of a plump girl who's spent the best years of her life in a clothes shop). The episode ends with her resolution to stop eating (Z, 35). There is a clear link between anorexia, the pressure of heterosexual female norms and of the male gaze, and the rivalry and insecurity generated by other feminine bodies connoted as ideal (Z, 33).

Elsewhere, Sonja feels humiliated for eating cheesecake in front of groupies, who she belatedly realizes only eat crispbread (Z, 75). As we will see further in the next chapter, relationships between women are complex in this text. Sonja reads the termination of her brief relationship with Johnny—he tells her he is now with Melissa—as confirmation that she is not thin enough (*Z*, 115). Melissa's own self-perception, a passage narrated from her point of view reveals, is bound up intimately with her appearance. Andrew Wright Hurley suggests, "[Melissa] has fallen for the beauty myth and has no political insight into how harmful it is."[46] The looks and reactions of other women, significantly, confirm her attractiveness, and Melissa herself is alert to other female bodies and faces.[47] On public transport, Melissa has to shut her eyes, and even considers traveling by taxi in future, so offensive to her is the ugliness of others. Sonja also seems to develop such horror for the bodies of others (*Z*, 135). As a model, Melissa is herself subjected to the pressure to look a certain way. She briefly rebels, by having her hair bleached blonde, but is advised by her agent to go back to the red the clients favor (*Z*, 92–93, 161): an episode that points up her limited agency.

Sonja's is a cautionary tale. Her eating disorder apparently spells success, initially. It brings about the necessary thinness, meaning Sonja corresponds to dominant ideals: she is now "wie eins von den Mädchen in den Modestrecken, wie eins von den Mädchen in der Welt" (*Z*, 168; like one of the girls in the fashion line-ups, like one of the girls in the world). Elsewhere, she reflects ironically that she has everything a girl (*Mädchen*) needs to have: her own money, friends, and the ability to fast (*Z*, 125). The beauty myth, then, is powerful and seductive. For Sonja, beautiful women are in fact clever because they are successful (*Z*, 169). Yet her obsession constitutes an illness. It colors her perception of the world (*Z*, 41). While in the grip of her disorder, she persuades herself she is fit and well, and her self-delusions increase in the course of the novel (*Z*, 55, 158). She eventually becomes aware of her "verzerrte Sichtweise" (*Z*, 223; distorted way of seeing).

Sonja's eating disorder involves self-infantilization, or retreat from adult femininity, thwarting her becoming. Indeed, Sonja struggles with being an adult, and actively wishes to revert to infancy (*Z*, 48–49, 75, 168; cf. *Z*, 178, 223). Her eating disorder leads her to retreat from her friends and to give up her creative ambitions (*Z*, 139, 145). In fact, Sonja suggests, girlishness is a condition of successful femininity: "ich bin ein schönes, junges Mädchen, wie es sich gehört für eine Frau" (*Z*, 147; I am a lovely young girl, as is fitting for a woman). Sonja's insecurity relates to her unstable childhood (*Z*, 19; cf. *Z*, 23). The questions of maturing and moving on are thus central to this text (see also *Z*, 20). Sonja's fragility is clear from the outset, when she despairs of her current existence: "was heißt hier echtes Leben? Irgendwie hab' ich keins. Ich muss heulen" (*Z*, 21; what does that mean, real life? I don't have one, somehow. I have to cry). Sonja is very much a subject in process. While the novel ends on a tentative note of hope, Sonja's progress is hesitant: her becoming is highly uncertain, in large part because of her anxiety in the face of cultural and social norms concerning feminine bodies and behaviors. Her relationship with her own body is based on a lack of respect (Z, 109). Hurley describes the novel as "a deeply ambiguous portrait of the empowerment that young women can derive from the creative consumption and production of music."[48] Sonja's relationships with other women are also tense and difficult, and they offer her limited support. The text exposes the shaping, or distortion, of will via mechanisms such as the media and the diet industry, but itself expresses willful critical awareness of these factors.

Sibylle Berg, *Ein paar Leute suchen das Glück und lachen sich tot*

Sibylle Berg's nihilistic, postmodernist work also exposes the lack of agency and authenticity that characterize life in the contemporary context.[49] Her first novel, *Ein paar Leute suchen das Glück und lachen sich tot*, presents a group of disconnected, disparate individuals who all come to unfortunate ends. Nora, who turns seventeen in the course of the narrative, suffers from an eating disorder. Nora's interior monologue documents her obsession with her weight and diet, which is reminiscent of Sonja's in Grether's text: Nora weighs herself every day to establish how much weight she has lost. She has eaten only cucumbers, apples, and lettuce for six months.[50] Later, she eats practically nothing, with even the occasional apple making her feel sick. As in Grether, the character's eating disorder leads to her isolation and detachment; her parents seem alien to her. But it also leads to a feeling of superiority over her classmates: "Als ich noch dick war, bin ich in der Pause immer aufs Klo gegangen, damit sie mich nicht ignorieren können. Jetzt stehe ich offen da und denke mal, daß sie mich beneiden" (*EpL*, 7; When I was fat, I used to go to the restroom during the break, so they couldn't ignore me. Now I just stand there, thinking about how they're envying me). As we will see further in the next chapter, weight is an area of tension and competition for girls and young women, here possibly projected or imagined, but nonetheless powerful.

Nora is engaged in an ongoing body project that is intimately bound up with her self-esteem. While she is pleased with her thin arms, and with the fact that her ribs now show, she finds her legs too fat (*EpL*, 7). She thereby exemplifies segmentarity and the never-ending identification of new "problem zones" on women's bodies. She finds flesh ugly, in line with Greer, Penny, and Power's claim that female flesh provokes disgust and fear in the contemporary context (*EpL*, 7). However, Nora's focus on her weight gives her an aim (*Ziel*), albeit one that is perverse and self-destructive. This counters the senselessness of existence, as she sees it. In a passage reminiscent of Baum (chapter 2), she reflects:

Daß ich bald mit der Schule fertig bin und dann irgendeinen Beruf lernen muß. Und dann würde ich heiraten und würde in einer kleinen Wohnung wohnen und so. Das ist doch zum Kotzen. Mit so einer kleinen Wohnung, meine ich. Das kann doch nicht Leben sein. Aber eben, wie Leben sein soll, das weiß ich nicht. Ich denke mir, daß ich das weiß, wenn ich schön bin. Ich werde so schön wie Kate Moss oder so jemand. Vielleicht werde ich Model. (*EpL*, 8)

[To think I'll be finished with school soon and will have to do training for some job. And then I'd get married and live in a small apartment and stuff. It makes me sick. The small apartment, I mean. That's no life. But I don't know yet how life's supposed to be. I think to myself, I'll know when I'm beautiful. I'll be as beautiful as Kate Moss, someone like that. Maybe I'll be a model.]

There is here a challenge to futurity and to assumptions about appropriate life courses involving coupledom and domesticity. For Nora, achieving "beauty" is a way of establishing some certainty, as well as more positive prospects: cruel optimism and the beauty myth combine to sustain this illusion. The reference to Kate Moss hints at the influence of celebrity culture on this young woman, recalling Grether as well as numerous feminist analyses. Later on, Nora expresses the view that the celebrity Pamela Anderson is fat, participating in the public scrutiny of female bodies that is the subject of ongoing feminist comment and concern (*EpL*, 17). On the one hand, then, Nora has a goal—a future-directed expression of will—but on the other, this aim, thinness and beauty, is clearly shaped by external factors such as dominant popular imagery, and involves compliance and submission.

Because of her eating disorder, Nora is referred to a counselor. However, she rejects this treatment, recalling Hegemann's Mifti. She dismisses the therapist she is assigned as fat and lacking in self-control. Nora thus shares the common popular assumption of fatness as connoting a failure of will. Describing herself as no longer fearful, Nora also claims she does not think about anything (*EpL*, 8). Her lack of reflectiveness is accompanied by an absence of agency and purpose, beyond losing weight. Nora travels, seeming aimless and adrift, like Jenny's protagonist. Nora's boredom and lack of curiosity are comparable with that of other of Berg's protagonists, and are linked to the writer's view of the postmodern condition. This involves—as in Zeh's *Spieltrieb*—mediation and inauthenticity. In this text, Nora "kennt ja schon alles. Hat schon alles gesehen. Die ganze Welt . . . Alle reden, um sich einzureden, was zu fühlen" (*EpL*, 68; knows everything already. Has seen everything. The whole world . . . Everyone talks just to kid themselves into feeling something). She self-medicates with alcohol, finding that red wine makes everything seem palatable and reasonable (*EpL*, 18).

Nora's passivity in her dealings with men accords with her aimlessness and alienation. She reflects, of a man she encounters: "Natürlich gehe ich mit ihm. . . . Was soll ich sonst tun" (*EpL*, 43; Of course I go with him . . . What else am I meant to do). Her detachment from her own body and desires becomes clear when she reflects: "Jeder kann mich haben. Es macht mir nichts. Es ist besser, als allein zu sein" (*EpL*, 44; Anyone can have me. Doesn't make any difference to me. It's better than being alone). Nora, then, is unable to pursue relationships founded on mutuality, and she drifts into a relationship with a young man who professes sadistic leanings (*EpL*, 64). Nora herself engages in sadistic activity, in what might be seen as an expression of will. However, she suddenly experiences nostalgia, or yearning for "Weihnachten. Nach ihrer Mutter . . . nach kleinen Häusern, wo Rauch rauskommt" (*EpL*, 76; Christmas. Her mother . . . little houses with smoke coming out of them). This impulse suggests this form of sexual activity does not accord with her desires. Instead, she experiences a wish for a return to a pre-sexual state, recalling Grether. Nora's pre-adult status is also underlined by her attachment to a toy sheep she carries round as a kind of talisman. When a child goes off with it, she takes leave of it: perhaps a suggestion that she is ready to mature and move on (*EpL*, 95). But Berg eschews comforting narrative trajectories, rejecting teleological stories of progress and success. Instead—like Baum, Jenny, Hegemann, and Roche—she stresses trauma and failure. Nora is hospitalized, and the narrative is typically laconic in relation to the causes of this: she has cut open her veins, she is severely underweight, and she is probably mentally unstable (*EpL*, 84).

Romantic relationships offer no salvation, either, as in Baum. Nora falls in love with a man called Tom, a development that seems to bring about recovery: she eats some of the hospital food without vomiting it up afterward and refrains from stealing sleeping tablets that will help her sleep and so avoid eating (*EpL*, 85). But the depiction of her sudden love for Tom is comic. The chapter heading "Tom und Nora verlieben sich und so ein Scheiß" (Tom and Nora fall in love and shit like that) is typically sardonic and mocking in tone. The pair rob a bank at Nora's suggestion, then travel to Venice. Nora's youth and thinness are at first flattering to Tom: "Er fühlt sich stark und potent" (*EpL*, 113; He feels himself to be strong and potent). But the relationship founders on Nora's immaturity and insecurity, and there are misunderstandings between her and Tom (*EpL*, 136). Nora self-harms and considers suicide; the narrator here explicitly points to her youth as leading to a lack of perspective (*EpL*, 113, 138).[51] While Tom resolves that Nora is the one for him, Nora reflects that the late musician Kurt Cobain would have been a better match for her ("Mit Kurt wäre ich wie ich. Mit Tom bin ich mir fremd" (*EpL*, 144, 145; With Kurt, I'd be myself. With Tom, I'm alien to myself). Nora is, however, needy, and jealous when Tom pays attention to another woman.

While she is not happy with him, she is not happy without him (*EpL*, 183). Tom sleeps with the other woman, and Nora is reduced to despair, becoming "ein Ding" (a thing). She finds a can of petrol and sets light to its contents, dying in agony (*EpL*, 188–89). If happiness is the aim of the will, and if even suicide can be seen to have happiness as its end, Nora fails in her quest (cf. *WS*, 3–4).

While alive, Nora at least possesses a measure of critical consciousness; she is aware of dominant discourses of femininity, as when she reflects on the depiction of women in film and on male domination of cinema (*EpL*, 132). The ideal cinematic girl is "kapriziös. Sie hat immer hohe Schuhe an, in denen sie völlig gut laufen kann, und enge Kleider. Sie hat die Haare hochgetürmt und sieht total verführerisch aus. Sie redet viel . . . Und sie macht ganz entzückend verrücktes Zeug" (*EpL*, 132–33; capricious. She always wears high heels, in which she has absolutely no trouble walking, and tight clothing. She has her hair piled up on her head and looks totally seductive. She talks a lot . . . And she gets up to mad stuff, in a delightful way). But Nora's fate, and Berg's typically sardonic, nihilistic take on her characters' fortunes, allow no room for hope. The text itself, though, acts as a spur to critical consciousness, a manifestation of willfulness, pleading for an awareness of the pathological, or pathologized, status of the young, female, embodied subject.

Sarai Walker, *Dietland*

Sarai Walker's first novel *Dietland* evinces such a critical consciousness in a more explicit and sustained way.[52] It concerns a young woman called Plum living in Brooklyn who gets caught up in a movement that opposes the diet industry. The group has links to an extremist feminist faction that takes gruesome revenge on rapists and other perpetrators of violence against women. Plum's journey from isolation and self-loathing to community and self-acceptance is at the center of this novel, which features satirical and dystopian elements. This journey is hard-won, and by no means straightforward. The transformation of Plum offers a counter-narrative to the conventional makeover paradigm, which involves losing weight and otherwise according with dominant ideals of feminine beauty, which the novel depicts as coercive and constraining. The novel explicitly problematizes makeover fantasies, critiquing neoliberal, postfeminist injunctions relating to body and beauty. It puts forward a collective feminist agency reminiscent of Ahmed's "alternative army of the wayward" (*WS*, 163).

The novel is concerned with the demonization of fat bodies in contemporary US society in particular.[53] Being fat, Plum is "every American woman's worst nightmare" (*D*, 102). Fatness is pathologized, viewed as the result or expression of trauma (*D*, 105). The novel exposes such othering and abjection, a move in line with fat studies and fat activism.[54] Plum is used to being looked at "with disgust," and being in public places is uncomfortable because of people's unkindness, even abuse (D, 4, 106–7). When Plum finally reacts to one aggressor, he punches her (D, 149–50). In response to a culture obsessed with fatness—the question "Do I look fat?" is everywhere to be heard—Plum reflects: "I was already fat. I was the worst that could happen" (D, 127). The word "fat" itself generates shame (see D, 48, 90).[55] Plum meets a former "headless plus-size model," whose body once appeared from the neck down in reports on the obesity epidemic ("America's looming holocaust"). This character illustrates the pathologization of the fat body, and the melodramatic and sensationalizing interpretation to which it gives rise (D, 140–41). Such pathologization makes for unhappiness. At the start of the novel, Plum is on antidepressants and leading a solitary, unsatisfactory existence: "my life wasn't real yet," she reflects (D, 6). She is in an arrested state. Although she is in her late twenties, she feels younger than women with "grown-up lives" (D, 7). Her failure to conform to dominant ideals concerning acceptable body shape hampers her becoming. Plum does not even experience herself as a woman: she is shocked during an ultrasound examination to learn that she has a womb and she later realizes that she had "never felt like a woman" (D, 167, 241). Femininity, then, is intricately bound up with ideals of slimness and attractiveness to men. Plum is "not a generic female" (D, 129): she occupies an "other" category.

Plum is on the one hand passive and isolated. On the other, the aim of future happiness drives her, in line with numerous philosophical understandings of the will: Ahmed notes that willing involves "positings of the positivity of the not yet thing" (WS, 32). Plum nurtures illusions of a future, thinner self. She is a member of a dieting group called "Waist Watchers," a satirical allusion to Weight Watchers, and also has plans to undergo weight-loss surgery. Her real name is Alicia Kettle, but her nickname ("a pearl, a plum—roundness defined me") throws into doubt her real identity: "Alicia is me but not me" (D, 38). Plum dreams of becoming Alicia: "*Burst!*" (D, 43). This is an allusion to adverts for slimming products, and the trope whereby a formerly large individual bursts through a picture of their former selves to reveal their new slender incarnation. It serves as a constant reminder in the narrative of the make-over paradigm and the body project. Plum's interpellation of the associated strictures becomes clear when she "feared [she] would stay a *before* picture forever" (D, 59). She imagines the other her will "dress in pretty clothes . . . travel . . . have a job that she likes [and] host dinner parties" (D, 107). Poignantly, this thinner self "will be loved" (D, 108). In Plum's current state, men find her repugnant or laughable. The trigger for Plum's depression was a boy's rejection of her when she was in college (D, 109, 112–15). In the course of the novel, Plum goes on a series of blind dates, all of which are humiliating, given the men's disgusted or disbelieving reactions to her body upon meeting her (*D*, 159–166). Plum has a privileged, if painful, insight into humanity's cruelty: Alicia would have no such insight (*D*, 159; cf. *D*, 197). Plum's job as an agony aunt grants further awareness. She doles out advice to teenage girls, whose concerns with their weight and experiences of self-harm and of abuse suggest the widespread nature of female suffering (*D*, 3, 8, 11). "Dieting, boys, razor blades," is how Plum sums up their concerns (*D*, 12). Becoming overburdened by the litany of problems, she deletes the messages in her in-box (*D*, 121, 124): a gesture that is liberating from Plum's point of view, but also disturbing, given the unanswered cries for help that are the result. As Plum later realizes, the letters she receives catalog the "trauma of becoming a woman" (*D*, 241), and she begins to write to her correspondents offering them a copy of a book and the chance to engage in discussion about it: that is, she undertakes consciousness-raising (*D*, 243).

As in Grether and as in Zambreno (see conclusion), celebrity is important in defining and upholding ideals of femininity in this context. The story of Marlowe, a former actor Plum meets, exemplifies the stylization of the celebrity body. Marlowe, who was famed for her appearance and especially her long, lustrous hair, tells Plum: "It took a committee to make me look the way I did" (*D*, 134). Marlowe rejects the strictures of celebrity. The press track her down and expose her in Italy, where she has been enjoying temporary anonymity, having cut her hair and gained weight. Subsequent coverage derides her as "ugly" and a "fat lesbian" (*D*, 137). Having lowered her "fuckability quotient," she loses her Hollywood career (*D*, 137). Marlowe writes a book on the topic of "fuckability," having earned a PhD, and she is now a writer and activist as well as the mother of a baby boy. Marlowe's is an exemplary tale that illustrates the perniciousness of the beauty myth, and the freedom to be gained from liberation from it. Marlowe takes Plum to a beauty and hair salon and a department store, where the rigors of feminine adornment Plum undergoes expose femininity as costly, sometimes painful, drag: "Being a woman means being a faker," Marlowe tells Plum (*D*, 145; cf. *D*, 160). Another character, Julia, masquerades as a conventional "woman," and her performance points up the performativity of gender, recalling Butler: "All makeup is drag," she tells Plum (*D*, 76). Julia has no breasts, like her sisters, having had them removed because of the risk of cancer, a detail that involves a challenge to conventional norms and ideals relating to the female body (*D*, 101). She later tells Plum she is passing for both thin and white, thereby introducing race into this narrative about embodiment and forms of privilege (*D*, 246).

Hollywood, the cosmetics industry, and advertising conspire to maintain a labor-intensive feminine ideal. The pervasiveness of images of ideally attractive female bodies is the object of satire: a pair of breasts "whizzed by" on the side of a bus (*D*, 219; cf. *D*, 222, 224, 225, 234), a detail that recurs, to savagely comic effect, to highlight the pornographization and segmentization of the female body. But it is the weight-loss industry that is subjected to the most vehement satire here. Early on in the novel, Plum is given a book called *Adventures in Dietland*, a memoir by a Verena Baptist that also acts as an exposé of the dieting movement founded by the author's parents, Baptist Weight Loss; Plum had once been a member. Excerpts of this book feature in the text, and they detail the duplicity and murkiness of the business, and the dubious ethics of the dieting industry as a whole. This industry is founded on fads and, in some cases, on deliberate deception and the exploitation of clients' vulnerability and self-loathing. In the book, "[Verena] devoted a whole chapter to liberating oneself from what she called Dietland. Dietland is about making women small, Verena wrote" (*D*, 64). This thesis recalls Marlowe's theorization of "fuckability"—"A fuckable woman doesn't take up space. Fuckable women are controlled" (*D*, 144)—and work by Penny, Power, and others. The "Baptist" plan has cult-like qualities. The program renders Plum chronically hungry, and she is racked with guilt when she cracks and eats (*D*, 56–57).

In contrast to the dieting industry, and to the contemporary makeover paradigm more broadly, Plum's mother has a "play-the-cards-you're-dealt mentality when it came to matters of the body" (*D*, 42). She sees physical attributes as "fixed, for the most part," and reassures her daughter she is beautiful as she is (*D*, 43). A comparable oppositional attitude is represented by the "fat feminist cunts," as they are described by a senior figure in the Baptist program, "with their 'Love Your Body' bullshit" (*D*, 57). But Plum herself succumbs repeatedly to the blandishments of the industry, in a kind of willing submission. After the forced closure of the Baptist plan by Verena, following her parents' death in a car crash, Plum gorges on cakes and gains weight. She joins Waist Watchers in college but becomes disillusioned with the program:

> I followed the diet plans outlined in books and magazines. I took diet pills, including one that was later recalled by the FDA after several people died. I took a supplement from a company in Mexico, but gave it up after it caused violent stomach pains. For all of my junior year, I drank a chocolate diet shake for breakfast and lunch, which turned my bowel movements into stones, causing hemorrhoids . . . I was too squeamish for bulimia and lacked the masochism needed for anorexia, so once I had cycled through every diet I could find, I went back to Waist Watchers. (*D*, 65)

Reading Verena's book affirms Plum in her desire to undergo surgery, since dieting apparently is ineffective: a response she acknowledges is not what the author intended (*D*, 65). Verena makes this clear herself when the women meet and converse ("Don't butcher yourself," *D*, 90). Plum's journey toward self-acceptance is faltering, and so it demonstrates the weight of the cultural pressures upon her, and the entanglement of forces at work in and on the subject.

Plum's journey is aided by other women, and willfulness emerges as a collective and contagious matter, in line with Ahmed: "a no is what can be given to others" (*WS*, 143). The novel features an underground feminist movement involving Julia, a PhD in women's studies who works undercover in a vast storeroom filled with makeup (*D*, 74–75). Targets of the movement's headline-grabbing actions include the editor of a UK newspaper that prints images of nude young women (*D*, 93). The editor is forced instead to print pictures of male genitalia, a move that proves "bad for business" (*D*, 94). London is described as "like one big red-light district," a description that echoes the author's own impressions of the capital (*D*, 95).[56] This and other actions mean that "the default Londoner, the implied viewer of everything, was no longer male" (*D*, 96). Through her contact with Verena and the women around her, Plum begins her transformation. Verena's house is dark red in color, and Plum is enveloped in a "womb of red wallpaper" (*D*, 85). The house represents an enclave that offers security and respite from patriarchal norms and from violence (*D*, 196). Verena begins with Plum a program of highly unconventional treatment and analysis. In particular, she challenges Plum's fantasies of a future, other her, asking: "What if this is your *real life* right now?" (*D*, 108). Plum at first resists Verena's intervention, persisting in her makeover fantasy (for example, *D*, 120). That is to say, she resists reality.[57] Yet in Verena's house, Plum undergoes a makeover of an unconventional kind: "I was different in a way that couldn't be seen. Made over" (*D*, 215). In place of willing submission to dominant norms, a form of willfulness erupts: Plum is "tired of being obedient" (*D*, 201). This process of self-liberation involves her coming to accept and even respect her body. It involves an eschewal of fantasies relating to the future and an assertion of the present:

> There was a phantom woman in my mind that I was comparing myself to, and I had to force her from the dressing room. When she was gone, I looked at my body, the body that had kept me alive for nearly thirty years, without any serious health problems . . . I had never appreciated or loved the body that had done so much for me. I had thought of it as my enemy, as nothing more than a shell that enclosed my real life, but it wasn't a shell. The body was me. *This is your real life. You're already living it.* I removed the clothes and stood naked before the mirrors, turning this way and that. I was round and cute in a way I'd never seen before. (*D*, 221–22)

Plum realizes that "*Alicia is me*" (*D*, 292). She develops a healthier relationship with her body and with food (*D*, 290). While her relationship
with food has long been anxious—"I spent my days tiptoeing around
food" (*D*, 101)—in Verena's house, she enjoys eating, and she begins
to cook for the other residents (*D*, 199, 207). In this setting, "there was
never any mention of calories" (*D*, 210).

The questions of normality and normativity are key to this text, and
they relate to the matters of will and willfulness. Plum is "other," and
yearns to be normal. Verena both relativizes and legitimizes her con-
ventionality: "[Alicia] wants to fall in love, get married, have babies, the
whole predictable triumvirate" (*D*, 130). Verena does not assume Plum
is straight, however (*D*, 108). Queerness appears as a viable possibility in
this text. Julia finds Plum beautiful and kisses her (*D*, 75, 139; see also
254): same-sex attraction features as a challenge to the male or mainstream gaze that elsewhere dominates. Plum's reactions to other women
themselves reveal normative assumptions. When she sees a woman with
a scarred face at Verena's house, she reflects that the place is a "freak
show" (*D*, 141). But she gets to know the woman in question, Sana, and
sees her beauty (*D*, 208). Sana engages with Plum in a discussion about
norms, in an exchange that also highlights the growing closeness between
the women:

> "We're different in a way that everyone can see. We can't hide it
> or fake it. We'll never fit society's idea for how women should look
> and behave, but why is that a tragedy? We're free to live how we
> want. It's liberating, if you choose to see it that way."
> The line that existed between me and most people didn't exist
> with her. I wanted to touch her face. (*D*, 200)

This encounter suggests solidarity between "other," or wayward subjects,
in line with Ahmed. Yet for all her new-found confidence, Plum is still at
the receiving end of humiliating and offensive behavior. She reflects that
while she has changed, "the world hadn't changed along with [her]" (*D*,
281). However, her laughter in the face of a yobbish attack suggests a kind
of sovereign transcendence (*D*, 284–85). The final word of the novel—
"Burst"—also affirms Plum's positive transformation. Interestingly,
Plum's body shape affirms female intergenerational connection:

> The women who came before me were black-and-white. My grand-
> mother, mother of my mother, died before I was born, but there
> are photographs of her . . . She's a teenager in [one] photo, her
> hair bobbed in the style of the 1920s. She and her sister are wearing
> polka-dotted dresses and both of them are round all over. Even as a

girl I saw myself in them. I knew we were connected, like a string of round white pearls stretching into the past. (*D*, 38).

If Plum has the surgery, she will no longer resemble her grandmother (*D*, 103). The novel affirms female connections and genealogy, and depicts the emergence of a collective feminist willfulness, as it tracks one character's progress toward self-actualization in defiance of injurious norms.

Conclusion

Body and will are closely aligned, even co-dependent, as this chapter has suggested. The unruly bodies in these narratives expose both the oppressiveness of norms relating to female beauty and the potential female embodied subjects hold performatively to resist, or rework, such norms. In Roche, disgust serves as a way to query norms relating to feminine propriety and hygiene. In Zeh, animality and intelligence are asserted over decorativeness. Even where, as in Berg and Grether, bodies are docile—or perhaps, rather, willful in a perverse way—the texts themselves expose the forces to which these bodies are subjected, critically highlighting the workings of culture and its imbrication with individual psyches and bodies. In Walker, there is a sustained challenge to the body project, the beauty myth, and the makeover paradigm, as an alternative form of "becoming" unfolds and the fat subject asserts herself. Ahmed writes of the body politic as a regulatory system, and frames disturbance of it in corporeal terms. In the Grimm story "The Willful Child," the child dies as a result of her disobedience. Her body is buried but her hand sticks out of the earth, connoting persistent, embodied willfulness (*WS*, 123). This chapter has foregrounded bodies that "stick out"—because they are excessive, unclean, "ugly," or disgusting—and disturb the surface of contemporary norms (Roche, Zeh, Walker). It has also examined bodies that comply and so become ill or threatened with death, thereby pointing up the perversity of those norms in a different, but no less effective way (Berg, Grether).

While the chapter has focussed on novels in which the body is at the heart of the narrative, corporeality and standards of beauty feature in most if not all the works I examine here. For example, Caitlin Moran's Johanna harbors an intensely private desire to be beautiful: "because it will keep me safe, and keep me lucky, and it's too exhausting not to be."[58] This reference to beauty as a guarantor of safety and fortune constitutes an acknowledgment of the centrality and the tyranny of appearance in constructions of femininity; it is "exhausting" not to live up to the ideal. Johanna sees herself in a mirror and realizes she is "not beautiful at all." But an assertion of bravado follows: "I am a poet, and a writer, and I deal with hearts and souls and words, and not meat and vanity" (57). This defiance is heartening. A stress on interiority and intellect is one possible response to the challenges posed by female embodiment. Yet the novels we have looked at suggest how difficult this project is, given existing norms and ideals, and especially given the image-driven nature of contemporary culture: femininity is spectacle, even or especially in the digital age.[59] Not least, the demands other women pose give rise to anxiety, tension, and competitiveness, as we will now see.

4: Sisterhood and Identification

THE TERM "SISTERHOOD" functions strategically here as a reference to a mythical "1970s feminism." It connotes a sense of shared political struggle among women, a notion that is not unproblematic but which is nonetheless crucial as a legitimizing and enabling condition of feminism. I have already mentioned claims that certain new-feminist texts ignore differences among women and so unwittingly reproduce hierarchies founded on race, class, and sexuality. This gesture might be strategically essentialist, but it also risks simplifying and reducing female subjects. However, such texts do also gesture toward internationalism and intersectionality.[1] And in any case, the issue of dividedness among women is arguably the more pressing one, as analyses of femininity in neoliberalism, and the literary texts under discussion, suggest. Ahmed's "army of the wayward" appears far from the point of assembly.

Beauvoir wrote in 1949 of the alienation of individual women from each other. How are relationships between women conceived and lived out in the context of neoliberal postfeminism? The nonfiction texts featured in chapter one of this volume note the importance of role models and of stereotypes. Natasha Walter, for example, underlines the significance of stereotypes such as male leader and female caregiver in shaping self-perception and ambition.[2] Representation is key here. Yet in the literary texts I have explored so far, excepting Moran's and Grether's, in which the protagonists find strength in female musical artistes, there is a distinct absence of role models in evidence. The mother-daughter relations featured in these texts are, on the whole, dysfunctional or distant.[3] Appearance causes tensions among women, as becomes even clearer in this chapter. Complex hierarchies and patterns of desire emerge. Such tensions and difficulties are symptomatic and representative of the neoliberal, postfeminist context, as Alison Winch suggests in *Girlfriends and Postfeminist Sisterhood*.[4]

Winch refers to "the complex emotions and systems of control that permeate female sociality in a postfeminist context" (9). In particular, she discusses the feelings of "competition and comparison" that neoliberal popular culture fosters and legitimizes (196). She argues: "technologies of oppression structure the gestures, conversations and interpersonal reflexivity enacted by and between women" (197). Yet to posit a utopian form of sisterhood, free of conflict, is not helpful, because it is illusory and because it prevents a better understanding between women from emerging (196). Winch claims, instead, that conflicts between women "could be approached dialectically as forms of energy and creativity." She adds, however, that in order for this project to come about, "we . . . need to devise a site of collectivity where these deeply exposing inner realms can be carefully brought to light" (197). For conflicts to be productive, Winch proposes that collectivity needs to arise in place of the antagonism and envy popularly depicted and actually experienced by and among young women. For this reason, "sisterhood"—or, at any rate, "identification"—remains necessary, at least as a goal: Ahmed states, "*we* is not a foundation but what we [feminists] are working toward."[5] Fiction, I will contend here, offers a "site of collectivity" where this ongoing project can occur. It constitutes, potentially, "a space of multiplicity and emergence where acknowledgments of difference can become a starting point for developing a sense of political solidarity."[6]

Identity and Identification

Sameness is not a precondition for collective action, nor does difference preclude attempts at mutual understanding. There is no (single, satisfactory) answer to the question of "female identity." Transfeminisms in particular make this usefully clear. Indeed, identity politics is giving way to ideas concerning becoming, and intersectional approaches are yielding to affective ones. Elizabeth Grosz, for one, challenges the centrality of "identity" in feminist theory, instead highlighting becoming and difference. While the notion of "difference" is fraught with complexity, Grosz affirms its significance. For her, difference is unpredictable and processual: "What difference means and how it is lived remains an open question, to be negotiated by each generation and geography in its own, unpredictable terms."[7] In *Becoming Undone*, Grosz also draws on Darwin to describe life as "the ever more complex elaboration of difference."[8] She asks how we can rethink subjectivity and the human using the Darwinian concept of constitutive difference, taking inspiration from Bergson and Deleuze (5).

Intersectionality has proved inadequate and constraining as a model: it demands the "knowing, naming, and thus stabilizing of identity across space and time."[9] Criticizing the "reduction of subjectivity to identity," Grosz challenges intersectional approaches, suggesting they may lead to unproductive fragmentation: "We must affirm . . . that . . . specification of identity in terms of race-class-gender-sexual orientation-and-ethnicity, must ultimately lead to individuality alone, to unique subject positions which then lose any connections they may share with other women in necessarily different positions" (89). Thus, a stress on intersecting oppressions may in fact lead to a weakening of solidarity. It also involves a misunderstanding of the nature of power and of how oppression works. In an intersectional view, "each oppression . . . is ultimately assumed to be determinable, recognizable, and separable from the other forms of oppression with which it engages" (92). Intersectionality, then, can lead to a rigid and static account of power and of oppression, as Jasbir K. Puar also suggests (see introduction).

If identity cannot (and should not) form the ground of a collective feminist project, and if intersectionality as an approach tends merely to shore up the fiction that is "identity," how can the "we" to which we are working toward even be conceived as realizable? "Identification," a term that suggests an ongoing, interrelational process that involves continuous differentiation, from self and other, might help.[10] Identification involves interactions between "individual" subjects, but also between subjects and culture, or the social imaginary. Rosi Braidotti evokes the ongoing construction of the subject in these terms when she addresses the question of social norms and their influence:

> Social and cultural norms or normative models are external attractors, stimulants or points of reference. They act like magnets that draw the self heavily in certain directions and stimulate the person accordingly. The social imaginary functions in terms analogous to discursive glue that holds the bits and pieces together, but in a discontinuous and contradictory manner . . . I do not see the impact of images or representations in terms of "internalization," because I find this theory too dualistic in the way it splits the self from society, the "inside" from the outside of the subject. I am far more interested instead in thinking about the extensive web of interconnections between the two. Power . . . is another name for this web of co-extensivity of self with society.[11]

Braidotti's reference to "this web of co-extensivity of self with society" is useful in its challenge to understandings of self and the social imaginary as discrete and static. It also undermines the idea of gender, for example, as imposed from without. It anticipates Ahmed's willfulness, which also raises the question of the particular versus the general and which also understands power as dynamic. Willfulness is not only or necessarily a matter of individual subjects engaging in oppositional moves: Ahmed highlights relationality when she describes willing as "a way we experience inhabiting a world with others."[12] She also criticizes the conflation of willfulness with individualism (WS, 150). To understand girls as willfully enmeshed in the social imaginary and in relationships with other female subjects is to see agency as relational and contextual.

This chapter discusses texts that have female relationships at their center, beginning with two novels by Elke Naters, *Königinnen* (Queens, 1998) and *Lügen* (Lies, 1999). These exemplify and to an extent endorse a view of female friendships as toxic and competitive. *Special* (2002) a work by Bella Bathurst, is even more despairing on this score, as we see next. Returning to Kerstin Grether's 2004 *Zuckerbabys*, we find female friendships which are tense and difficult, but nonetheless important to the narrator's development. In the final three texts I discuss, Emma Jane Unsworth's 2014 *Animals*, Zoe Pilger's *Eat My Heart Out* (2014) and Rachel B. Glaser's *Paulina and Fran* (2015), female bonds are fraught with ambivalence and hostility, but they also constitute sites of intense intimacy, need, and desire. In this way, fiction creates an arena such as Winch posits as necessary: a space in which a holistic view of feminine connections can be played out and affectively experienced. In many of these texts "same-sex"-desire features. In all cases, it is ambivalent, distorted, or repressed, as I discuss further in my conclusion to this chapter, when I address the question of queer and its relationship to ideas of transgression and refusal. These fictions together manifest a female willfulness that is at once collective and wayward: femininity is a matter of voluntarism as well as of subjection, of individuation as well as of co-optation.

Elke Naters, *Königinnen* and *Lügen*

Elke Naters's *Königinnen* is narrated from the points of view of two female characters, Gloria and Marie, who are ostensibly friends. But their relationship involves envy, dissimulation, and resentment. Marie is relatively young, at thirty, and for most of the novel single. Gloria, on the other hand, has a partner and one child, and by the end of the novel is expecting a second child. However, Gloria's partner and child are sketchily evoked and appear comically irrelevant. While the novel ultimately affirms the relationship between Gloria and Marie as key to both women's lives, it is not clear how far this affirmation is sincere. The irony of the narrative offers a strategy through which female relationships are rendered both trivial and central. The novel is set in, and satirizes, a context in which women are rivals for status and male attention. The women occupy a consumerist, commodified world in which labels and brands hold great weight. Appearance is a central concern for them, as well as a marker of status. Gloria goes shopping to improve her mood. Despite her precarious finances, she buys expensive shoes, deceiving herself about their cost. The bathetic ending of the first chapter points up the superficiality of her worldview: "Das einzige, für das es sich immer lohnt, viel Geld auszugeben, sind Schuhe . . . Und wenn man gute Schuhe trägt, dann sieht alles andere auch gleich aus, als wäre es von Helmut Lang. Und nicht von H&M" (The only thing it's always worth spending lots of money on is shoes . . . And if you wear good shoes, everything else looks like it's from Helmut Lang, too. And not H&M).[13] Such passages tie in with work by Penny on women in capitalism and also evoke neoliberal cruel optimism. The characters here are flat and interchangeable, their voices barely distinct. The readable, affectless quality of the prose aligns it with *Popliteratur*.[14] Like Berg's *Ein paar Leute suchen das Glück und lachen sich tot*, this novel evokes a postmodernist ennui (*K*, 10–11, for example).

Women's relationships are from the outset evoked in terms of rivalry and tension. The opening paragraph, narrated by Gloria, informs us:

> Ich sitze mit Marie im Cafe, und Ala kommt herein. Sie tut so, als wäre ich nicht da und setzt sich neben Marie und erzählt ihr unwichtiges Zeug. . . . Ich höre, wie sie zu Marie sagt: *Du hast wunderschöne Schuhe an.* Ich wette, wenn ich diese Schuhe getragen hätte, hätte sie gesagt, deine Hose rutscht dir runter . . . Ala war meine beste Freundin. (*K*, 7)

> [I'm sitting with Marie in the cafe, and Ala comes in. She acts like I'm not there and sits down next to Marie, starts going on about this and that. . . . I hear her saying to Marie: "I love your shoes." I bet if I was wearing those shoes she'd have said, "Your trousers are falling down" . . . Ala used to be my best friend.]

We learn that similar tensions arise when Gloria meets Marie together with a friend named Susan. The proliferation of names here is comedic and suggests the interchangeable nature of these friendships, which are temporary and disposable. There is a lack of sympathy or care between female characters (*K*, 11, for example). According to Gloria, Marie is fickle and only around when she needs comforting after a breakup. Yet she is the only friend Gloria really has.[15] Female friendships are thus in short supply. Shortly after this reflection, Gloria learns Marie has been seen with Martin, a friend of Gloria's, a revelation that causes further tension and disruption. Competition for male attention and approval is crucial to the dynamic the novel evokes. From Marie's point of view, Gloria is only interested in her when things are going badly, so she can experience *Schadenfreude*: "Sie ist die beste Freundin, wenn es mir schlecht geht" (*K*, 106; She's the best friend in the world when I'm having a hard time). She concludes that it is better to have a man than a friend who cannot bear her being happy in love (*K*, 107). The women do eventually meet again, however, and the final paragraph of the novel expresses Marie's pleasure in her friend's company: "Ich bin so froh, daß sie da ist . . . Ich bin so froh, daß ich so eine großartige Freundin habe, die so eine köstliche Melone mitgebracht hat" (*K*, 151; I'm so happy she's here . . . I'm so happy I have such a great friend who's brought along such a delicious melon). The detail of the melon provides bathos, comically undercutting the sincerity and validity of Marie's feelings here. Her final reflection, on the necessity of having a friend like Gloria, is also dubious. The novel ultimately affirms the precariousness and superficiality of relationships, including or especially those between women, in a consumerized, urban world, in which values, and politics, appear to be missing.

Naters's follow-up novel is comparable in its view of female friendship as at once central and toxic. *Lügen* tells of two long-time friends, Augusta and Be. Augusta, the narrator, is in thrall to Be, who is capricious and manipulative. Be leaves her husband for a woman. Her self-declared feminism is based on "falsehoods," and the lesbian relationship she embarks on turns out only to involve a new form of *Realpolitik*.[16] Augusta's reaction to her friend's new relationship reveals both homophobia and suppressed lesbian desire. She recalls a dream she had in which she was having sex with a "fette Lesbe" (fat lesbian), then wondering:

> Was machen die, denke ich mir. Binden die sich Gummischwänze um und ficken sich gegenseitig? . . . Ist das ekelhaft.
> Ich muß auch daran denken, wie ich und Be, als Kinder, noch ganz klein, Sex hatten. Wir haben uns ausgezogen und in meinem Kleiderschrank eingesperrt und uns befummelt. Glaube ich. Was wir genau da drin gemacht haben, weiß ich nicht mehr, weil es dunkel war. Zu dunkel, um sich daran zu erinnern.[17]

> [What do they do, I wonder. Do they put on rubber dicks and fuck each other? . . . Disgusting.
> I also have to think about how when Be and I were children, still very little, we had sex. We got undressed and locked ourselves in my wardrobe and groped each other. I think. I don't know what we got up to in there any more, because it was too dark. Too dark to remember.]

Margaret McCarthy points to the link the novel establishes between lesbian desire and the yearning for a maternal, nurturing presence, an ideal the text challenges especially through the depiction of mother-daughter relationships as sites of duplicity and deceit.[18] I will return to this observation in the conclusion to this chapter.

The novel, whose title indeed highlights deception, deals with the characters' adjustments to their changing situations, and with the very idea of change: Be feels Augusta's view of her is rigid, for example (*L*, 85). The question of whether Be has really changed, and what she is really like, is in fact key to this novel (for example, *L*, 60, 66, 165). In the end, the narrator appears to accept Be as she is and to be grateful to the latter: Be's recklessness provides her with an instructive spectacle (*L*, 191). The end of the novel is cautiously optimistic. Friendship with both Be and Pit, her girlfriend, and a romantic relationship with Pit's brother, appear to await Augusta: "[Ich] könnte . . . einen Freund haben und zwei

Freundinnen, und wir hätten eine Menge Spaß und viel zu lachen, bis an unser Lebensende. Das wäre mal schön" (*L*, 192; I could have a boyfriend and two girlfriends, and we'd have loads of fun and laugh a lot, till the end of our days. That'd be nice). Yet the grammar here hints at the fragility of these dreams.[19] What emerge ultimately are the precariousness and the difficulty of relationships among women in the neoliberal, postfeminist context. This depiction is critical: Naters's satirical works slyly, willfully undercut associations of femininity with care and nurture, at the same time asserting the importance of such values, along with the necessity of degendering them: "Caring relations remain a fiction, but one worth imitating and internalizing," McCarthy remarks. In her view, the novel suggests that "individuality and shifting power relations can coexist with deep bonds and solidarity"—albeit in the subjunctive mood.[20]

Bella Bathurst, *Special*

There are very few such suggestions in Bella Bathurst's first novel, *Special*, which concerns a group of teenage schoolgirls on a trip to the countryside: "a way of using up the time between exams and the end of term."[21] The novel is narrated from the points of view of Hen, Ali, and Jules. The shifting viewpoints point to the complex, relational model of the self that emerges in this novel. This collective identity is fraught with anxiety. The narrative ends in death and catastrophe: Jules falls from the roof during a confrontation involving Hen and another character, Caz, when the various tensions between the girls come to a head. Only one character, Ali, experiences a positive development. In this sense the text accords with the negativity of the novels explored in chapter 2. As Berthold Schoene notes, the novel "highlights disorientation and failure."[22]

Special charts the struggle for self-definition the girls undertake alongside and in opposition to each other. Its title points to the struggle to forge a distinctive self and attain status. Becoming is a painful matter. Summing up her discomfort, Jules declares: "Hate being thirteen. Thirteen's unlucky and crap and it's so sort of in the middle of things. It's so *not anything*" (*S*, 100; cf. *S*, 105). Adolescent awkwardness, here, is an uncomfortable matter. When she dresses up to go out, Ali thinks: "Jules looked like a simulated woman" (*S*, 131). The struggle to be or appear adult takes its toll. When Ali reads out fairy tales, "children's books," for the other girls' pleasure, they experience a moment of relief (*S*, 244). Children need "the solidity of adults," but that is shown here as lacking (*S*, 292). As in other texts, the girls receive little support or understanding from the older generation. Role models are conspicuously absent: the two teachers on the trip seem repellent and ridiculous to the girls. Hen's mother is immature and unstable, recalling Lucy in *Das Blütenstaubzimmer*. Schoene describes this character as "directionless[ ]" and as "a femininity junkie" (139). He further suggests that "adult womanhood in *Special* is a traumatic delirium of arrested development" (138), a reading that gains weight in light of the image of the female accident victim that features at the start of the novel.

The girls collectively define smoking, drugs, men, and drink as crucial to enjoyment (*S*, 16). Smoking constructs a group identity: "By the end of the second year, the group of those who smoked had acquired solidity and definition" (*S*, 94). Schoene observes that this solidity is illusory, as is the broader ideal to which the girls aspire: "taking their cue from popular magazines and guided by each other's fantasies of womanhood, they subscribe to an entirely imaginary and ultimately dead-end ideal of feminine glamour, revolving around sex, alcohol and clothes" (137). Dissimulation, duplicity, and bravado are the norm among the girls (for example, *S*, 15–16, 134). The struggle for status dominates much of their lives. Physical appearance is key in this contest for superiority. Izzy is unattractive: "the scapegoat and the punchbag . . . it was always necessary to have someone to hate" (*S*, 18; see also *S*, 171). Ali explains the process of othering to Izzy, remarking: "There's a theory that people need scapegoats" (*S*, 52). The other, here, is the site of projection as well as abjection: Hen sees her own "disgustingness" reflected in Izzy (*S*, 242). Normality is here, too, a difficult and oppressive ideal. Ali, for example, is a loner, and so deemed not-normal, as Izzy informs her:

> "All that going off on your own. Climbing trees and stuff. People think it's weird."
> Ali found herself becoming angry. "It's not weird. It's just what I like to do. They're the weird ones."
> "They're not. They're normal. It's us who's weird."
> "Well, if that's normal, then . . ." Ali was having difficulty with Izzy's use of the word "us." She started walking faster. (*S*, 53; ellipsis in original)

Ali thus rejects an alliance with the equally "weird" Izzy, suggesting ejection from the mainstream means isolation rather than solidarity with other others.

Conflict is ever-present between the girls: Ali reflects on her antipathy to "the endless arguments, the slow corrosive pickpickstabstab of claim and counter-claim" (*S*, 29). Real communication is impossible in this context, where Ali can only hope for "a series of audible misconnections" (*S*, 51). When Jules is furious with Hen, she conducts a frenzied interior monologue haranguing her, rather than addressing her directly (*S*, 71–72; cf. *S*, 216, 230). Power relations are shifting and tense, as Hen finds out: "Now, abruptly, she had become the excluded" (*S*, 88). Hen, who is from Scotland, had for a long time been blind to the others' silent mockery of her pride in her background and her pleasure in telling others about it. When she becomes aware of having been ridiculed, she experiences shame and humiliation (S, 91). Vulnerability, in this context, is an invitation to attack (S, 210). The relationship between Caz and Jules in particular exemplifies such harmful dynamics. Jules feels inferior to Caz, who appears mysterious and glamorous (S, 105–6). Jules also desires Caz, as I discuss further in chapter 5. Another girl, Vicky, has "a thing about Caz," leading her to dote and simper (S, 209). Hen, for one, feels she will "never be as good as Caz" (S, 242), who is an object of envy as well as of desire.

The question of feminism, and the related issues of sisterhood and identification, surface when Caz declares herself uninterested in "woman stuff" (S, 110). Jules queries this position, citing "girls . . . having jobs and things. . . . And stuff about people sticking together" (S, 110): that is to say, female professional advancement and solidarity. Caz's reply reflects a different perspective:

> "what people—us, girls—really actually want is to make themselves up, put on their blindingest clothes, do the stuff with the heels and the hair and the lipstick. And then they want to walk into a room, looking as dead fuck-off gorgeous as they can ever look, and for every other girl in the room to look at them and think 'Bitch'." (S, 110–11)

Female solidarity is in this view an illusion, trumped by the competition for male attention. Caz qualifies this view, saying it does not apply "here," only "outside. At parties. The world, where men are," and she goes on:

> "That's the way it works. Everybody pretends the other stuff, stuff about friendship and kindness and looking after each other and all the rest of it, but actually, really, what they're actually thinking is, she's got better legs than me or better tits than me or better hair than me or whatever. And then they're thinking, I want those tits or those legs or that hair, I want all that stuff that she's got . . . I'll hang out with that person just so I can be close to it. And they know they'll never be six foot or a decent blonde or rich enough to slice their tits up and stick in implants, so they hate each other instead. That's how it works. That's how it is." (S, 112)

For Caz, women stick together except when it comes to "men or sex or important stuff" (S, 113). The girls subsequently discuss the view of men as inferior to women. When Jules argues that women are better than men, Caz objects (S, 113). The tense, competitive relationships between the girls bear out Caz's claims. For example, Jules reacts to Hen's eating disorder with anger: "You can starve yourself to death if you like. We don't care. You're so boring these days" (*S*, 227). Seeing Jules covered in vomit, having passed out after coercive sex, Caz does not try to help her, merely "staring down at her friend" before leaving the scene (*S*, 147).

Caz also problematizes the ideals of individuality and choice, noting that girls are interpellated by dominant discourses, or, as she puts it: "You don't even *know* what you like [when choosing clothes] . . . You buy stuff because you know it's going to get right up your sister's nose" (*S*, 114). Caz concedes that some of her views come from her sister, only exemplifying further the constructedness of subjectivity and agency. The discussion between Caz and Jules thus touches on the issues of choice and consumerism. It is notable that Jules asserts her agency through consumer choices ("I don't buy things for other people! I buy them for me, right?") (*S*, 115). As Schoene notes, the novel situates itself in a postfeminist milieu, also embedding the narrative "within a pre-feminist history of female disorientation . . . and madness [through its former-asylum setting]" (139). The girls have "imbibed the post-feminist message of gender equality," and this has led not to heightened self-esteem, but to "a fatalistic lack of pride in their femaleness" (135). This reading ties in with an understanding of postfeminism as involving the simultaneous taken-for-grantedness and repudiation of feminism.

The girls form a tense, unstable grouping, one that is defined against the "other sex," boys and men, who are mysterious. Jules reflects that having been away from male company, she no longer knows how boys "worked": "Blokes, she knew, came with a different set of instructions to girls" (*S*, 117). Heterosexual femininity involves performance: Caz is "different in the presence of men" (*S*, 140). Feminine masochism is suggested when, having been raped, Jules blames herself (*S*, 152). Boys occupy distinct spaces, demarcated as theirs. Of the record shop it is reported: "Girls didn't come here. Girls weren't meant to come here" (*S*, 56). The girls, in turn, are "alarming" to men, with their "pack mentality . . . power . . . imagination" (*S*, 205). And the widely held view that "women were safe and men were unsafe" (*S*, 250) proves dubious in this bleak novel. As mentioned, there is no *Bildung* here, not, at least, for the majority of the characters, and Jules's prediction comes true:

> There was going to be no redemption, no improvement, and no one to lift her up. This is how it was, this is how it was going to continue. Things didn't get better, people didn't suddenly discover the lost treasures in each other . . . She'd spent her whole life trying not to be herself, and it hadn't made any difference at all. All she'd ever wanted was to be special . . . But she . . . wasn't even right. (*S*, 160)

Jules in fact dies. Hen, too, has nothing to look forward to: "she was dreading everything" (*S*, 172). Only Ali, the loner, meets a man she feels she can trust, and opens up in a life-changing encounter (*S*, 206, 250–51). Sisterhood appears here highly problematic and unlikely, given the insecurity, ambivalence, and hostility of the girls. And yet in Jules's timid defence of feminism, and her—albeit twisted and complicated—desire for Caz, there are suggestions, at least, of possible alliances between women that may also involve desire. But more obviously, the text challenges ideals of feminine "caring" behaviors, and—in keeping with other works under discussion—asserts the abject, disgusting, and baleful, insisting on the messiness of sociality and of identification.

Kerstin Grether, *Zuckerbabys*

The female relationships evoked in Kerstin Grether's novel *Zuckerbabys* are also fraught with tension. Allita, for example, is older than Sonja, and Sonja reflects that their friendship depends on the former's maturity and stability.[23] This is not an equal relationship, then, and Sonja wonders why Allita wants a friend who is so much younger than her (*Z*, 83). The relationship involves envy, rivalry, and tension (*Z*, 175). As in Bathurst, young women react to each other's eating disorders with a mixture of scorn, disgust, and envy. Allita tells Sonja brutally, "Krieg mir bloß keine Essstörung" (*Z*, 43–44; Just don't go getting an eating disorder on me). When members of the band Museabuse confront Sonja with her eating disorder—one of them pulls a blanket off her and describes her emaciated body as resembling "ein Skelett" (*Z*, 209; a skeleton)—she counters with insulting observations about their own obsessions and complexes. Weight is a site of feverish competition. Such brutality and hostility tie in with Winch's understanding of neoliberalism as inimical to sympathy and intimacy among women. As we have seen, Grether's protagonist occupies a culture saturated with imagery, and she struggles to define herself in this context. Sonja's mother does not offer a role model, and is instead associated with Sonja's concerns around weight and shopping. The importance of images and of representation—of identification—is clear in this novel in the many cultural references it features, and in Sonja's reaction to the texts she is exposed to. Sonja at one point seems to enter into an advertisement for "real life," a moment that points to the contemporary mediation of experience (*Z*, 47). She feels her life has become "eine rasante Bravo-Foto-Lovestory" (*Z*, 48; a wild photo love story, like you'd get in *Bravo*). On the whole, dominant contemporary representations of femininity are not at all enabling here, but rather oppressive and distortional.

Questions of normality and normativity are central to this text, as they are to the ideas of sisterhood and identification. Grether's narrator feels herself to be outside, and apart. She resolves in future to conform, to become "Teil einer Normalität" (*Z*, 22; part of normality). The tension between individuality and conformity surfaces when Sonja urges herself to be honest about the thin groupies who apparently have no independent wishes or ambitions: "Ja, ich will so sein wie diese idiotischen Freundinnen. Auch wenn sie nie etwas auf die Reihe kriegen und sich immer nur über ihre Typen definieren und noch nie in ihrem Leben ein gescheites Buch zu Ende gelesen haben" (*Z*, 76–77; Yes, I want to be like those idiotic girlfriends. Even if they never achieve anything and just define themselves through their guys and have never read a good book right through). Here, Sonja appears torn between fitting in to a dominant norm of femininity—as decorative, empty, and possessing no ambition—and her own wish to achieve in creative and career terms. When Kicky suggests Sonja is too artistic and strong for Johnny, the latter responds with anger:

> "Es reicht immer noch nicht? Willst du behaupten, ich hätte mich immer noch nicht genug angepasst? Sag mal, das kann nicht wahr sein. Wie hoch muss der Grad der Anpassung eigentlich sein, um in der Scheißgesellschaft der Männer mitmachen zu dürfen? Ab wann gilt man endlich als angepasstes Mädchen?" (*Z*, 120)

> ["It's still not enough? Do you mean to say I still haven't fitted in enough? Tell me that can't be true. How high does the level of conformity have to be, then, in order to be able to join in with the shitty society of men? At what point exactly do you start to be considered a girl who fits in?"]

She thus queries the level of adaptation, or rather self-abnegation, that is required of a "girl."

Questions of conformity and difference thus haunt the narrator. Sonja watches Kicky and Ricky, two girls from the band, observing how connected they are, despite or because of their differences.[24] They exert a magnetic pull on Sonja, who becomes close to them. Kicky advises Sonja to develop a thicker skin (*Z*, 88). Her work for the band, and experiences on tour with them, appear as partial prompts for Sonja to address her eating disorder. The end of the work is not entirely optimistic, however, as already implied. While Sonja has started eating, Kicky, having been told by her management that she needs to lose weight, has "symbolically" stopped.[25] And Sonja's struggles with food are far from over (see *Z*, 245). But nonetheless, a kind of progress appears here, albeit of a faltering and timid kind, and a "gut feminism" that focuses on embodied responses to cultural pressures manifests itself. While sisterhood is not an easy matter, Sonja's connection to Museabuse is important to her development, and the text itself offers a female-dominated space of reflection and relation.

Emma Jane Unsworth, *Animals*

Naters, Bathurst, and Grether suggest a fundamental and fatal divideness among girls and women, one fostered by celebrity culture, popular images of women, consumerism, and commodification. Yet they also affirm relationships among girls as women as powerful and central, even as these are distorted or derailed by such forces. Novels by Unsworth, Pilger, and Glaser insist even more forcefully on female intimacy, simultaneous eschewing sentimentality: Pilger and Glaser in particular stress grotesque and bizarre forms of dependence, dominance, and power play.

In chapter 2, I discussed the importance of Laura's relationship with her friend Tyler in Emma Jane Unsworth's novel *Animals*, and how it connects to the novel's treatment of will and willpower. Tyler is both an accomplice and an antagonist to Laura, reflecting and provoking her opposing desires. In its intensity and centrality, their relationship illustrates both the seductions and dangers of female relations, especially as these coexist with, and possibly threaten, heterosexual bonds. Tyler's possessiveness, and the fact that the friendship seems to be in conflict with Laura's plans to marry, bear out this reading. With Tyler the narrator experiences "kinship," or "that doppelgänger effect that can go either way: to mutual understanding or mutual destruction."[26] Thus, difference is not the challenge here, but rather an excessive similarity, as the reference to the myth of the *Doppelgänger* implies. This is an important point, since it challenges the obsession with difference of certain feminist theories, and suggests a relative, contextual view of the matter is necessary.

For much of the novel, the characters' relationships are held in a delicate, if tense, balance. Laura alternates between taking Tyler and Jim with her on visits to her family home, to ensure fairness; Jim is the easier guest, given Tyler's unpredictability (*A*, 53). Tyler is an awkward, or willful, figure. She questions norms relating to family and inheritance: the kinship between her and Laura can be read as queer in its challenge to the primacy of heterosexual bonds, and in the suggestion that Tyler may desire Laura. As the following exchange between the friends demonstrates, Tyler raises questions about the status of friendship and sexual relationships in contemporary culture, at the same time covertly airing her jealousy:

> "The whole idea of marriage *is* preposterous, though, in the modern age," Tyler went on.
> "Everything's preposterous when you look at it too long," I said
> . . .
> "But there's no ceremony for *friendship*, is there? Does friendship mean nothing in this world? Nothing to *you?*"
> . . .
> "Believe me, if I could marry you too, Tyler, I would."

Would I? Probably not.
"Did you know there are now as many unmarried parents as married parents in the UK? Things are changing. You don't have to fuse the nuclear family any more." (*A*, 81–82)

Laura is forced to defend and justify her decision to marry Jim and therefore, according to Tyler, "ruin" her friend's life. She explains her motivation as "love," and marriage as constituting "progress," and she asserts her will in this matter: "I want to marry Jim. I have not been coerced or conditioned" (*A*, 82). She also explains her wish to get married in terms of a desire to be part of "a team against the world," as experienced with her own family (*A*, 82–83). Tyler responds:

> "Teams are awful. Families are awful. People are awful. Why perpetuate the awfulness?"
> "So why don't you live alone? Why have me around?"
> Neither of us said it but it was there, unspoken. . . . *We used to be a team.* (*A*, 83)

Tyler's challenge to the "awfulness" of the social order is thus motivated by her feelings of rejection. This conflict surfaces again over an awkward meal, in which a discussion about drugs serves as an outlet for the tension between Jim and Tyler (*A*, 111).

In fact, Jim is unfaithful to Laura and their relationship breaks down. Laura's connection to Tyler also founders. The text withholds a resolution, offering neither heterosexual marriage nor a potentially queer relationship as the "answer" to Laura's questions about life. As we have seen, Tyler appeals to an aspect of Laura that she finds hard to resist: the urge to drink excessively and postpone "adulthood." The conflict concerning Tyler and the associated destructive lifestyle comes to a messy conclusion. Tyler spikes Laura's drink and urges an academic of their acquaintance to have sex with her friend, in an aggressive gesture that suggests displaced desire. This episode acts as the trigger for Laura's resolution to move out of Tyler's apartment. When it appears Tyler's turbulent life might yet suck Laura in again, she in fact moves in with her parents, opting for monkish solitude and tranquillity (*A*, 236). Tyler's self-diagnosis is that she is dead, stagnant (*A*, 224). However, Tyler arrives at her sister's wedding with a girl called Valerie. While the nature of their connection is not explicit, it appears that a lesbian relationship may have granted her a kind of resolution.

Within the novel, there are reflections on questions of agency and sisterhood. There is an explicit challenge to individualist ideas of agency when Tyler makes a dismissive remark about an image of a scantily clad woman in a men's magazine. Laura begins: "I thought we agreed it was wrong to slam individuals for the perpetuation of –"

> "Oh, you think her real name's 'Vikki'? She's a symbol! An allegory! That's all we have, and people celebrate these symbols as though we don't need a complete economic restructure. I despair, I really do. It's all completely fucked."
> "You watch porn!"
> "Well, that's different—that's already there, like meat. You might as well." (*A*, 114)

This discussion brings to mind Braidotti's description of the subject's relation to the social imaginary, which operates by means of "external attractors, stimulants or points of reference"—or symbols and allegories, in Tyler's formulation. Individual subjects are enmeshed in such a web of symbols. Tyler's complicity with this imaginary—she consumes porn—points up the complex nature of agency. This very discussion, part of an ongoing exchange between the characters, evokes self-questioning, ever-evolving female, feminist subjects. As discussed in chapter 2, the novel combines a complex exploration of conflicted, intense friendship with cultural analysis pertaining to difference, desire, and identification. And although the narrator is finally alone, she at one point explicitly meditates on female solidarity even as she asserts her changeful, or aimless, self:

> Where were my allies? My sad captains? Those moonsick girls I drank with over long winters . . . Those times when we were all strangers and everything was so far away but all we needed to do was run towards it. I had not grown much. I had not reached anywhere. I was still running. When I wasn't lying down. (*A*, 107–8)

This vision of a group of strangers running toward a distant goal evokes Ahmed's wayward army, suggesting the possibility, however distant, of a collective feminine willfulness.

Zoe Pilger, *Eat My Heart Out*

Zoe Pilger's *Eat My Heart Out* engages explicitly and satirically with feminine—and feminist—connections, also exploring generations and genealogies of feminism. It tells of a young woman named Ann-Marie—who "went crazy during [her] university finals"—seeking to establish a life in London post-university.[27] The tone of the novel is by turns flippant, random, and grotesque. The author herself has termed the contemporary context "post-feminist," and such an understanding informs the text.[28] The novel features a prominent second-wave feminist writer and academic as a key character. This figure's work concerns the passivity of the female subject, recalling Beauvoir: "To wait is a woman's prerogative, according to Stephanie Haight . . . To wait and see what a man will do for you" (*EMHO*, 2). Haight in some ways challenges Ann-Marie, whom the author describes as "in thrall to the myths of post-feminist culture."[29]

Haight's pronouncements have an uncertain status in the text, however. Assertions such as "Hysteria is the corralling of women's natural jouissance under patriarchy" read like parodies of, for example, Hélène Cixous (*EMHO*, 88). In this exchange between Haight and Ann-Marie, the reference to second-wave "sistahood" suggests an outdated and self-aggrandizing figure:

> "Erm, Hello? Man was woman's *god*. He only got knocked off his pedestal—metaphorically died, if you will—back in the '60s and '70s when the sistahood, in which I played a key part . . ."
> "Yes," I said.
> "After the death of the patriarchal god, a void opened up."
> (*EMHO*, 173; ellipsis in original)

Haight's writing as quoted in the narrative is anecdotal and unscholarly (*EMHO*, 107), though the novel also hints at her academic background and activity. A character called Marge attended Haight's course on "feminist rereadings of the Hegelian unhappy consciousness at Harvard" (*EMHO*, 43). Academic discourse is the target of satire.[30] The text's uncertain stance with regard to Haight and her theorizing is complicated by the fact of Haight's PhD on "romantic masochism in the work of Simone de Beauvoir" echoing Pilger's concern with "romantic subjection" in her own doctoral thesis (*EMHO*, 15).[31] While an extract from Haight's nonfiction book seems to function as a parody of populist feminist writing—it claims, "The whole cultural atmosphere is tuned to keep women falling" (*EMHO*, 17)—her thinking is not lacking in theoretical sophistication. During her first meeting with Ann-Marie, Haight relates her view of agency. In answer to the heroine's question, "Why are men such fucking bastards?" she replies: "It's not the men's fault. It's The Symbolic" (*EMHO*, 40).[32] She also offers diagnoses of contemporary culture, referring, for example, to "this Sadeian generation [Ann-Marie's], reared on internet pornography" (*EMHO*, 157). She sums up contemporary women's position as "caught between the housewife and the whore," and bemoans "the post-feminist whirly-pool" (*EMHO*, 162, 190). Haight's cultural status becomes clear at a gathering of older people Ann-Marie attends; a female book critic avers her importance and influence (*EMHO*, 195). Stephanie Haight is thus a curious creation. She spouts what might be termed received feminist wisdom, but she is also at points complex and compelling. She is artificially youthful—perhaps having undergone cosmetic surgery (*EMHO*, 14)—and so at odds with the stereotype of the unadorned, hairy feminist to which chapter 1 alludes.[33] "Undeniably beautiful," she is apparently complicit with the patriarchal norms she challenges: Haight describes "normative femininity" as "a perversion" (*EMHO*, 40, 90). Haight is also a cultural product, or brand, who advertises her own work nakedly (*EMHO*, 215). Her background is the subject of myth: Haight gives different versions of it at different times (*EMHO*, 267–7, 275).[34] She is thus suspect and untrustworthy.

The protagonist's relationship with Haight is complex and ultimately warped. She first encounters Haight in the Soho restaurant where she works, and her initial reaction implies intimate identification and even love at first sight: "I felt an acute sense of recognition. Maybe this was the *coup de foudre?*" (*EMHO*, 40). Ann-Marie's relationship with Haight involves attraction, flirtation, and power play. She turns up at Haight's house shortly after their first meeting, and their conversation encompasses questions of sexuality, normativity, and the need for role models. Ann-Marie tells Haight of a series of films she has made with her gay friend Freddie about suicidal women writers. Haight comments:

> "Queens can be just as oppressive as normal men."
> I laughed, nervously. "Surely there's no such thing as normal?"
> "Oh, but there is." She blew on her coffee. "Go on."
> "I guess he got the idea from me because I was always going on about how there are no strong women role models, you know? No one who we want to aspire to." I reddened. "Apart from you, of course." (*EMHO*, 84)

Haight does indeed in some ways assume the role of mentor to Ann-Marie, purchasing her a copy of *The Second Sex* (*EMHO*, 269). Haight's apparent desire to encourage Ann-Marie in her goal of being a writer ties in with this view (*EMHO*, 141). But the intensity of their relationship is matched by its randomness and ridiculousness. The intimacy that at times emerges is undercut by the surreal nature of its depiction, as well as by Ann-Marie's own ambivalence. When Haight tries to engage her in an art project, Ann-Marie observes: "She looked old. 'No,' I said" (*EMHO*, 150). Haight's age here appears to be a determining factor in Ann-Marie's rejection of that figure (possibly as a potential partner). Ann-Marie is subsequently forced by Haight to do her cleaning, and the power relations involved are uncomfortable. Ann-Marie is compelled to engage in this "hyper-feminine" act as part of a humiliating initiation rite of some kind. A bizarre voodoo ritual also takes place (*EMHO*, 152–62). Haight's attempt to restore Ann-Marie to a time before "gender normativity" fails, in an episode that suggests the failure of the second-wave feminist project

(*EMHO*, 178). While Ann-Marie claims that Haight is her "girlfriend" and she is now "gay" (*EMHO*, 169, 167), she makes these claims provocatively to her ex-boyfriend Sebastian, and there is scant suggestion of desire. Instead, a weird form of dependence emerges (*EMHO*, 171). Haight declares love, but Ann-Marie is ambivalent at best (*EMHO*, 204). Haight later tells Ann-Marie to leave, and gives her a substantial sum of money (*EMHO*, 247). But she resumes contact, and so a lack of clarity about the nature and extent of this attachment prevails (*EMHO*, 253).

The relationship between these two figures involves an engagement with the question of generations of feminist thought. Haight accuses Ann-Marie, for example: "The problem with you post-feminist girls is that you love with all your hearts what you know in your heads to be wrong. You love it ironically" (*EMHO*, 175–56)—but Ann-Marie protests that she truly loves Beyoncé, the singer who triggers this exchange. Female or feminist connections are thus fraught with ambivalence. Haight is involved with one of her protégées, Gabriella, who calls her "Mummy" and asks if Ann-Marie is "her new daughter" (*EMHO*, 208). Her friend Marge suggests that a damaging pattern is at work in Haight's relationships with younger women (*EMHO*, 42).[35] Haight retorts that Gabriella was "just a life model" and would have remained so "if I hadn't pulled her out of that phallocentric head space and turned her into an artist in her own right" (*EMHO*, 42). Marge and Haight discuss feminist waves or movements, as well as issues of feminist genealogies and obligations:

> "Gabriella's from a later world," said Marge . . . "She's Third Wave." She bent her fingers in parentheses. "If that is a thing at all."
> "Maybe she doesn't wanna be part of any *wave*, Marge," said Steph . . . "Maybe she's not into *waves* . . ."
> . . .
> Marge went on . . . "She's a paradigm of selfish fucking neo-liberal individualism, Stephanie."
> "We all wanted to be individuals, Marge, remember? We all wanted to be *ourselves*. That's why we got involved. We didn't want to be what our mothers –"
> "Yes, but we sought solidarity! . . . Do artists have the right to disavow their foremothers? To pretend that Second Wave feminism never happened?" (*EMHO*, 43)

Haight accuses Marge of wanting younger women to "defer" and "pay homage" to older generations of feminists (*EMHO*, 43). This discussion raises the question of the tensions between "neo-liberal individualism" and feminist connection. It also touches on the issue of academic versus non-academic feminisms. Marge proclaims that she entered the academy for Haight, seeming to feel betrayed. She accuses Haight of peddling outdated ideas, referring in this connection to Shulamith Firestone and Jessica Benjamin, and terming her a "*populist*," to which Haight retorts: "Bite me" (*EMHO*, 44).

This novel is thus highly ambivalent about feminisms. While the text in various ways troubles gender normativity and binarism—not least by referencing such terms (see also *EMHO*, 19, 20, 108, 196)—female solidarity and sisterhood are targets of satire. A girl called Allegra befriends Ann-Marie at college, coming to her room with "a box of post-feminist cupcakes" (*EMHO*, 12). The college as a setting itself serves as a critique of feminist separatism. This Cambridge college was "supposed to be proud of its all-girls tradition, [and was the] owner of the second largest feminist art collection in the world" (*EMHO*, 12).[36] Returning there, Ann-Marie sees:

> Girls who looked stricken, traumatised, raped, weird, mad, old before their time. . . . Girls who had given up on men by the age of eighteen. Girls with death in their eyes. Girls with bunches at the age of eighteen. They were not ironic bunches; they were just bunches. The place reeked of arrested development and chronic perfectionism. The women–only college [had] an atmosphere of despair. (*EMHO*, 272–73)

While her college friend Allegra "toasted to our new-found sistahood," she later gets together with Ann-Marie's boyfriend, which leads to a violent scene (*EMHO*, 12, 124). "Sistahood" appears temporary and provisional, as well as infantile and unwholesome.

Yet the novel also critiques a postfeminist context that sexualizes and commodifies female bodies. Ann-Marie finds herself in a queue, and when she asks what is going on, she receives the answer: "it's like a neo-burlesque social innovation start-up? It's a pop-up?" (*EMHO*, 142). The use of trendy terminology signals a skewering a faddishness. This episode alludes to the revival in recent years of the burlesque form. Ann-Marie is assured: "It's not like stripping . . . It's like art" (*EMHO*, 143). In a savage mockery of neoliberal, postfeminist discourse, the organizer of the event proclaims: "Unlike yesteryear when us girls could sparkle soft, we're now fully entitled to sparkle as hard as we possibly can!! As though our lives depend on it! . . . Our lives do depend on it" (*EMHO*, 144). The roaring of the crowd "assumed the intensity of a fascist rally," a description that suggests the coercive power of such injunctions to "sparkle"— that is to say, of neoliberal, pseudo-feminist incitements to say yes. This grotesque scene—which involves men with their members exposed acting as gauges of the performers' appeal—offers a biting commentary on the ways in which the female body becomes spectacle.

Like Baum and Hegemann in particular, Pilger does not offer a "useful" trajectory in her novel. While it seems Ann-Marie does accept her break-up with Sebastian and can even see it as empowering (*EMHO*, 264), she forms no convincing plan for her life. Toward the end of the novel, Ann-Marie claims she intends to do an MA "in poetry," but this assertion lacks weight: "Yeah, that's what I might do." When Haight objects that creativity cannot be taught, Ann-Marie replies that she wants "some direction" (*EMHO*, 269). Asked at a religious gathering about her journey, she states, "I don't have one of those" (*EMHO*, 287). She is urged to read Kahlil Gibran: a mockery of new-age ideals relating to self-improvement and progress. It is notable that Ann-Marie has a distant relationship with her mother, like most of the protagonists I examine (*EMHO*, 194). Like Roche's Helen, she comes from what she sees as a "broken home," and she seems obsessed with her parents' wedding (*EMHO*, 238, 222). The scatological references in the novel are striking, as are the frequent mentions of meat (see, for example, *EMHO*, 179; *EMHO*, 235). These act as avowals of embodiment and flesh. This is, like Roche's, a disgusting novel, and like Hegemann's and Baum's work, it is surreal and grotesque. It challenges second-wave assumptions as to the empowering nature of feminist sisterhood. It both supports and undermines postfeminist understandings of female connections as toxic and competitive; the grotesque and satirical elements of the novel allow for the development of a willfully critical stance on these matters.

Rachel B. Glaser, *Paulina and Fran*

Paulina and Fran by Rachel B. Glaser also features grotesque and satirical elements. The novel tells the story of the relationship between its titular protagonists, who meet at art college in an unnamed, small American town and who remain in contact for a number of years. This ambivalent relationship involves hostility, love, and desire. The novel's title indicates its centrality to the text. Emma Jane Unsworth praises the book as "a beautifully complex and brutal exploration of female friendship."[37] Ultimately, the relationship between the women fails to develop into a partnership, as it is suggested it might, owing to a complex mixture of fear, misunderstanding, and internalized homophobia. The text takes a sardonic view of its protagonists, yet it mounts a delicate evocation of their relationship. The tension between irony and intimacy enriches and complicates this notable exploration of female relationality and sexuality.

Paulina is a monstrous creation: selfish, whimsical, and driven by her own desires. Early on, for example, "She felt a big ambition, a great horniness, the conviction that she was a genius" (*PF*, 2; cf. *PF*, 114). She is confident in her looks: "She wasn't beautiful, she knew, but she was striking" (*PF*, 2). Her behavior is in general inconsiderate, even destructive (see *PF*, 28–29). Appearing to lack family—she borrows someone else's life story (*PF*, 144)—she appears as pure ego, or will.[38] When she attends a fellow student's funeral, her reactions are typically self-centered and hard-hearted (*PF*, 116). She eventually establishes a hugely profitable line of hair care products, despite her blatant lack of professionalism, and grows rich, in a satirically rendered rags-to-riches tale. The moral of this tale is deliberately unclear, but the novel does seem to suggest that relationality is the key ingredient in a life. Pauline prizes intimacy, or at least sex, more than professional or financial success: "Each development [in her business] was momentous, but Paulina grew used to it. She was still looking for good people to sleep with" (*PF*, 180).

Yet this proves a challenge. Her relationship with Fran ultimately fails to develop. Relationships between women at the art college are also, for the most part, shifting and tense (for example *PF*, 3). Paulina's judgments of others are harsh and terse: "Sadie was obvious" (*PF*, 4). In general, the college is the site of rivalry, power play, and tension, as well as of satirized engagements with art and the art world. The relationships between Paulina and her friends Sadie and Allison in particular undergo numerous shifts and reversals. On a college trip to Norway, Paulina is "freed from Sadie and Allison" and she "spent the long bus rides breaking down their personality flaws for Fran's entertainment" (*PF*, 25; cf. *PF*, 6, 47, 50, 60, 62, 70). But she is equally keen to dissect Fran for Sadie's entertainment when she emails the latter (*PF*, 31). These relationships are volatile and painful, but they are also crucial and compelling. Relationships with men interrupt and disrupt female relations, at least from Paulina's point of view: "She didn't want Sadie to have a boyfriend because she didn't want to have to listen to her talk about him" (*PF*, 47). Promiscuity, in this milieu, is rife (for example, *PF*, 5). Paulina treats men casually. Indeed, she thinks: "no man could ever make her happy for very long" (*PF*, 118).

The novel is largely devoted to the perspectives of its two main characters, although Julian, Paulina's and then Fran's boyfriend, is also focalized, in this case to provide a further view of Paulina, for example: "It excited him to be around [Paulina]. Her moods were so erratic. He could not control her" (*PF*, 39). Here, masculine excitement arises from the inability to gain mastery, a notable detail in light of ideas relating to masculine control as the norm. The novel is also queer in its subversion of heterosexual romance as the defining narrative of female existence. It acknowledges queerness in the depiction of boys Paulina knows who are "unlike the mainstream gays one got used to," and in one character's pronouncement that "everyone is gay" (*PF*, 8, 9). But most of all, it does this through the depiction of Paulina and Fran's mutual attraction. When Paulina sees Fran at a party, she is at first dismissive, but "now she saw that the girl's face was beautiful" (*PF*, 12). Remembering that Fran is friends with "one of Paulina's enemies," her feelings darken: "She wanted to be her, or be with her, or destroy her. She watched Fran's breasts bounce in her dress" (*PF*, 12). Later, the desire to "be" Fran emerges again when Paulina observes the other woman's beauty, "yearning to switch faces and bodies with Fran" (*PF*, 112). Desire, envy, and identification are here bound up with each other: "[Paulina] felt drawn to Fran and repelled by Fran. She felt superior to all women and started walking quickly away from Fran" (*PF*, 113). Fran, in turn, deems Paulina "compelling and strange" on the trip to Norway, and "very quickly, the girls formed a familiarity" (*PF*, 21).

Paulina is tyrannical, demanding exclusivity: "Being with Paulina was like being under Soviet rule, [Fran] thought during a few outrageous moments, but it was worth it" (*PF*, 27; but cf. *PF*, 111). Paulina is fearsome, and too exacting in her affection (*PF*, 78). The relationship is nonetheless, in its early stage, empowering; the girls together create a spectacle that affirms their narcissism: "'We must be very beautiful to feel this beautiful,' Fran thought" (*PF*, 27). Paulina cherishes dreams of the pair dominating their college, and then, in future, "growing even more sophisticated and successful" (*PF*, 27). Their attraction is at first mediated through a fantasy about a Viking who would ravish them (*PF*, 24; cf. *PF*, 30), that is, through a heterosexual erotic narrative, and both are attached to men when they first converse (*PF*, 22; see also *PF*, 33, 42–43). Fran is indeed obsessed with a student called Marvin (*PF*, 44, 57, 67, 85). But the possibility of unmediated attraction and action is hinted at already in Paulina's assessment of Fran at the party. When Fran learns from another student that Paulina was "a big lesbo" at her previous college, and had been thrown out of that institution, having seduced "every girl there," her own fascination grows: "Just when it seemed like Paulina could not be more interesting to Fran, something like this would emerge" (*PF*, 28).[39] At the end of the Norway trip, they embrace, "Paulina's breasts pushing against Fran's" (*PF*, 38). The active nature of Paulina's embodiment and desire emerges here.[40]

Fran's unconscious attraction to Paulina, in turn, is hinted at by an artwork she creates featuring the pair of them; its "lesbian undertone" attracts comment from her fellow students ("I was just being surreal, she told them in her head" [*PF*, 57–58]). Fran, then, does not recognize her own desires, and disavows them, while her art—and others—discern them. The muted, circuitous fashion in which the relationship develops exemplifies the workings of repression, individual and cultural, even in a post-queer milieu. Fran takes up with Paulina's ex, Julian, and the unfixed nature of the libido becomes clear when, "With her eyes closed, Julian was everyone, Paulina and Marvin, the world wanting Fran" (*PF*, 74). She later spends the summer with Julian in a state of domestic boredom that is nonetheless comfortable (*PF*, 94–99). Paulina takes up with a man called Mystic, to whom she "wasn't very attached" but for whose validating gaze she is grateful (*PF*, 100). Matters are complicated when Fran kisses Marvin at a party, and Paulina tells Julian, also seducing him (*PF*, 104–6). The text presents a complex dance of attraction, repulsion, ambivalence, envy, and desire.

Repression also comes to the fore when, following the revelation of Fran's involvement with Julian, Paulina realizes: "She loved him [Julian]. She loved both of them [Julian and Fran], but this thought snapped back into the dark unknowing place of her" (*PF*, 87). Paulina's self-deception is clear: "She hadn't really liked Fran as an equal she told herself" (*PF*, 89). The final part of the sentence—paradoxically under-lined by the lack of punctuation separating it off—points up Paulina's unconvincing attempt to deny her feelings. Her intense reaction to Fran later at a party again suggests the unknowable and mysterious nature of her own feelings.[41] Fran and Paulina do eventually kiss, having danced competitively for male attention at a party.[42] They have sex in a toilet, an episode whose power and centrality for both parties is underlined by the narrator: "Though it lasted about eight minutes, the girls would think of this moment so often that it became notched in their mem-ory, a place they got stuck thinking" (*PF*, 126). But the encounter is terminated when Paulina pulls away, filled with "cold fear" (*PF*, 127). While Fran pleasurably imagines further similar encounters, and Paulina "could picture a whole life with Fran," she, Paulina, immediately seeks out a man to whom she gives "the longest blow job in human history" (*PF*, 128). Her "fear" and her attempt at displacement or repression suggest her discomfort with intimacy, and particularly with lesbian inti-macy. Fearing rejection, she also tells herself Fran has likely realized the encounter was a mistake and that "[Fran] wanted her lovers to be male" (*PF*, 129). Fran, meanwhile, stands despondent outside Paulina's door (*PF*, 130). A relationship thus fails to form at this point.

When Paulina is the subject of discussion post-college, Fran speculates that Paulina may end up with a female partner. She subsequently blushes, revealing shame and persistent desire (*PF*, 158). The women's post-col-lege years are characterized by distance, but once again their relationship becomes mediated by a man, Julian, whom both begin seeing. Paulina even writes a message for Fran on Julian's back, so that he becomes, lit-erally, a means of communication. Fran turns up at Paulina's apartment building at the time specified in this message, but leaves; because Fran has changed her hairstyle, Paulina fails to recognize her in the security camera recording, and so never even knows she came that far. This is a romance in the sense that the intensity and specificity of the characters' desires are affirmed, but it is a failed romance, as indicated.[43] When Fran realizes one of her co-workers is in a relationship with a woman, she is forced to con-front her attachment to Paulina, and the possibility that lesbian relation-ships are "natural" and viable:

> Fran stared at them. Was it possible they were *together*? They couldn't be. Fran would have heard about it. Fran would have been able to sense a vibe from Jane, a gay vibe. Fran got lost looking at Deena's lips. . . . As Fran watched Jane and Deena talk and laugh, it seemed so natural, something she and Paulina could have been, long ago in the college town, without Julian, or Marvin, or any jerk with nice eyes. (*PF*, 200–201; cf. *PF*, 211–12, 214–15)

Yet Fran is also struck by the fear that were she to meet Paulina again and kiss her, she would realize she wasn't "attracted to girls" (*PF*, 230). The reignition of their relationship thus founders in part on her obsession with identity categories.

But the novel does not allow for any simple reading. The novel's play with point of view, its flip, savage tone, and satirical and grotesque elements mean that its central characters, and especially Paulina, are in part caricatures, and the text disavows sincerity. Julian emerges as the best option for Fran, arguably, with Paulina a mere distraction. But the pathos the narrative grants Paulina, and the tension that runs through the novel as it traces the complex affective patterns at work in this "same-sex" relationship, mean that it does not allow for an overlooking of queer desire and relationality. The novel tantalizes and frustrates as it offers up the possibility of such desires and relations as, potentially, defining.

Conclusion

All of these novels, in different ways, depict relationships between girls and women as crucial, conflicted, and often painful. They bear out Winch's assessment of the effects of neoliberalism on feminine connections. In Naters, relationships between women are subjected to satire and are at once central and trivial. In Bathurst, the tension and toxicity that characterize the girls' relationships prove fatal. In Grether, young women offer each other limited support as they contend with the pressures imposed by their context. In Unsworth, Pilger, and Glaser, intensity or desire come strikingly to the fore—but in all cases, these are complicated and problematic. Pilger's novel additionally thematizes questions of generationality and feminist sisterhood, here given caustic treatment. I have suggested that fiction can flesh out accounts of neoliberalism and postfeminism. These texts, in tracing the complex dynamics between female subjects—employing literary means such as shifting points of view, satire, and the grotesque—open up space for an affective acknowledgment of these relations. The assertion in these texts of the richness and complexity of female friendships and relationships makes them challenges to a mainstream culture that trivializes and reduces connections between girls and women. The point is not to understand such bonds as only ever positive and enabling, but rather to explore and evoke the full spectrum of affective responses possible between women.

Yet the treatment in these texts of lesbian desire seems to suggest its impossibility and undesirability. Where such desire is featured, it is repressed, short-lived, or not lived out at all. In these novels, "queer" is not, cannot be, a site of resistance—this in keeping with Puar's criticism of simplistic associations of queerness with transgression.[44] The texts do not establish such an association, nor are they interested in the potential of lesbian feminism to challenge patriarchal tenets.[45] McCarthy's observation regarding the lack of maternal care in Naters, and lesbian intimacy as a possible substitute for such nurture, is suggestive, given that in the novels I explore, mother figures are largely distant or absent. Hegemann's Mifti desires a woman who reminds her of her dead mother, as we will see in the next chapter. In Helen Walsh's *Brass*, also discussed in chapter 5, there is an implied link between the absent mother and the lesbian desires of the daughter. In depicting lesbian attraction as a matter of substitution, these texts refuse to affirm, never mind celebrate, desire between women. In this sense, they can be seen as symptomatic of postfeminist neoliberalism. But at the same time, they demonstrate the inevitably circular, near-impossible nature of resistance to this order, and the structuring of desire by culture. They expose the precariousness of affective ties in neoliberalism, and speak to the need for the continuous working toward a "we."

5: Sex and Desire

THERE IS AMONG feminist commentators widespread concern about the pornographization of culture and the sexualization of young girls, as we saw in chapter 1. On the one hand, the assertion of female sexuality is important and necessary, as is the avoidance of unhelpful moral panics. On the other, the vulnerability of girls and young women to sexual assault, and the reduction of women to their bodies, require acknowledgment and action. Sex and desire thus raise the matters of agency and volition. They are also obviously linked to the questions of body and beauty: as chapter 3 demonstrates, the prevalence of eating disorders and low self-esteem among young women in the Western world is bound up with normative ideals regarding sexual attractiveness. Sex and desire may also challenge or affirm sisterhood and identification, entailing emulation, rivalry, hostility, or attraction between female subjects. This book's chapters thus form an interlinked investigation into contemporary feminine willfulness. If not necessarily or only oppositional, this willfulness is at the least troublesome and, occasionally, optimistic.[1]

Framing Female Desire

The tension between affirmations of female desire and the requirement to protect and appropriately advise young women raises the matters of will and willfulness. If the thousands of contributors to the Everyday Sexism project are to be believed, young women experience sexualization and harassment routinely.[2] The social will renders them docile. But what happens when the girl or young woman herself desires? Is her desire willful in Ahmed's sense? In *Daddy's Girl*, Valerie Walkerdine suggests so: "the little girl who is not nurturant, but displays a sexuality too different, active, animal, is one who constantly threatens the possibility of the rational order."[3] Elsewhere, she points out that the girl as an erotic object challenges the notion of the innocence of the child.[4] Yet Walkerdine also acknowledges the systematic sexualization and scrutiny of girls: "There is an erotically-coded and ubiquitous gaze at the little girl."[5] Affirming female desire, and especially the sexuality of girls and young women, can serve to legitimize views of girls as appropriate targets, or fair game, so to speak. Natasha Walter points out the vulnerability of girls and the dubious status of the idea of "choice" in this context. She further observes that the contemporary celebration of promiscuity in Western cultures exists "alongside a continuing attachment to monogamy," and so is not necessarily progressive.[6] Sexualizing practices are not always empowering or liberating, though neoliberal discourse may imply that they are. In *Female Chauvinist Pigs: Women and the Rise of Raunch Culture*, Ariel Levy makes an extended case for this view. Analyzing various instances of what she terms "raunch culture" in the United States, she argues that the internalization of chauvinistic, hyper-sexual behaviors on the part of women is damaging and limiting.[7] We might argue that at present female desire is impossible: if a young woman expresses her sexuality, she is a slut, if she represses it, she is a prude.

In a highly sexualized or pornified culture, female desire is paradoxically, or logically, the object of diminution and distortion. In Kerstin Grether's novel, *Zuckerbabys*, Sonja's extreme self-consciousness makes her unprepared for the self-exposure that sex with her boyfriend Johnny, who pays her a surprise visit, would involve. She feels that she has not properly packaged and presented her body:

> Vielleicht gibt es auch noch eine Hand voll Mädchen in der westlichen Welt, die nicht so sind. Die einfach glücklich die Ärmchen ausstrecken und sich das Hemdchen hochziehen lassen und sich das Höschen ausziehen—ohne darüber nachzudenken, ob sie auch eine gute Figur dabei machen. Ich gehöre nicht dazu. Ich bin schon ganz verdorben in meinem Kopf von der vielen Hochglanzfotografie.[8]

> Maybe there are still a handful of girls in the Western world who aren't like that. Who just stretch out their little arms and let their little top be lifted up and take off their little panties—without thinking about whether they're looking good. I'm not one of them. My head's been completely messed up by all those glossy pictures.

Objectification and sexualization lead to paralyzing self-consciousness, and the inability to desire. Female desire, in this view, is malleable and vulnerable: not so much a threat to the the social order as its shadowy trace. Expressions of active female desire may constitute manifestations of willfulness, then. Rosi Braidotti indeed views desire in active and affirmative terms, arguing that being "outward-directed and forward-looking," it has to do with "the creation of new possibilities of empowerment." She stresses, therefore, the "embodied subject's capacity for encounters and interrelation," as well as "desire and yearning for interconnections with others."[9] In this way, Braidotti's view of desire offers parallels with her discussion of a nomadic ethics.[10]

Queer desire in particular may appear "forward-looking," in its resistance to a patriarchal, heterosexist order, as Ahmed suggests in her discussion of lesbian feminism.[11] Yet "queerness-as-sexual-identity" is a dubious model, as Jasbir K. Puar argues, serving falsely to fix queer subjects. Queerness as "assemblage," on the other hand, moves away from binarism and rigidity to underscore "contingency and complicity with dominant formations."[12] Sexuality, then, is not to be understood as constitutive of identity, or as necessarily oppositional. Elizabeth Grosz puts forward a comparable view. Grosz refers usefully to "the vagaries of taste, desire, appeal and intensification that make up sexuality."[13] She frames Darwinian sexual selection in both queer and aesthetic terms. Sexual selection, she suggests, "may be understood as the queering of natural selection, that is, the rendering of any biological norms, ideals of fitness, strange, incalculable, excessive," and further contends that the process "unveils the operations of aesthetics . . . as a mode of enchantment" (132). Viewed in this light, sexuality is inherently "queer," since it does not take into account norms or ideals—at least not necessarily—and it involves artistic seduction and pleasure. Such a view counters a pornifying, yet paradoxically desexualizing, "raunch culture," as well as a position that would insist on drawing a distinction between queer and nonqueer subjects and acts.

The contemporary fiction I explore evinces willful, sometimes perverse reactions to the objectifying tendencies of such a pornified and reductive culture. Caitlin Moran's 2014 *How to Build a Girl*, Charlotte Roche's 2008 *Feuchtgebiete* (*Wetlands*), and Helen Walsh's *Brass* (2004) are all in different ways concerned with affirming female desire against a rigid and restrictive context: in Moran's case, by exposing masculine dominance of the cultural imaginary and of the sexual arena; in Roche's, by challenging sanitized versions of female embodiment; and in Walsh's, by evoking active, queer desire, which it nonetheless shows to be ethically problematic. The other three texts I examine also probe and undermine heterosexism and pornification: Bella Bathurst's 2002 *Special* by emphasizing shame, confusion, and disgust in the face of these norms, and Zoe Pilger's 2014 *Eat My Heart Out* by skewering traditional assumptions relating to gendered power relations. Finally, Helene Hegemann's 2010 *Axolotl Roadkill* offers an unsettling view of desire as bound up with fantasy, lack, mourning, and violence. If for Ahmed, the willful subject is one whose will accords with her desire, then Hegemann's text in particular shows this accordance to be potentially problematic (cf. *WS*, 85). Yet the novels' collective exposure of desire as potentially obstructive and awkward raises useful questions about the status of sex in the contemporary era, as I will argue in my conclusion to this chapter.

Caitlin Moran, *How to Build a Girl*

Moran's novel involves a frank focus on (hetero)sexuality. Sex and sexuality are crucial to its young narrator's "becoming." This first-person narrative begins with the fourteen-year-old narrator lying in bed next to her sleeping brother, masturbating, an activity that she finds relaxing and pleasurable.[14] In terms of the link, or perceived link, between appearance and sex, it is notable that Moran's protagonist is fat. Her weight and her sexuality come to the fore in a passage that suggests both frustration and defiance:

> If you're going to be a fat teenage girl, it becomes hard for people to guess how old you are. By the time you're in a 38DD bra, people are just going to presume you're sexually active, and have been having rough, regular procreative sex with alpha males on some wasteland. Chance would be a fine thing. I haven't even been kissed yet. I want to be kissed so much. I am angry I haven't been kissed. I think I would be really good at it. (*HBG*, 21)

Her thin cousin Meg, in contrast, "has been fingered five times" (*HBG*, 22). As a "fat girl," however, Johanna has internalized views of herself as undesirable (*HBG*, 231). But unlike Grether's and Walker's protagonists and like Roche's Helen, Johanna is comfortable asserting her sexuality. She is confident she will be "good" at kissing. She even reflects that sexual activity will "make sense" of her (*HBG*, 193). Sex is thus central to her self-understanding and integral to her ambitions:

> "When I get to London [Johanna tells her dog], that is when I will start being me."
> Quite what that is, I have no idea. There isn't a word for what I want to be yet. There isn't a thing I can gun for. The thing I want to be hasn't been invented.
> Obviously, I know *some of* what I want to be: primarily, I want to move to London, and be hot . . . I want everyone . . . to want to have absolute, total sex with me. (*HBG*, 29)

The passage continues in this vein, the hyperbole obviously comic. But the stress on the "rioting" hormones of the teenage girl grounds the subject in embodied and desiring terms (*HBG*, 30). The assertion of female sexuality and desire—especially on the part of a "fat" girl—is striking in the light of views that pliability and plasticity are the contemporary feminine norm. Johanna later indulges in "medieval" sexual fantasies, inspired by her reading on witchcraft (*HBG*, 177–78). The vagaries and vicissitudes of desire emerge, in line with Grosz.

Having eventually confirmed that kissing is "brilliant," Johanna finds that it brings about a joyful self-transformation: "you are Christmas Day; you are the Moon Shoot; you are field larks" (*HBG*, 211, 223). Desire leads to pleasure and is even constitutive of the subject. Along with writing, sex spells the materialization of the protagonist's identity: "Having sex, and printing words. I was slowly assembling, into vision, at the end of a telescope" (*HBG*, 224). For her, sex means a return to the intensity of the mother-baby bond. Paradoxically perhaps, it simultaneously affirms her status as an adult woman (*HBG*, 224). This reflection suggests at once an infantile symbiosis with a male yet maternal other, and a confirmation of adulthood. In any case, Johanna appears to find sex empowering, as a form and expression of agency.[15] Given her sense of mastery and control, she imagines herself as the "S" in any "S/M" scenario (*HBG*, 277). She is put out when she is positioned as the "M" in a decidedly unerotic scenario that recalls sibling tussles (*HBG*, 278). For while sex and sexuality are central and vital to Johanna, they are also matters of confusion, given Johanna's youth and inexperience as well as the cultural contradictions attaching to female sexuality that become evident to her. Johanna does not yet know what she wants: she is "learning so many new things about [herself], every day" (*HBG*, 278). Once she has lost her virginity, Johanna embarks on "a massive Shag Quest," with James Bond as her role model (*HBG*, 231). This deployment of a masculine model makes for a subversion of traditional paradigms, and highlights Johanna's sexuality as deviant, by some accounts. Johanna learns how to gauge male attitudes to women, how to access a "stockpile of received wisdoms and beliefs" (*HBG*, 233). Desperate to amass knowledge and experience, she becomes aware of a double standard: "the only way I can gain any qualifications at this thing—sex—that is seen as so societally important and desirable, is by being a massive slag—which is *not* seen as societally important and desirable" (*HBG*, 234). Moran thus refers to the phenomenon that has come in recent years to be known as "slut-shaming." "Slut" is indeed a term Johanna reclaims "in a shame-busting exercise" that deliberately challenges this trope (*HBG*, 235).

The novel thus critiques male-centered acts and representations of sexuality, as a frank and depressing account of oral sex suggests (*HBG*, 237–38). Feminine self-denial appears the norm in this context. Johanna has "no template" for female pleasure; the sex act is structured around male satisfaction (*HBG*, 239).[16] Johanna notes that this is a time "before internet pornography" (*HBG*, 239). This observation brings to mind Moran's own view that a proliferation of pornographic modes is now possible.[17] If the world were run by women, there would be no sex industry, Johanna also reflects. She thus points up the links between power, heterosexual masculinity, and the commodification of bodies and acts (*HBG*, 196). This male-dominated order means female pleasure is in short supply and not a priority for Johanna's sexual partners.[18] Johanna's unfortunate experience with a character she refers to as "Big Cock Al" leads her to the following observation about feminine voicelessness in sex:

In later years, I find this is called "physical disconnect," and is all part and parcel of women having their sexuality mediated through men's gaze. There is very little female narrative of what it's like to fuck, and be fucked. I will realise that, as a seventeen-year-old girl, I couldn't really hear my own voice during this sex. I had no idea what my voice was at all. (*HBG*, 243)

During this episode, Johanna is made desirous by Al's desire, rather than experiencing any herself. The encounter, which occurs when Johanna is a child, causes her to develop acutely painful cystisis: a comical if unsettling challenge to romanticizations of sex. Female corporeality is indeed, as in Roche—though in a lesser way—almost defiantly unglamorous, as when Johanna develops diarrhoea and finds her period has started: "*Carrie* in my pants—this is my most glamorous and successful day ever" (*HBG*, 117).

Heterosexual relations here are in general fraught with doubt and uncertainty, as Johanna's relationship with one Tony Rich also suggests. But Johanna does experience love for a musician called John Kite (*HBG*, 143). With him, Johanna talks unrestrainedly and feels "normal" (*HBG*, 145; cf. *HBG*, 152). John Kite is from a difficult background and understands poverty and precarity (*HBG*, 167–69). With him, Johanna experiences happiness and a realization that "[the] point of life is joy" (*HBG*, 306). Despite her fear that she has sabotaged their friendship by suggesting sex, their relationship does in fact remain intact, though the sex is deferred (*HBG*, 309–36). Thus, friendship appears as important as sex, or as more important: a notable detail, given the contemporary stress on sex, which is perhaps now giving way to other forms of subversion, or prompting rejection—a matter to which I will return. For this heterosexual protagonist, incidentally, "kissing a girl is weird"—though the addition of the follow-up comment "Well, this girl, anyway" tempers such heterosexist squirmishness (*HBG*, 293). The depiction of Johanna's secretly gay brother is crude, however. While the joke may be on Johanna for not recognizing the heavy hints relating to his sexuality (*HBG*, 338), closetedness as a trope feels dated. But Moran's fat, curious character, who learns to affirm her own desire in defiance of the slim, passive, pornographic ideal, issues a willful call to readers to reimagine their own pleasures.

Charlotte Roche, *Feuchtgebiete*

The author of *Feuchtgebiete* Charlotte Roche has publicly criticized what she sees as the anti-sex position of older feminists such as Alice Schwarzer. She is in favor of pornography and the sex industry, and her public persona has given rise to a reputation for frankness.[19] The protagonist of Roche's *Feuchtgebiete*, Helen, is similarly unashamed in her desires. If many young women are filled with self-loathing and shame, then Helen represents a figuration that would challenge this paradigm. She willfully refuses to hate herself or deny her desires. She takes pleasure in her own body and is opposed to the widespread sanitization of female corporeality. What is striking here is the coexistence of distressing or gross elements and the erotic. This combination raises questions about the voicing of female desire and the status of sex and sexuality in the contemporary context. Sexual explicitness—or raunch—is not necessarily productive in this context, given its pervasiveness. What is more disturbing, or troublesome, is the assertion of disgust and disgustingness, in line with the ideas of failure and refusal presented in chapter 2.

Helen does on the one hand assert desire and pleasure, however. Her challenge to norms relating to female hygiene is bound up with her erotic inclinations. Helen's mother is obsessed with hygiene, and subjected to satirical treatment.[20] For Helen, excessive cleanliness is unattractive. She cultivates her bodily smell with the aim of attracting men, rejecting the commonly held view that manufactured perfumes are erotic and even referring to "Vergewaltigung durch Hygienefanatiker" (*F*, 19; rape by hygiene fanatics, *W*, 14). Women who are too packaged are not appealing:

> Gepflegte Frauen haben Haare, Nägel, Lippen, Füsse, Gesicht, Haut und Hände gemacht. Gefärbt, verlängert, bemalt, gepeelt, gezupft, rasiert und gecremt.
> Sie sitzen steif wie ihr eigenes Gesamtkunstwerk rum, weil sie wissen, wie viel Arbeit darin steckt, und wollen, dass es so lange wie möglich hält.
> Solche Frauen traut sich doch keiner durchzuwuscheln und zu ficken. (*F*, 106)

> [Well-kept women get their hair, nails, lips, feet, faces, skin, and hands done. Colored, lengthened, painted, peeled, plucked, shaved, and lotioned.
> They sit around stiffly—like works of art—because they know how much work has gone into everything and they want it to last as long as possible.
> Those type of women would never let themselves get all messy fucking. (*W*, 105)][21]

Helen's defense of an unadorned, "natural" kind of sexuality accords with critiques of restrictive feminine norms that Greer, Penny, Power, Walter, and others put forward. Despite Roche's disavowal of earlier feminisms, Helen's assertion of the importance of knowing her own body recalls conscious-raising efforts of the 1970s. Helen's curiosity about her own body makes for an ongoing investigatory project; she regularly explores her own vaginal discharge, for example (*F*, 51). She is not content with a limited perspective on her vagina, asserting: "Ich will bei mir alles so sehen wie ein Mann" and "Es kann ja nicht sein, dass ich beim Sex die Beine für einen Typen breit mache, um mich zum Beispiel ordentlich lecken zu lassen, und selber keine Ahnung habe, wie ich da unten aussehe, rieche und schmecke" (*F*, 50; I want to see everything on me the same way a man sees it; There's no way I can spread my legs for some guy—to get thoroughly eaten out, for instance—without knowing myself how everything looks, smells, and tastes down there, *W*, 47, 46). At the same time, Helen's appeal to the male gaze arguably undermines any claim to feminist subversion.

However, the novel's elaborate descriptions of masturbation do insist on female pleasure. Helen masturbated in the shower "schon als ganz junges Mädchen" (*F*, 24, when I was younger, *W*, 19).[22] Her description of her Venus mount as the most important part of her body highlights the significance of her sexual organs, which she finds comforting and pleasing (*F*, 36). Katie Jones observes the detailed nature of the text's depictions of masturbation and argues: "Although this purely mechanistic view [of sexual pleasure] might not be the most desirable way to think about sex, it has a certain gender-political usefulness: *Feuchtgebiete* asserts . . . that women should and do want physical satisfaction."[23] Helen also describes one lover's technique for pleasuring her orally, thus countering a mainstream stress on penetration as the goal of heterosexual sexual intercourse (*F*, 72). Her reflections on sex during menstruation also challenge taboos in this respect (*F*, 109). Helen's distaste for the crucifix and religious poster on her wall indicate an historically Christian context, as well as Helen's rejection of this legacy; her mother, incidentally, is a Catholic (*F*, 31–32). When she discovers a Bible in the drawer, Helen's reaction is humorously scornful (*F*, 96). Such details suggest rejection of a set of ideologies that have demonized or erased female sexuality.

Nevertheless, and in line my discussion of Helen's willful contradictoriness in chapter 2, she otherwise remains bound to dominant discourses, as when she reluctantly removes her body hair. She refers to the practice as "Quatsch" (*F*, 10; crap, *W*, 3), and as a waste of time (*F*, 47). She still feels bound to engage in it, however, despite having earlier been happy with her body hair. While shaving round her anus, her reluctance to undertake the task makes her sloppy and causes her to injure herself (*F*, 10). She quotes advertising slogans ironically: "Alles das Ladyshaven schuld. Feel like Venus. Be a goddess!" (*F*, 10; Blame it all on lady-shaving. Feel like Venus. Be a goddess, *W*, 3).[24] The female subject negotiates with dominant discourses. The novel demonstrates this process of coercion, resistance, and complicity. Elsewhere, during Helen's encounters with an Ethiopian man, hair removal is erotic. The man carefully shaves her, prompting desire in Helen (*F*, 55). Helen considers that if men want shaven women, they should take on some of the work. She points out the dominance of male gazes and pleasures when she claims: "Frauen wäre es doch ohne Männer ganz egal, wie sie behaart sind" (F, 57; In the absence of men, women wouldn't care at all how hairy they were, W, 54). She suggests both partners in a heterosexual pairing should shave each other in mutually pleasing ways. Helen at once complies with heterosexual norms and seeks to reshape them. The contradictoriness of this figure, already noted, is both vexing and productively willful. For all her defiance Helen does experience shame relating to bodily functions and pleasures, for example (F, 110–11, 38).

Perhaps the most problematic aspect of the text's depiction of female sexuality lies in its depiction of prostitution. Roche's protagonist employs female prostitutes—like Walsh's, as we will see. Her visits to brothels stem from her curiosity: "Ich bin jetzt öfters im Puff zur Erforschung des weiblichen Körpers" (F, 114; I go to brothels a lot now to explore the female body, W, 115). The text's depiction of a black prostitute is highly disturbing in its simultaneous erasure of blackness—the woman looks exactly like Helen, but "in Schwarz" (F, 115; She looked like a black version of me, W, 116)—and fetishization of the black body (F, 123–24). The reductive accounts of female others are troubling, as in Walsh (see F, 126–27). One might see Helen's female chauvinism as an attempt to beat patriarchy at its own game. In asserting female desire, and the potential for female agency within the contract established by the sex-work industry, the text unsettles assumptions to the effect that only men want sex without commitment and are capable of objectifying other bodies. In any case, the novel leaves the sex industry intact as a given, in line with Roche's stated views on the matter. Jones suggests, in this connection, that the text "deliberately sidesteps the question of gendered power relations" (249): Helen is baffled by the exercise of male power over women in sexual relationships, when she hears tell of it. She is also ignorant of white privilege. Jones notes:

> Roche presents us with a narrator who is in turns naive and knowing, and who chooses to analyse only the effects and not the causes of sexual behaviour. In this way, she is able to bypass more complex questions concerning the social and cultural construction of sexual fantasies and gendered power relations altogether, in favour of a reimagining of the female body from a more basic, if somewhat simplified, physical foundation. (249–50)

However, as chapter 3 suggests, the novel's challenge to dominant models of femininity as clean and demure is useful, if contradictory and confused. Helen notably experiences her body as a totality, refusing the segmentation of bodies that Penny and Power argue is common to mainstream representations of female bodies (see chapter 1). She views her piles as a test of her sexual partner's desire:

> Wenn einer mich liebt oder auch nur geil auf mich ist, dann sollte doch so ein Blumenkohl keine Rolle spielen. Außerdem habe ich schon so viele Jahre, von fünfzehn bis heute, mit achtzehn, trotz eines wuchernden Blumenkohls sehr erfolgreich Analverkehr. . . . Ja, da bin ich stolz drauf. (*F*, 9)

> [If somebody loves me or is even just hot for me, something like the cauliflower [piles] shouldn't make a difference. And anyway, I've had very successful anal sex for many years—from the age of fifteen up to now, at eighteen—despite the ever-expanding cauliflower. . . . Yep, I'm proud of that. (*W*, 2)]

Helen describes how she exposes lovers to the sight of her anus during her first sexual encounters with them. She challenges her sexual partners, and the reader, to feel disgust. For her, sex and disgust should not go together. Unlike her mother, who advocates washing after sex, Helen embraces sperm, reasoning: "Wenn man Schwänze, Sperma oder Smegma ekelhaft findet, kann man's mit dem Sex auch direkt bleiben lassen" (*F*, 26; If you find cocks, cum, or smegma disgusting, you might as well forget about sex, *W*, 20). Yet the novel itself is disgusting. It thus issues a challenge to a context in which sex—or a particular way of representing sexual acts—is omnipresent and all-pervasive. As Helen Hester suggests in her reading of the novel, sex in the contemporary imagination is arguably no longer a privileged locus of transgression. The willfulness of *Feuchtgebiete* is more convincingly located in its disgustingness, and its subversion of sanitized, pornified norms relating to female embodiment and sexuality.

Helen Walsh, *Brass*

Natasha Walter describes Helen Walsh's Liverpool-set debut *Brass* as a "striking coming-of-age story."[25] Ahmed, notably, sees willfulness as "that which is striking" (*WS*, 47). The protagonist Millie's sexuality, in particular, stands out here. The impact of the book is in large part down to its depictions of sex, and in particular to Millie's sexual encounters with prostitutes. In this way, Millie recalls Roche's Helen, as well as Hegemann's queer protagonist, Mifti.[26] For Ahmed, "a queer will might be what you want to have if you are to have what you are not supposed to want" (*WS*, 80). The novel asserts Millie's queer will, but also questions sex and desire on ethical grounds. It is both pornographic and anti-pornographic, evincing a willful ambivalence on the matters of the sex industry, promiscuity, and porn itself.

The novel opens with Millie's narration of her encounter with a young female prostitute, "a child in the eyes of the law" (B, 1). Her appreciative description of the girl's appearance involves an assertion of the female gaze. This encounter is problematic in feminist terms, involving exploitation. Millie considers briefly fleeing but: "as my mouth falls upon her cunt and the smell of rubber smacks me in the face, I resume my role. Guiltlessly. As a punter" (B, 3). The graphic descriptions of sex, as in Roche, are potentially shocking, as is the objectification of the other woman: "I manipulate myself hard and selfishly, the whore becoming nothing but a body. A cunt in a magazine" (B, 4).[27] Millie's sexuality is phallic. Her repeated references to her sexual organs recall discourses around male sexuality.[28] Millie makes the comparison herself: "If I were a lad I'd be steel hard" (B, 209). Such a queering of dominant paradigms is subversive, or at any rate noteworthy. It involves a refutation of assumptions to the effect that women are less libidinous than men and that female sexuality is mild and unthreatening. Millie describes eyeing a woman desirously: "I drag my eyes down her entire . . . frame. . . . My eyes fuck her and feel her, everywhere" (B, 81–82). Arguably, her desire for men, expressed in such terms, is even more "striking" (for example B, 170).[29]

Millie's female gaze is cruel. In the context of a culture in which young women experience extreme pressure related to their appearance, Millie's complicity with the body project is troubling in feminist terms.[30] At the same, time, the vagaries of desire emerge here, perhaps usefully. Millie is both alive to female appearance and critical of mainstream constructions of it, as when she compares two women on a bus:

> She's quite a honey this big-breasted blonde piece, and she bears all the hallmarks of someone who is incapable of finding a bloke who will offer her respect and commitment. She's mainstream. Universally attractive. Big blue eyes, large breasts, honey-hued skin, a cute button nose and a Colgate smile. There's nothing to her. As Billy would say, a pure spunk deposit. Her mate though . . . She's a skewed beauty. Pure Vogue material. And straight as fuck. Ah well, Millie. (B, 36–37)

Millie's desiring gaze is at once objectifying and radical, asserting queer desire as livable. Yet there is no female solidarity here (see also B, 211). Millie empathizes instead with all the ugly men of the world, frustrated by the plethora of provocative images around them (B, 77). While such a lesbian perspective adds to the discourse on objectification and interpellation, in aligning herself with a male perspective, Millie supports the dominance of the male gaze. Her attraction to young women recalls masculine models of predatory sexuality (for example, *B*, 208). She watches teenage girls playing sports and reflects on their "hypnotic sexual potency" (*B*, 124). But the episode ends with Millie feeling sad, as she recalls that she herself was once "fourteen and carefree . . . a kid" (*B*, 126). Desire is ethically dubious in this case, as Millie seems to realize. She is troubled by her desire for prostitutes, too, at least briefly:

> My mind meanders over to the streets of Liverpool 8. Skinny whores with bad complexions, girls who reek of cheap perfume and rubber and the street. I can't help myself. The very notion stirs something so deep in my groin that I should be shocked—troubled, at least, that I should itch so greedily for such a wretched thrill. But instead I feel alive—drunk and fearless and wonderfully, fervently alive. (*B*, 92)

She also refers to buying sex as "sheer filth," and experiences "[a desire] to degrade myself and be degraded" (*B*, 99, 103). Her encounter with a prostitute involves a strange intimacy: "Whore and punter united, as intimate as newlyweds" (*B*, 105). However, Millie ends up feeling "spent and unloved" (*B*, 107). Moreover, she experiences empathy for the sex worker (*B*, 108). Millie's attempt to engage in "filthy," degrading sex does not satisfy her, perhaps because it does not involve true intimacy, or because it is excessively intimate. In any case, it appears Millie's and the text's bravado coexists with ethical concerns about the sex industry.[31]

Millie's friend Jamie also remonstrates with her in the matter of her desires, asking her to imagine having a daughter and seeing "some fat aul' perve leching her" (*B*, 22; see also *B*, 56). Millie responds that she does not see herself as a mother, rebuffing Jamie's suggestion as to a maternal perspective. Millie's rejection of family and futurity ties with the ideas of failure and refusal that chapter 2 discusses. In Millie's disavowal of family—she claims not to "go in for all that family stuff" (*B*, 79)—and in her outsider-ness, she is, like Hegemann's Mifti, an awkward figure. Millie's peer group does not appeal to her (*B*, 41). She finds their youthful idealism hypocritical: "You just know that ten years down the line, most of them will be carting their GAP kids around in the Renault space mobiles, all munching away on McDonalds Happy Meals" (*B*, 116). Thus Millie disdains mainstream ideals, founded on heteronormativity, reproductive futurism, and global capitalism. In a challenge to conceptions of femininity as naturally maternal and selfless, Millie also refutes maternity and asserts her own desires over the well-being of others. Millie claims provocatively that she views mothers as sexual objects.[32]

While according to Millie most teenage girls are unaware of their sexual potential, she herself lived out her sexuality from a young age (*B*, 195,

196). Millie rejects a "coming-out" paradigm when recounting her sexual history, refusing to fix or define her orientation: "And then there were the girls. Which just kind of happened" (*B*, 198). She discovers a porn magazine featuring lesbian sex—this on the night her mother left, though she denies there is a connection.[33] She wonders now: "Who knows, if I'd never set eyes upon Lara and Dawn I may have skimmed over such a moment of realisation [of desire for women] and evolved into a healthy uncomplicated heterosexual" (*B*, 199). The ironic reference to hetero-sexuality as healthy and uncomplicated challenges heteronormativity. It is notable that mainstream porn serves as an induction to queer desire here. Despite the male gaze, such material can provoke deviant desires in a female viewer. Millie takes on a pornographer's gaze as she looks at other women, who "suddenly became candidates for Escort, Men Only, Mayfair" (*B*, 201). Millie herself, however, remains outside of such cat-egorization.[34] If "willfulness can be the refusal to be housed by gender" (*WS*, 149), Millie's genderqueer stance makes her unruly. The text in fact references queer theory (*B*, 24; see also *B*, 167), and also situates Millie's lesbian desires in a broader context in which these are not acceptable, or at least not standard. Millie's quest for gratification is difficult (*B*, 2, 61). She envies a man she sees soliciting: "as a man, and a man with a car, he has privileges that I can only dream of" (*B*, 93). The status of lesbian desire as novelty act or titillation is clear. Women on nights out "love playing up to that whole girl on girl thing. They use it as a pulling mechanism" (*B*, 88). But most do not follow through, experiencing "dis-belief and disgust" at Millie's attempts to go further. Thus lesbian desire emerges in the novel as at once complicit and transgressive, recalling Puar.

On the matter of pornography, there is a comparable ambivalence or awkwardness. Pornography is a source of amused disappointment: "That was *it*? Pornography? The boys club [*sic*] that had dared to exclude me. And that was what it amounted to?" (*B*, 199) On the other hand, its effects can be powerful and damaging, Millie concedes grudgingly:

> My love affair with wank mags and lap dancing bars lasted all of twelve months, and I'm glad in a way that it's over now. In hindsight I can see what a distorted view of the world it lent me. I don't buy into all that received feminist wisdom that holds porn responsible for every ill perpetrated on women by men, but there's no doubt that pornography impinged on my sense of reality. Implicit in its appeal is the idea that all girls are gagging for it, that they crave to be treated like filthy indefatigable whores as much as they crave to be pampered like princesses. That glamour models and lap dancers—they do what they do for the love of it. Not for the money. They *crave* sex. I truly believed that for twelve months. And when I discovered otherwise, the realisation crushed me. (*B*, 201–2)

Thus, Millie does come to a critical view of pornography, and the novel suggests the damaging effects on human relations of a pornified view of women. It also implies that Millie undergoes development. At one point, she seems to reach a nadir: "I'm crying for me" (*B*, 109). When she is diagnosed with gonorrhoea and herpes, this seems to represent a turning point: Millie looks in the mirror and feels estranged from herself (*B*, 127). Sexual abstinence brings about a kind of self-satisfaction. Millie also claims she has reinvented herself as "the model daughter" (*B*, 156).[35] However, the text ultimately remains willfully open: the end of the novel, which sees Millie poised to meet her mother again after many years, feels cursory. Millie's awkward challenge to sexual and gender norms finds no clear narrative resolution.

Special, Bella Bathurst

Bathurst's *Special* also exposes dominant constructions of gender and sexuality as unhelpful. As we have seen, the novel probes the complex and often hurtful conflicts among a group of teenage girls. The questions of appearance and of perceived sexual attractiveness are key factors in this dynamic. Queer desire is shameful in this context. The alleged desire of a female teacher for Caz gives rise to awkward jokes: the teacher becomes a scapegoat for unacceptable inclinations.[36] Jules herself experiences an ambiguous but powerful attraction to Caz: "For a second Jules felt desire so strong that she could scarcely breathe. But though she looked at Caz with passion, it was not love that Jules felt. It wasn't even close" (*S*, 36). Jules catches sight of what this hidden element of her feelings might be: "Something uneasy swam through the corners of her mind and then vanished" (*S*, 37). The text does not name this "something uneasy." Its unmentionable quality points up the power of the taboo surrounding queer desire. Later on, Caz and Jules climb the ropes in the gym in a competition, in front of their teacher and the other girls. The mixture of anger, desire, and physical effort arouses Jules, and "she knew suddenly, appallingly, what had happened" (*S*, 122): she experiences orgasm. The experience leads to horror and shame.[37] Her internalized homophobia explains the fact that Jules consents to a sexual act with a boy: "to prove she wasn't a lesbian" (*S*, 139). The narrative evokes this encounter in squalid and violent terms. Sex is a matter of disappointment. The male member is grotesque and absurd (*S*, 144). The experience does not correspond to Jules's imaginings of intercourse: "All this disjointed groping and prodding, all this noise" (*S*, 145). She feels extreme pain as the boy penetrates her, and the encounter leaves her "tangled up and sad" (*S*, 145, 153).

For this group of girls, desire is a matter of disgust, confusion, fear, and shame. Hen worries, for example: "maybe I'm into dead people" (*S*,

39). She experiences revulsion at thought of the teacher Miss Naylor having sex (S, 79). Sex also provokes frenzied interest. Ali reads aloud from books pertaining to sex: favored topics include "sado-masochism, the myth of the vaginal orgasm, and anything at all which involved the word clitoris, throbbing, or gusset" (S, 109). However, "discussion of rape or lesbianism . . . reduced the room to silence"—a silence owing to "boredom, discomfort or longing" (S, 109). These two taboos are linked in this observation. The suggestion that rape is the object of longing is troubling. Ali's reflection elsewhere that "she was too ugly to get raped" (S, 250) similarly implies a lurid teenage understanding of the phenomenon of rape as an expression of desire or a tribute to attractiveness. Sex is also a site of dissimulation and bravado: Jules, a virgin at the time of speaking, claims to be "bored of sex at the moment" (S, 134; cf. S, 170).

The shaping of desire by culture is hinted at by the quotation from a feminist text that Ali reads out:

> The classic sexual position . . . is . . . the missionary position. The woman lies passive, the flattened receptacle for the penis, no more active or participatory than an insect on a dissecting board. The act of penetration is all; the penis's pleasure is the aim and goal of the act. The penis is thrust, weapon-like, into the wound of the vagina, whilst the woman, in order to escape the demeaning charge of frigidity, simulates the false promise of satiation. The woman is entered, sometimes violently, usually too early for her own pleasure. (S, 111)

This fictional feminist text points to phallocentrism, the structuring and shaping of desire under the sign of the phallus, in a manner that recalls Luce Irigaray. But it is dismissed by Caz as boring, and fails to have a perceptible impact on the girls; Jules's sexual encounter comes after this reading. The novel thus seems to point to the inefficacy of feminist discourse—or at least, of feminist academic discourse—in allowing a rethinking of female sexuality and agency. Mainstream, normative depictions are more compelling. Caz brings a porn magazine to school. To Hen, "the pictures were fascinating, but somehow scary as well. She stared at the women's sculpted pubes. Hers didn't look anything like that. Was that how they were supposed to be?" (S, 125). The anxiety provoked by pornographic images, and their damaging effects, become clear. Hen is suffering from an eating disorder. Her disgust at food blends with her unease in the face of the pornographic imagery: "The images wouldn't stop crawling into her mind, the creeping baked beans, the cream, the raw hideous slits like wounds" (S, 127). This linkage is suggestive: Hen's fear of adult female physicality may, then, be a factor in her eating disorder.[38] For Hen, significantly, "fancying people, desiring them, seemed a faraway notion" (S, 253).

Male sexuality is similarly a site of competition, but is framed in more predatory terms. The boys at a local college keep knickers as trophies from their conquests, having devised an elaborate scoring system. Discovering this, Hen is troubled: "All the need and all the lies were starting to make [Hen's] head hurt" (*S*, 198). The boys view girls' bodies as objects to be conquered. Caz undergoes a distressing encounter with one of the college boys, following which Hen sees her looking uncharacteristically unkempt and crying (*S*, 200). We learn later than she was humiliated: tied to the bed then left, for other boys to come and gawp at (*S*, 269–70). This was deemed to be just as Caz seemed "a bit of a slapper" (*S*, 269). The impossible paradox of young women's sexuality further emerges when Caz later encourages admiring male looks and lands the girls in a dangerous situation. One man accuses Jules of "playing games" and the girls of being "slags" (*S*, 265–66). The girls' confusion and unease coexist with their attractiveness. The novel points up the contradictions and complexities attending to young women's sexuality. Their discomfiting sexuality becomes apparent when the driver who gives Caz, Hen, and Jules a lift into town seems unnerved by his passengers, "with their thick feral reek of perfume and their naked clothing" (*S*, 136). This study of young girls, which ends with Jules's demise, suggests a pessimistic view of girls' *Bildung*. But one character, Ali—an outsider—does establish a connection with a man. She appears to forge a way out for herself via this heterosexual connection. The relationships between the girls, on the other hand—desirous or hostile and competitive—are toxic. The novel suggests the influence of dominant discourses, including pornography, on female relationships and sexualities, implying that illness, repression, and isolation are the result.

Zoe Pilger, *Eat My Heart Out*

Chapter 4 discusses Pilger's *Eat My Heart Out* in terms of sisterhood and identification. The novel's depiction of sex and desire is also notable, and willful, however. At the start of the text, Ann-Marie has broken up with her boyfriend Sebastian, who has formed a relationship with Allegra, the sister of one of Ann-Marie's friends. The tense mesh of relationships the work evokes underlines the complexity of human connections, the object here of grotesque and surreal treatment. The text features queer characters and ambiguous attractions.[39] It involves a critique of heterosexual romantic love as delusional and damaging (see *EMHO*, 98). Explaining the influence on her of Simone de Beauvoir, and the origin of the text, Pilger states:

> *The Second Sex* changed the way I look at the world and it changed my life. I started a PhD on romantic love and femininity and wrote a novel, *Eat My Heart Out* . . . Why do we allow ourselves to be

objectified, abused, and humiliated, in the media and in life? Is sub-
missiveness a condition of being loved and desired? Young women
have recently become interested in feminism once again, and the
questions posed by this visionary book [*The Second Sex*] seem more
relevant than ever. A new wave is coming.[40]

The text skewers postfeminism, as I outline in chapter 4. It also unsettles
ideas relating to feminine submission and masculine dominance in sex.

The novel begins with the protagonist in pursuit of a man, Vic. She
"rides him," and refuses to get off. When she claims he likes women to
say "No," he refutes this: "No" (*EMHO*, 6). Male sexuality, then, is not
necessarily predatory and rapacious. Ann-Marie's pursuit of Vic appears
random and grotesque. Against his will, she performs oral sex on him,
in a reversal of conventional power relations and practices (*EMHO*,
64–65). In conversation with her mother, she later terms herself a "rap-
ist" (*EMHO*, 71). The questions of power, control, and consent undergo
teasing treatment:

> He threw me against the wall and gripped my neck so that I couldn't
> breathe.
> "Stop," I croaked.
> He loosened his grip.
> "No!" I screamed. "Tighter!"
> He tightened his grip.
> "You're not supposed to do what I say," I rasped. (*EMHO*, 100)

Desire is contradictory and hard to convey or decipher. The feminist slogan "No means no," intended to assert the importance of consent in heterosexual sexual intercourse, appears inadequate. Contraception is also a
thorny matter, as emerges during their first sexual encounter:

> Vic was surprised when I rolled away from his hairy body and pro-
> duced a packet of Performa condoms from my handbag. I snapped
> one on his penis efficiently.
> It immediately began to die.
> "Would you rather we didn't use them?" I said.
> "Yeah. Thanks. It's just that I don't like the sensation of
> condoms."
> "Well, I don't really like the sensation of abortions." I sat up. "I
> don't really feel like having a foetus ripped out of my womb, thank
> you very much."
> There was silence.
> I felt for it, but now it was dead.

He got out of bed and stood over me. "Why do you humiliate me?"

I waited.

"Hit me, then," I said.

He exhaled, agonised. He lay down again.

Soon he was snoring.

I moved into the crook of his arm. I felt so happy then. (*EMHO*, 8)[41]

Later on, Ann-Marie insists that she does not want to use protection, however, favoring "bareback" intercourse. Vic protests she will present him with a pregnancy. She suggests he withdraw, but he demurs. She then avers: "I want your disease" (*EMHO*, 67). This is an example of the skewed, contradictory logic of the protagonist and the work, which is set on troubling commonsense—mainstream or feminist—assumptions. Ann-Marie terminates the relationship abruptly with Vic, telling him "So wait." The male partner ends up waiting, in opposition to Stephanie Haight's argument that is it is women in Western culture who conventionally engage in this activity (*EMHO*, 134). Vic carves Ann-Marie's initials into his stomach, having lost his mind (*EMHO*, 233).

Gender relations in this novel are the targets of black humor, then, as is feminism (see also chapter 3). Ann-Marie sees a fortune teller, who tells her client:

"You want to be tough and alone like a man. Sleep with men like a man sleeps with women."

"No," I said.

"Yes," she said.

"You lost him because you wanted to be like him. To be better than him."

. . .

"No!" I shouted. "Equal!"

. . . "Men and women can never be equal," said the women. "It's not written in the stars." (*EMHO*, 113)

Equality and difference emerge as slippery terms. The surreal narrative raises these questions in order to derail easy assumptions. Power relations are similarly problematic, as already suggested. Meeting a man called Dave, Ann-Marie asks if he is either "S" or "M," assuring him he must be one or the other, "because that's how human nature works" (*EMHO*, 226). Haight's work involves a view of female sexuality, in particular, as involving inferiority and passivity. The references to burlesque and to the postfeminist climate of hypersexualization suggest that women in contemporary culture are pornified and flattened. Haight writes: "Women use the weapons of the weak. We are coquettish; we preen. We are less then ourselves in order to get more for ourselves. What some scoundrel 'feminist' academic recently called erotic capital' (*EMHO*, 107).[42]

Yet an instructive conversation about power takes place between Haight and Ann-Marie. Ann-Marie reads aloud from Haight's book, and then objects: "Why does it always have to be one or the other? . . . I mean, Stephanie—are you master or are you slave?" "I'm both," said Steph, sucking ravenously on her fag. "We're all both"' (*EMHO*, 270). The novel, which involves a mockery of feminist academia, art, and discourse, thus ultimately challenges the idea that there can be an "outside," and insists with gleeful perversity on the embeddedness of subjects in skewed power relations. The castration of the Oxford don toward the end of the novel is to be read as a macabre fantasy of feminist revenge that at once asserts and undermines feminist challenges to phallocentrism. The text's treatment of sex and desire ties in with its perversely willful stance on the matter of femininity in the contemporary context.

Helene Hegemann, *Axolotl Roadkill*

As chapter 2 suggests, Helene Hegemann's *Axolotl Roadkill* is a queer text. For example, the designation of a customer in Lidl as a "heterosexuelle Kommunikationsdesignerin" (heterosexual female communication designer) challenges heteronormativity by labeling the straight subject, rather than assuming that it is the queer who is deviant and in need of categorization.[43] A similar refusal of heterosexism occurs when Mifti's half-brother Edmond is declared gay by a man who appears to be his lover (*AR*, 131). Mifti counters that he is in fact "stockbisexuell," as is Mifti herself (*AR*, 133; as bi as they come, 130). This description, "stockbisexuell," gives bisexuality a taken-for-granted status. Pseudo-Darwinist explanations of human sexual behavior appear dubious when Mifti's friend Ophelia wonders: "Kann es denn sein, dass alles nur Chemie oder Biologie ist? Wäre dann nicht nur die Fortpflanzung der Sinn des Verliebens? Warum verliebe ich mich dann generell nur in Frauen? Aber will trotzdem immer noch brutalen Sex mit Männern?" (*AR*, 29: Is it possible that everything's just chemistry or biology? Then wouldn't the point of falling in love be only reproduction? So why do I only ever fall in love with women? But still want brutal sex with men?, 23).[44] The queerness of desire emerges, in a manner that recalls Grosz. Mifti herself is in love with a 46-year-old woman, Alice. Ophelia dubs this state of affairs sick. Mifti agrees and elsewhere describes Alice as perverse (*AR*, 44, 176). This cheerful embrace of abnormality is highly queer, in J. Halberstam's sense (see chapter 2). Mifti and Alice had sex when Mifti was fourteen or fifteen, and Mifti sees in the older woman her dead mother. Mifti's claim that her feelings for Alice have nothing to

SEX AND DESIRE ◆ 135

do with homosexuality (*AR*, 168)—a description that mockingly paraphrases Ophelia's earlier claim that her relationship with a male DJ has nothing to do with heterosexuality—acts to free feelings from categorizations such as "gay" and "straight": itself a queer move that challenges the "Heteromatrix" that Hegemann's text explicitly refers to elsewhere (*AR*, 177; heteromatrix, 175).

The queerness of this text resides not only its depiction of a (disturbing) "same-sex" relationship, however, but also in its challenge to reproductive futurism (see chapter 2). The text's treatment of desire stresses mourning and lack and brings to mind ideas of failure and refusal. Desire also has complex and troubling links to family histories and dynamics. Alice is the subject of obsession for Mifti, but details about her and about the relationship become slowly and indirectly apparent, through the prism of memory and fantasy (for example, *AR*, 36). The following passage, which mixes third- with second-person modes focuses on fear, dissolution, and loss:

> Sobald wir beginnen, etwas für andere als uns selbst zu tun, lösen wir uns aus dem Gefängnis in unserem Inneren. Alice hasst sich selbst, aber das ist ja das Geile, ich sehe, dass sie durchdreht und sich zunehmend selbst zerstört. Ich habe so große Angst, dass ich nicht mehr denken kann. Ich will alles tun, um dich weiterhin kennen zu dürfen. Wenn du nicht mehr mit mir ficken willst, ist das völlig in Ordnung. Jetzt bist du aus meinem Leben verschwunden. (*AR*, 9)

> [As soon as we begin doing something for others, we release ourselves from the prison inside of us. Alice hates herself, but that's what's so awesome: I can see she's losing it and increasingly destroying herself. I'm so scared I can't think any more. I'll do anything to still have the privilege of knowing you. It's no big deal if you don't want to fuck me any more. You've disappeared out of my life now. (3)]

Relationality appears at first freeing in this passage, which then goes on to stress Alice's self-destructiveness, which is attractive to Mifti, perhaps paradoxically. Mifti asserts her fear and her longing but then downplays the importance to her of sexual activity with Alice. The final sentence confirms Alice's withdrawal from her life. These shifts and reversals suggest a tantalizing and frustrating dynamic. Later Alice appears in a dream Mifti has, and is associated with a vision of wholeness:

> Alice war auch da. Sie war kein Mensch. Sie hat ihr Gesicht zurechtgerückt, zart über meinen Handrücken gestrichen und mir vergegenwärtigt, dass sie und ich wirklich sind—echte Individuen

oder wie man das nennt, in einer echten Gesellschaft, mit echten Wünschen, die nicht einfach so aus unseren echten Körpern rausgeschnitten werden können. (*AR*, 28)

[Alice was there too. She wasn't human. She adjusted her face, stroked the back of my hand tenderly and reminded me what she and I really are—real-life individuals or whatever you call it, in a real-life society, with real-life desires that can't just be sliced out of our real-life bodies. (22)][45]

The implication is that this wishful fantasy, which suggests the intactness and integrity of desires, is at odds with reality. Individuality and sociality remain fantasies in this vision of fragmentation, in line with Iris Radisch's discussion of the text as challenging bourgeois subjectivity (see chapter 2).

Wholeness remains a fantasy in the novel. Mifti recalls sharing a sensation of plenitude with Alice beside the sea. She had been experiencing disassociation from her body but her encounter with Alice, and with the sea, appeared to provide relief (*AR*, 166–67). This respite was, however, temporary. A further encounter with Alice—likely hallucinated—again stresses loss. Mifti asks Alice accusingly if she knows what she has done, and Alice points to her own function in Mifti's psychosexual development:

Wärst du alt geworden, hättest du irgendwann zurückgeblickt und erkannt, dass die Erinnering an deine ganze glückliche Jugend eigentlich nur aus mir besteht . . . Und dann hättest du dir eingebildet, dass ich eigentlich gar nicht existiert habe. Ich wäre nur noch irgendeine unangemessene, runtergekommene Person gewesen, durch die du lernen musstest, dass Hingabe zu Selbstverlust führen kann, und dieser Selbstverlust nichts mehr mit Liebe zu tun hat, sondern nur mit Autoaggression. Merkst du, wie du jetzt gerade transzendierst? (*AR*, 40–41)

[If you'd got old you'd have looked back at some point and realized that the entire memory of your whole happy youth consists only of me. . . . And then you'd have told yourself I never even existed. I was only some inappropriate fucked-up individual through whom you had to learn that devotion can lead to loss of self, and this loss of self has nothing to do with love any more, only with auto-aggression. Can you tell how you're transcending right now? (35)]

Alice is explicitly figured here as a product of fantasy. The association of desire with self-loss is significant in light of queer notions of failure and self-divestiture. The importance of fantasy emerges again later when

Ophelia questions whether Mifti should ever see Alice again, given how damaging the attachment is. She tells Mifti of the medieval notion of a fantasy place where love could be fulfilled, and refers in this connection to her own youthful experience of love for an actor. When Mifti protests that Ophelia is reducing her feelings by likening them to a teenage crush, Ophelia explains further how profound her imaginary relationship with this actor was: it even socialized her (*AR*, 44). But Mifti insists on the reality of her feelings for Alice. She claims that sex with Alice was "perfekt" and "reibungslos" (*AR*, 45; perfect[ ], smooth[ ], 40), in opposition to the usual awkward rigmarole. However, the novel never depicts sex between Mifti and Alice directly: it remains mediated through memory and narration. Mifti also declares that she wishes for a continuation of the status quo, stating that she is not jealous of Alice's many other lovers. However, she would object to Alice owning a pet or becoming pregnant, an event that would cause her to shoot herself (*AR*, 45). Mifti's attachment to Alice is rooted in her feelings for her mother, as Mifti is herself aware. Alice, however, has no insight into this aspect of her appeal for Mifti, and Ophelia suggests that if she did, the knowledge would cause scruples to awaken in the older woman (*AR*, 45).[46]

Mifti addresses Alice later on in a passage that links desire to writing and to remembering:

> Alice, ich denke jetzt gerade im Moment an dich und ich werde weder damit aufhören, dein Gesicht zu sehen noch damit aufhören, diese Dinge, hinzuschreiben, denn sonst ist alles weg, diese Direktheit ist dann weg und dieses Glück. Trotzdem werde ich nie wieder etwas mit dir zu tun haben, weil du mich nämlich offenbar, egal ob nur die Umstände dazu geführt haben oder nicht, nicht mehr lieben willst. Es gibt Komplikationen, denn ich benehme mich wie ein Kleinkind. Das hier alles trifft die Situation wahrscheinlich gar nicht, es gibt naheliegenderweise Schattierungen, Grauabstufungen, es gibt dich immer noch nicht, komm endlich raus, du verdammte Allerweltshure. (*AR*, 67–68)

> [Alice, I'm just thinking about you right now and I'm not going to stop either seeing your face or writing these things down, because otherwise it'll all be gone, this directness will be gone and this happiness too. But I'm still never going to have anything to do with you again, because you obviously don't want to love me anymore, regardless of whether the circumstances are to blame or not. There are complications, because I tend to act like a little child. All this is probably way off the mark, of course there are shades of grey, but you're still there somewhere—why don't you come out, you hackneyed old whore? (62–63)]

Desire is here impossible because it is one-sided. Ultimately, Mifti's account falters, becoming uncertain of its own representative powers, and she ends up insulting the love object. The novel indeed associates desire with destruction: Mifti fantasizes about tying Alice up, and placing a caged rat on her chest, to eat away at the victim (*AR*, 92). She writes a letter in which she expresses the wish to look like Alice so that Alice can be confronted by her own disgusting self, in an apparent criticism of narcissism that is fuelled by sadism (*AR*, 146). The end of the novel sees Alice tying Mifti up. This encounter involves disorientation, loss of self, and degradation, and precedes the final element of the novel, a hate-filled letter from Mifti's mother that apparently seals Mifti's fate as an unloved child.

The novel queers desire, then, and it also relativizes sex and sexuality, sometimes treating these with humorous detachment. Hester Baer notes that although sex and desire form central themes of the novel, they are rarely linked to pleasure, "instead providing a focal point for Mifti's anxiety and liminality."[47] Viewing a man in a club, Mift fails to experience her usual "sexuelle[ ] Gelüste," experiencing instead "ein paar emotionale Zuneigungsattacken" (*AR*, 23; sexual yearning . . . a bit of an emotional affection attack, 17).[48] She does experience lust for a man later. The resulting sexual encounter is couched in terms of passivity and randomness, however, and is blackly comic: "[ich lasse mich] aus diversen Gründen wahnsinnig lange in den Mund ficken" (*AR*, 58; I let him fuck me in the mouth for an incredible length of time, for various reasons, 53). Indeed, Mifti apparently views sex with detachment, even distaste. She has issues with genitals and finds sex animalistic and anti-intellectual (*AR*, 95–96). A sexual encounter with a taxi driver involves "Ekel, pure Geilheit, Egoismus," among other things (*AR*, 112; Disgust, pure lechery, egoism, 109). Desire and sex are not cohate or coexistent. Desire cannot be pinned down to "einen konkreten Anspruch" (*AR*, 103; a specific demand, 100). What emerges in this novel, ultimately, is the unstable, unfixable nature of desire: as queer, as endlessly deferred and displaced, as always mediated.

Conclusion

The novels by Moran, Roche, and Walsh affirm female desire, asserting it against dominant norms and ideals. Moran's fat, desirous protagonist, Roche's libidinous and unhygienic Helen, and Walsh's rapacious Millie are all willful figures. But all are subjected to, or complicitous with, male-dominated acts and representations. In the case of Moran's protagonist, her inexperience means she fails to secure pleasure for herself. Roche's Helen is a contradictory figure, and Walsh's Millie is also awkward and ambivalent. Transgression is no easy matter. In Bathurst, Pilger, and

Hegemann, desire is distorted, repressed, or relativized. In Bathurst, pornography and homophobia lead to despair and depression. Pilger's grotesque novel stresses insanity and violence alongside or over desire, and Hegemann too subverts Ahmed's "happy stories" relating to heterosexual, or indeed queer, fulfillment.[49]

All of the texts, barring Moran's, give voice to queer desire, bringing to mind Ahmed's linkage of willfulness and queerness. Given the historical prohibition on queer desire, "a queer history of sexuality might cover some of the same ground as the history of the faculty of the will" (*WS*, 9). Yet as we saw in the last chapter, queer is not necessarily or only a site of resistance. In Hegemann and Walsh, most notably, queer desires and inclinations are more or less pathologized. Queer here does not act as a locus for privileged, subversive forms of being. The association of queer with failure and perversity is potentially troubling, in that it might lend weight to heteronormative assumptions concerning the healthiness or otherwise of queer relationships. But as with Rachel B. Glaser's *Paulina and Fran*, and with Kate Zambreno's *Green Girl*—to which I shortly turn, in my conclusion—these depictions of "same-sex" relations are usefully intense and intensive. This is not to say that depictions of queer *Bildungen* which gesture toward security and permanence would not be welcome.[50] But queer is not an end-point. And all the novels, in different ways, also suggest the shaping of desire by culture, as well as its vagaries and vicissitudes, and in this way, perhaps, are "queer" in Puar's sense. The status of sex as a taboo appears questionable in a number of these texts, too. It might indeed be that the bodily realities of defecation, say, are more shocking, or "striking"—to refer to Ahmed (*WS*, 47)—than sexual activities, in a culture that favors plastic and pornified depictions of female corporeality. And it might be that fantasy, rather than bodily activity, is a more promising site of transgression. If this is the case, what kinds of fantasies or figurations might usefully undermine postfeminist and neoliberal strictures? My conclusion suggests that green girls and trainwrecks might prompt such productive subversions.

Conclusion: Green Girls, Trainwrecks, and Willful Politics

T HE TEXTS I HAVE EXAMINED in this study reveal a spectrum of feminine becomings. Failure, refusal, disgust, and bile feature strikingly in these willful literary responses to postfeminism and neoliberalism. In the course of writing this book, I came across Kate Zambreno's 2011 novel *Green Girl*. This text holds an emblematic status as far as my project is concerned, and demands a special emphasis. *Green Girl* engages with the concerns of this book in important and instructive ways, offering an important case study in terms of contemporary literary constructions of and engagements with femininity. The novel's aesthetic illustrates strikingly the ways in which literature itself can provoke becoming, as my introduction suggests. This conclusion therefore discusses Zambreno's novel under the headings agency and voluntarism, body and beauty, sisterhood and identification, and sex and desire, also reiterating and crystallizing the concerns of previous chapters. It argues that the green girl, and the related figure of the trainwreck, are provocative and useful figurations. Finally, it turns to the questions of feminist art, criticism, and activism today, in light of Ahmed's theorization of willfulness as "a style of politics."

Green Girl: Agency and Voluntarism

Green Girl concerns Ruth, a young American in London who is adrift and as-yet unfixed.[1] The novel self-consciously thematizes the creation of its protagonist. The narrator is a mother-author: "I am trying to push her [Ruth] out in the world" (*GG*, 3). This self-reflexiveness involves a postmodern emphasis on the constructedness of text. It also highlights the struggle for self-definition in which the protagonist—an archetypal neoliberal girl—is engaged. Ruth's job in a department store, where she sells a celebrity-endorsed perfume wittily called Desire, points up the commercialism and consumerism of the age, and the power of celebrity and branding (see *GG*, 184–86). Affect, here, is to be packaged and sold: "Would you like to sample Desire?" (*GG*, 7). The text archly quotes and subverts sales patter. It also exposes and mocks the neoliberalist make-over paradigm (*GG*, 45–48, 89). Ruth, who is in "her last gasp of girl-hood" (*GG*, 3), is undergoing "becoming" in this context. The process is anxious and faltering.[2] The novel explicitly foregrounds becoming, then, and like texts such as Baum's and Hegemann's, it suggests how arduous and precarious a process that is (GG, 81, 229). Ruth's status and identity are uncertain. Her accent is neither American nor British; she is not a tourist, but "something in-between" (GG, 79). She is also apolitical, uncommitted (GG, 93). Her lack of stability makes her appealing to others: the novel suggests a widespread voyeuristic fascination with "the unstable girl-woman": "She is such a trainwreck. But that's why we like to watch" (GG, 13).[3] It thereby provides a perspective on many of the novels I discuss, raising questions about their reception as possibly voyeuristic—a point to which I will return when I discuss the figure of the trainwreck, an emotionally unstable girl or young woman.[4]

The "green girl" is a reference to a line spoken by Polonius to Ophelia in Shakespeare's *Hamlet*. The novel quotes this line: "You speak like a green girl, / Unsifted in such perilous circumstance" (GG, 49).[5] The green girl represents a type (see for example GG, 43). Mediatedness is crucial to the experience of such girls, in a manner that recalls Berg, Grether, and Zeh: "They are in the film of their lives. They are playing themselves. There is a soundtrack always playing. A camera always following them and eyes oh eyes always watching . . ." (GG, 65; ellipsis in original; cf. GG, 104). The female subject is alienated from herself, interpellating the gaze of others. She is unable to inhabit an authentic state of being. Indeed, for the narrator, "being a girl is like always being a tourist, always conscious of yourself, always seeing yourself as if from the outside" (GG, 229; cf. GG, 142). This focus on exteriority, and on others' perceptions, has negative implications and effects. Agency and volition are difficult matters for young women: the term "girl" connotes marginality: "[Ruth and her friend Agnes] are part of the demimonde in London, foreigners working humiliating jobs on the high streets where they are 'girls.' Shopgirl. Coffeegirl" (GG, 25). Their condition is one of precarity and cruel optimism.[6] Ruth is a compliant neoliberal girl. The references to performance and disguise suggest not so much a liberating Butlerian performativity as a fundamental inability to challenge set roles and an estrangement from the self (GG, 5, 7, 8, 11, 13).[7] Ruth does evince occasional critical awareness of her condition (GG, 42). More obviously, however, she lacks agency, or will. In particular, norms relating to feminine propriety and politeness prevent her from being truly herself.[8] She is also interpellated by consumerism and fashion: an "arsenal of voices" tell her to buy a dress (GG, 33).[9]

Ruth's situation as a temporary worker is precarious, but on the other hand, her precarity seems willful: she routinely walks out of jobs (GG, 39). We find a perverse rejection of appropriate life courses and choices, as in Baum and Hegemann. There is no vitalism here, but rather a questioning of the term "life," and the evocation of an anxious, restless form of affect:

> Ruth wants to escape . . . She doesn't want to be. She doesn't want
> to live. She wants to lose herself, lose herself in the crowd . . . The
> violence of life she observes, blankly. She watches it all unfold. She
> is not there. A series of shocks and sensations. All along she is trying
> to figure out life, life, a life which has lost all meaning. Yes, life. Ahh,
> life. And what about that? Is there nothing else? Life, death, nothing
> else? (*GG*, 70)

Affect here—that "series of shocks and sensations"—is emphasized over
stable notions of self, according with the importance of affect and sensation in contemporary feminist thought. The death drive manifests itself:
Ruth elsewhere imagines herself dying and dead (*GG*, 84–85). Her "nihilistic streak . . . that impulse to ruin everything" (*GG*, 145) ties in with the
questions of failure and refusal that have been important in this study, and
in particular with fiction by Bathurst, Baum, Berg, Hegemann, and Jenny.

Green Girl: Body and Beauty

The novel foregrounds "the rituals of busied femininity, the elaborate cleaning and preparation of the body" (*GG*, 85; see also *GG*, 135).
Glamor and grime coexist in the flat Ruth shares with Agnes: concealer
and perfume mask spots and body odor (*GG*, 141). The performance of
desirable heterosexual femininity becomes apparent. Ruth does not eat
properly, and an unhealthy concern with weight is in evidence (see *GG*,
24, 33). Her sweaty clothes prompt a desire for glamor: "Oh to be pol-
ished, a seamless image, a film still" (*GG*, 19). Indeed, she successfully
achieves this effect (*GG*, 21). The narrator highlights the identification of
self with image as something specific to girls (*GG*, 67). Imagery is dominant in the text and in Ruth's world. Ruth absorbs dominant iconogra-
phy, even merging with it (*GG*, 29).[10] As in Grether especially, imagery
prompts anxiety, threatening the self. Ruth looks at American *Vogue*, staring at a picture of one model so intently that it feels as if "she knows her
intimately, like she is another self" (*GG*, 61).[11] Images challenge the self,
but they also offer temporary respite from the rigors of becoming woman.
Celebrity magazines offer the chance to adopt "other names other faces.
. . . and breathe" (*GG*, 153). This observation invites consideration of
imagery not only as part of damaging "bombardment," but as a more
ambiguous force, since it involves complicity and identification.

Fashion, consumerism, and consumption are integral to Ruth's self-
definition. A dress in Liberty speaks to her:

> Is that me? (Who am I?)
> Is that me? (Who do I want to become?)
> The dress is giving Ruth an identity crisis. (*GG*, 32)

While consumer goods appear to offer alternative selves, in fact they grant no security, instead creating panic. The beauty myth is pernicious, in particular because it does not allow for negativity: "No one wants to be a cosmetics ad when depressed" (*GG*, 58). This observation accords with notions of failure and bile as integral elements of a willful feminine response to the social order. Yet Ruth is a "willing accomplice to this farce," making herself up as beautiful and happy—this in response to the male gaze, which is ever-present (*GG*, 58). This exposure is testing and troubling, at least sometimes. Feminine ambivalence about being looked at is strikingly crystallized here:

> Look at me
> (don't look at me)
> Look at me
> (don't look at me)
> Look at me don't look at me look at me don't look at me don't look. (*GG*, 59)

A man observes Ruth in a café and draws her, "a beautiful sight" (*GG*, 98). The male gaze, and masculine representation, come to the fore. The gulf between what the idealizing male artist sees and the messy interiority the novel invokes involves a challenge to sanitizing and sentimentalizing representations of womanhood. The novel recalls John Berger's claim that "Men look at women. Women watch themselves being looked at."[12] Ruth observes a shopgirl who is aware of her "to-be-looked-at-ness," a reference to Laura Mulvey (*GG*, 98).[13]

In opposition to dominant representations of girls as pretty and unthreatening, the novel insists on disgustingness. Ruth and her friend Agnes, having sex, are "gorgeous and disgusting":

> I look lovingly at all of their flaws they are too consumed to now notice. How their curly pubic hair peeks, pokes out from their panties. The hairs on their nipples they pluck when they remember. How cute their ripples of cellulite on their baby white thighs . . . The red bumps on their rough upper arms. How beautiful they see each other now, in their altered glow, how banal their surroundings. Yet how gorgeous I too find them, gorgeous and disgusting. (*GG*, 221; see also *GG*, 63, *GG*, 204)

Ruth cuts her hair, arguably in an attempt to shed the carapace of conventional beauty, becoming "ugly, ugly, ugly"—but this is remedied when her hair is styled in a salon, and so apparently there is no escape from the beauty myth (*GG*, 162–67). The text also evokes a kind of gut feminism.

Ruth is embodied in a fretful way (see *GG*, 55, 99, 131). Bodies prolifer-
ate in the tube and the department store (*GG*, 4; see also *GG*, 101–2).
Ruth's stomach is unsettled, "a fire-breathing belly. A seething sputtering
ball of stress. A volcano spilling over messy anxieties, sensitivities, fears"
(*GG*, 53).[14] Ruth's body thus issues unruly, "unfeminine" responses,
recalling Roche as well as moments in Moran, Pilger, and Unsworth.[15]

Green Girls: Sisterhood and Identification

The novel also ties in with work on feminine bonds in neoliberalism. Other
women are complicated and threatening: Ruth's co-workers at the store are
"terrible girls" who appear hostile (*GG*, 4, 53–54). Ruth observes other
women with a feeling of superiority, displaying no sisterhood (*GG*, 5). As
with other mother figures I examine here, Ruth's late mother was remote:
"always perfect, an indestructible fortress" (*GG*, 19). Following her death,
Ruth felt "free"—albeit "terribly free" (*GG*, 20). There is a dearth of role
models here, beyond the Hollywood stars and models who embody ideals
of feminine physical perfection. Ruth's relationship with Agnes is fraught
with ambivalence (*GG*, 25). As in Bathurst and Grether, appearance is key
to women's relationships. Ruth and Agnes beautify themselves together:
"their favorite mutual activity" is "the grooming of themselves" (*GG*,
204).[16] The relationship between Ruth and Agnes is precarious, condi-
tional, recalling Naters (*GG*, 217). Agnes has sex with Olly, a man Ruth
likes, in an encounter that began as a threesome involving all of them (*GG*,
146). This prompts a breakdown in Ruth: "She feels deep inside that she
hates Agnes. And that maybe Agnes harbors a greater hatred for her, a hate
and a love both so intense it confuses her" (*GG*, 159). Such intensity is
reminiscent of Glaser's Pauline and Fran. Like that pair, Ruth and Agnes
have sex. They fail to form a couple, though, and apparently eschew queerness: Agnes later refers to a man she assumes is gay as a "poof" (*GG*, 237).
She starts seeing rich men and plans to move to a more central, comfortable
apartment (*GG*, 262). Their intimacy is thus fragile and temporary. The
novel suggests consumerism and individualism hamper relationships. The
remote figure of the mother stands as an emblem for the lack of older role
models, here as elsewhere, and invites renewed challenge to the dividedness
among generations of women that appears to be fostered by the neoliberal,
postfeminist present. That the narrator is Ruth's "mother," as suggested, is
especially striking, given her ambivalence, a matter to which I will return.

Green Girls: Sex and Desire

Ruth dreams of a fantasy male lover, referred to as "HE"; this figure relates to a man in her past who abused her (*GG*, 14, 36–37, 180).

Heterosexual romance is thus couched in terms of regressive fantasies of subjugation: "She prays to be preyed upon" (*GG*, 37). Ruth's fantasy regarding her past boyfriend is explicitly framed in terms of self-delusion (*GG*, 43). Her sexuality involves narcissism rather than active desire. When she masturbates, she conjures up her own face, imagining herself as beautiful in another's eyes: "Her fantasies are of being witnessed, of being watched" (*GG*, 61). Actual sexual encounters are matters of passivity. Having sex with a stranger in the back room of a bar, Ruth is "still, like a doll." Her responses are mechanical, and scripted (*GG*, 107–8; see also *GG*, 212). The text recalls Berg and Jenny in its evocation of female passivity. Ruth has a relationship with Rhys, "a nice boy" (*GG*, 191), but it founders on the fact that he is too nice: "She desired a beast" (*GG*, 208). Her later relationship with an older man, a "Svengali" figure (*GG*, 249) ceases following a party at which she is revealed to be insufficiently adult for his circle, and out of her depth (*GG*, 249, 253–54). As for lesbian desire: when Agnes flirts with Ruth, the latter initially does not respond (*GG*, 65). When they do kiss, it is as part of the show they put on for male observers, as "lesbians just for the night" (*GG*, 125). A threesome is aborted when Ruth begs off and passes out (*GG*, 146). The drug-fueled sex in which Ruth and Agnes engage is to an extent celebrated by the narration: "They are innocent babies. Polymorphously perverse" (*GG*, 221). Yet on the whole, sex and sexuality are matters of disgust and confusion here.[17] Like much of the sex depicted in Lena Dunham's television series *Girls*, sex here is awkward at best: a deflationary move in the light of the dominant pornographization of female sexuality.

A Green, Girlish Aesthetic

"Sometimes she narrates her actions inside her head in third-person. Does that make her a writer or a woman?" (*GG*, 27). Zambreno finds a self-reflexive, layered voice to articulate the tensions between surface and interiority, between irony and sincerity, and between beauty and disgust, affirming wholeness even as her novel conveys fragmentarity and superficiality. It also thematizes the (self-)narration of women, as the above quotation suggests. Ruth records her experiences, "takes pictures in her mind" (*GG*, 73).[18] But her entries are superficial, and once again the narration insists on the negativity beneath the mask: "What is it with young women and exclamation points and smiley faces! So afraid of appearing somber, always wanting to appear light and happy and sparkling, even when they are dying inside. Not ever being able to escape the mask that smiles" (*GG*, 74). Ruth's writing founders on the fact that she is not fully formed (*GG*, 74).[19] The novel thus foregrounds the narratives that are *not* written, given the lack of stability of some would-be narrators.

A further layer of complexity arises through the suggestions that this text is autofictional: "I experience horror at my former self," the narrator asserts (*GG*, 57)—even as she claims also to give birth to Ruth. She watches Ruth's breasts, comparing them with her own, which are "maternal and massive and saggy" (*GG*, 109). The tension between irony and sympathy, subjectivity and objectivity, also means that the matter of subject positions, of "identity," reveals itself to be complex. The narrative features epigraphs, so the text is a collage of allusions. One epigraph cites Emily Dickinson, and a line from the poem in question occurs to Ruth on the next page ("from somewhere") (*GG*, 82–83). The narrator thus "knows" more than the protagonist, but still keeps track of Ruth's thoughts, not always unsympathetically. There is also satire, however, as when the narrator, commenting on Ruth's lack of political awareness, riffs: "She is volunteering for her own Party of One. The Me Party . . . My seductive little solipsist" (*GG*, 93).[20] Ruth's life story involves "the usual list of traumas self-inflicted" (*GG*, 199), so that her trials—those of a white Western woman—are relativized. This narrative ambivalence emerges powerfully here:

> I want to choke these youngsters just to hear them make a sound not banal or repeated or well-behaved. If I choked Ruth she would make a squeaking sound, like a rubber doll. But I won't choke Ruth why would I choke her I love her. If I did choke her it would be in a loving way, like the poster of the Heimlich maneuver you see hung up in school cafeterias and auto shops, the two faceless figures doubled over together in a violent embrace. I would choke her to get at her insides. (*GG*, 94; cf. *GG*, 156, 162)

There is, then, a tension between intimacy and irony, ambivalence and sympathy.[21] Affect comes into play, and an embodied form of knowing and narrating: "I taste the salt of Ruth's tears. I confirm their veracity" (*GG*, 151).

Zambreno's narrative is self-consciously literary, and self-consciously "feminine." Zambreno is also the author of *Heroines*, a text that fuses memoir with literary criticism and history. Here, Zambreno asserts that literary culture, and culture more broadly, disdains female embodiment and experience: "We live in a culture that punishes and tries to discipline the messy woman and her body and a literary culture that punishes and disciplines the overtly autobiographical (for being too feminine, too girly, too emotional)." And she encourages resistance to this culture, and reappropriation of it: "Fuck the canon. Fuck the boys with their big books. For, after all, we must be our own heroines."[22] In *Green Girl*, Zambreno has created a heroine who is "messy," emotional, and embodied. Her plaidoyer for feminine heroines finds expression in this novel, which also thematizes autobiography and involves complex affective dynamics. Ruth is irritating.[23] Her very vexatiousness, and that of Zambreno's complex, multi-layered narrative as a whole, exemplify the idea of literature as dialogue: that is to say, as becoming.

Becoming Willfully

As we have seen, identity has given way to becoming, intersectionality to assemblage. On the matter of definitions, Grosz asks:

> A more interesting and far-reaching question than, "How can we include the most marginalized social groups and categories in policies that are directed to easing their social marginalization?" is "How can we transform the ways in which identity is conceived so that identities do *not* emerge and function only through the suppression and subordination of other social identities?"[24]

That is to say, if "we"—societies—think of identities not as fixed and as exclusively defining, then a more fluid and liberatory understanding of the self and of social organization is possible. To stress becoming is ever more vital now, if one accepts that neoliberalism and postfeminism are governing features of the contemporary era, and that these involve rigid and reductive accounts of female subjects in particular. Lindy West writes:

> Women matter. Women are half of us. When you raise women to believe that we are insignificant, that we are broken, that we are sick, that the only cure is starvation and restraint and smallness; when you pit women against one another, keep us shackled by shame and hunger, obsessing over our flaws, rather than our power and potential; when you leverage all of that to sap our money and our time—that moves the rudder of the world. It steers humanity toward conservatism and walls and the narrow interests of men, and it keeps us adrift in waters where women's safety and humanity are secondary to men's pleasure and convenience.[25]

That is, women's humanity needs fully to emerge, as Beauvoir suggested in 1949 and as Ahmed argues in 2017.[26] "You" in the quote above could mean "you men" or "you women and men" ("When you raise. . ."): women are possibly compliant with the humiliating project West describes. "We" here means first "we humans" ("half of us"), and then "we women" ("we are insignificant"). This double use of "we" asserts women's full human status, but also their enforced deficiency.

If, as Braidotti contends "politics is . . . maybe primarily the management of the social imaginary," and if "careful, patient revisitations" are required to undo the structures of domination, then we must revisit the social imaginary again and again, carefully and patiently, for shifts to occur toward a recognition of women's humanity and wholeness.[27] I have argued for the importance of literary studies and of the humanities more broadly in this process.[28] Cultural concerns related to writing and creativity have been my focus, and I have framed these in terms of willfulness. Grosz describes art as "the formal structuring or framing of . . . intensified bodily organs and processes which stimulate the receptive organs of observers and coparticipants."[29] If we see art not only in terms of fixed, officially sanctioned works, and more as a matter of flow and process, appealing to and involving the sensual and the affective, then it comes to seem vital to Braidotti's revisitations and her proposed agenda. This conceptualization of art accords with a Deleuzian view of "becoming" and with Braidottian nomadism, as well as with notions of circularity, sensation, and virality that have been alluded to throughout.[30] This book sees the novels it discusses as the structuring of bodily and affective intensities: a kind of excess emananating from the culture that offers us not only discrete insights into issues such as embodiment, sexuality, and agency, but also the chance to engage in a mode of becoming. The texts are willful, in Ahmed's terms, and their willfulness is potentially catching.

Activism, Academia, Politics

Ahmed suggests that willful subjects can recognize each other, potentially to form "an alternative army of the wayward" (*WS*, 163). But how? When thinking about the feminist politics of willfulness today, I need at the very least to acknowledge the importance of the Internet, and specifically of digital feminisms.[31] The literary texts themselves are largely uninterested in the Internet, even those dating from the last few years. That may be seen as a reaction to the dominance of social media, in particular, as a way of young people defining themselves in the contemporary context. In broader feminist terms, however, the Internet is crucial today. Jessica Valenti notes the explosion of online feminism.[32] There are numerous examples of campaigns that the Internet has helped fuel, such as Everyday Sexism and Pinkstinks. Feminist phenomena that involve physical gatherings, such as SlutWalks and One Billion Rising, also benefit from the Internet in terms of garnering publicity and support. As Hester Baer has noted, "the . . . use of digital media has altered, influenced, and shaped feminism in the twenty-first century by giving rise to changed modes of communication, different kinds of conversations, and new configurations of activism across the globe, both online and offline."[33]

On the question of activism, Kira Cochrane suggests that contemporary feminism is "generally more active than academic"—a good thing, if one agrees with Caitlin Moran, for example, that academization can have a deadening effect. Moran argues that feminism has become too obscure, too academic, to engage most women. She avers, "Feminism is too important to only be discussed by academics."[34] Valenti states comparably: "I think feminism should be accessible to everybody, no matter what your education level."[35] Taking on board Dawn Foster's exhortation to "lean out," and the structural factors that shape people's access to education and intellectual activity, these are valid assertions. But it is perhaps more useful to see academic activity of various kinds—including teaching and work carried out in the name of outreach, widening participation, or impact—as in dialogue, at least potentially, with broader social currents and shifts. Ideas that may arise in the context of a higher-education setting as the product of debate, discussion, or publication can be motivating and transformative. Angela McRobbie claims: "Research can help to make a kind of 'clamour' which in turn can be used to challenge widespread misconceptions."[36] Valenti, for example, discusses the concept of intersectionality in her popular book, which draws on her academic studies. The academy itself, however, is hardly a pure space in feminist or antiracist terms, as Ahmed suggests in her work and in her working life (*WS*, 144–46).[37] It also relies on "normative genres and categories for and of evaluation."[38] Willfulness may well erupt in this context as in others.

This book has created a willfulness archive relating to the present, bringing together female protagonists who in various ways lean out. As Ahmed notes, "Political rebellion might require becoming unwilling to be able" (*WS*, 177). Ahmed points out how willfulness is gendered, as we have seen. She draws attention the familiar figure of the unruly young female. Zambreno's novel also acknowledges the shopworn familiarity of this trope, which is itself instructive. If it is easy to dismiss messy trainwrecks of girls, then it is worth asking *why* it is so easy, especially given recent reports of a high incidence of mental illness among girls and young women today.[39] That very dismissal is suspect. For Ahmed, "The willful subject might be striking in her appearance not only because she disagrees with what has been willed by others, but because she disagrees with what has disappeared from view" (*WS*, 16). It is worth looking again, to see "what has disappeared from view": what is not the subject of comment, but should be. Given the stylization of feminists as disagreeable killjoys, such trainwrecks, who are "willfully unhelpful," are at the least striking in feminist terms (*WS*, 152–54). Cochrane writes about the importance of humor to contemporary feminism, but she also acknowledges the compliance comedy potentially involves, and she appeals to Ahmed's feminist killjoy as a figure that causes genuine trouble.[40]

In her 2016 *Trainwrecks*, Sady Doyle examines the cultural fascination with women who are self-destructive and out of control, and she speculates: "the trainwreck might turn out to be the most potent and perennial feminist icon of them all."[41] While this figure functions often as a deterrent that silences women—this is a world in which "the only alternative to being made a spectacle or a trainwreck is to disappear"—the line between trainwreck and triumph is in fact unclear (90, 218). The female figures Doyle explores are troublesome and often innovative, in line with an understanding of willfulness as constituting potentially productive disturbance. Doyle states: "There is no 'ideal girl'" (212). Instead, she asserts, "The only thing that exists is *us*, in a world where there are no normal girls" (256). This book has willfully argued that becoming woman involves failure, refusal, and bile, as well as vitality, affirmation, and desire. It has thereby underlined the totality of human experience as messy and variegated. Ideals and norms must give way to the insight that we are all, in some measure, green girls and trainwrecks: imperfect, vulnerable, and defiantly, invariably, nonstandard.

Notes

Introduction

[1] Simone de Beauvoir, *The Second Sex*, trans. H. M. Parshley (London: Vintage, [1949] 1997), 295.

[2] See here, for example, R. W. Connell, *Gender* (Cambridge: Polity Press, 2002), 4.

[3] Cisgender subjects are the focus of this study, which can only fleetingly acknowledge the significance and implications of emergent trans activisms and theories.

[4] Sara Ahmed, *Willful Subjects* (Durham, NC: Duke University Press, 2014).

[5] See here Elizabeth Grosz, *Becoming Undone: Darwinist Reflections on Life, Politics, and Art* (Durham, NC: Duke University Press, 2011), 186.

[6] Ibid., 92.

[7] Rosi Braidotti, *Metamorphoses: Towards a Materialist Theory of Becoming* (Cambridge: Polity Press, 2002), 68.

[8] Affect has been defined as "those . . . visceral forces beneath, alongside, or generally *other than* conscious knowing" that constitute "persistent proof of a body's never less than ongoing immersion in and among the world's obstinacies and rhythms, its refusals as much as its invitations." Gregory J. Seigworth and Melissa Greg, "An Inventory of Shimmers," in Melissa Greg and Gregory J. Seigworth, eds., *The Affect Theory Reader* (Durham, NC: Duke University Press, 2010), 1.

[9] Sinikka Aapola, Marnina Gonick, and Anita Harris, *Young Femininity: Girlhood, Power and Social Change* (Houndmills, UK: Palgrave Macmillan, 2005), 1.

[10] Catherine Driscoll, *Girls: Feminine Adolescence in Popular Culture and Cultural Theory* (New York: Columbia University Press, 2002), 9.

[11] Aapola, Gonick, and Harris, *Young Femininity*, 1.

[12] Driscoll, *Girls*, 5; cf. Marnina Gonick, *Between Femininities: Ambivalence, Identity, and the Education of Girls* (Albany: State University of New York Press, 2003), 6.

[13] Marion de Ras and Mieke Lunenberg, "General Introduction: Alice in Wonderland. Girls, Girlhood and Girls' Studies in Translation," in *Girls, Girlhood and Girls' Studies in Transition*, ed. Marion de Ras and Mieke Lunenberg (Amsterdam: Het Spinhuis, 1993), 1.

[14] Valerie Walkerdine, "Girlhood through the Looking Glass," in de Ras and Lunenberg, *Girls, Girlhood and Girls' Studies*, 9. Subsequent references provided parenthetically in text.

[15] Gonick, *Between Femininities*, 5.

[16] Driscoll, *Girls*, 303.

[17] Ibid., 304–5.

[18] de Ras and Lunenberg, "General Introduction," 2.

[19] Bascha Mika, *Die Feigheit der Frauen: Rollenfallen und Geiselmentalität: Eine Streitschrift wider den Selbstbetrug* (Munich: Goldmann, 2012), 101. My translation; unless otherwise noted, all translations are my own.

[20] Sherrie A. Inness, introduction to *Millennium Girls: Today's Girls around the World*, ed. Sherrie A. Inness (Lanham: Rowman and Littlefield, 1998), 9.

[21] Gonick, *Between Femininities*, 4.

[22] Anita Harris, introduction to *All about the Girl: Culture, Power, and Identity*, ed. Anita Harris (New York: Routledge, 2004), xviii.

[23] Myra Marx Ferree, *Varieties of Feminism: German Gender Politics in Global Perspective* (Stanford: Stanford University Press, 2012), 176.

[24] As Carrie Smith-Prei and Maria Stehle also note in *Awkward Politics: Technologies of Popfeminist Activism* (Montreal: McGill-Queen's University Press, 2016), 47.

[25] Kathy Davis and Mary Evans, "Introduction—Transatlantic Conversations: Feminism as Travelling Theory," in *Transatlantic Conversations: Feminism as Travelling Theory*, ed. Kathy Davis and Mary Evans (Farnham: Ashgate, 2011), 2.

[26] Christina Scharff, "Passages to Feminism: Encounters and Rearticulations," in Davis and Evans, *Transatlantic Conversations*, 117.

[27] Christina Scharff, Carrie Smith-Prei, and Maria Stehle, "Digital Feminisms: Transnational Activism in German Protest Cultures," *Digital Feminisms: Transnational Activism in German Protest Cultures*, special issue of *Feminist Media Studies* 16, no. 1 (2016): 11. They allude here to Jasbir K. Puar, "Homonationalism as Assemblage: Viral Travels, Affective Sexualities," *Jindal Global Law Review* 4, no. 2 (2013).

[28] Haun Saussy, "Exquisite Cadavers Stitched from Fresh Nightmares: Of Memes, Hives, and Selfish Genes," in *Comparative Literature in an Age of Globalization*, ed. Haun Saussy (Baltimore: Johns Hopkins University Press, 2006); Saussy suggests that globalization *is* Americanization, not just owing to a uniform consumer culture, but because of the shaping of economic and political decisions on a world scale by the perceived needs of the United States (25).

[29] Smith-Prei and Stehle, *Awkward Politics*, 12, 59. They also note: "The local and the national matter, but local and national politics shift in the context of digital circulations and new kinds of localities emerge" (45).

[30] See Paul Jay, *Global Matters: The Transnational Turn in Literary Studies* (Ithaca, NY: Cornell University Press, 2010). See also the essays in Elisabeth Herrmann, Carrie Smith-Prei, and Stuart Taberner, eds., *Transnationalism in Contemporary German-Language Literature* (Rochester, NY: Camden House, 2015).

[31] Saussy, "Exquisite Cadavers," 5. Subsequent references provided parenthetically in text.

[32] Lauren Berlant, *Cruel Optimism* (Durham, NC: Duke University Press, 2011), 4.

33 Smith-Prei and Stehle, *Awkward Politics*, 177.

34 Rosalind Gill and Christina Scharff, introduction to *New Femininities: Post-feminism, Neoliberalism, and Subjectivity*, ed. Rosalind Gill and Christina Scharff (Houndmills, UK: Palgrave Macmillan, 2011), 5. Cf. Alison Winch's definition in *Girlfriends and Postfeminist Sisterhood* (Houndmills, UK: Palgrave Macmillan, 2013): "an aggressive form of capitalism that opens up every area of life to exploitation for profit and limits democratic restraints on corporate and financial freedoms" (2).

35 Gill and Scharff, *New Femininities*, 5; Heather Savigny and Helen Warner, "Introduction: The Politics of Being a Woman," in *The Politics of Being a Woman: Feminism, Media and 21st Century Popular Culture*, ed. Heather Savigny and Helen Warner (Houndmills, UK: Palgrave Macmillan, 2015), 18.

36 George Monbiot, "The Zombie Doctrine," *Guardian Review*, April 16, 2016, 19: "So pervasive has neoliberalism become that we seldom even recognise it as an ideology."

37 Gill and Scharff, *New Femininities*, 7. Cf. Scharff, Smith-Prei, and Stehle, "Digital Feminisms," 6.

38 Claire Charles, *Elite Girls' Schooling, Social Class and Sexualised Popular Culture* (London: Routledge, 2014), 26.

39 Dawn Foster, *Lean Out* (London: Repeater Books, 2015), 21; see also Sheryl Sandberg, *Lean In: Women, Work, and the Will to Lead* (New York: Alfred A. Knopf, 2013).

40 Gill and Scharff, *New Femininities*, 3.

41 Ibid., 3–4. Cf. Savigny and Warner, who note that "postfeminism" is often used to signal both an historical break from "second-wave" feminism and a backlash against feminism (*Politics of Being a Woman*, 3).

42 Gill and Scharff, *New Femininities*, 4.

43 Laurie Penny, *Meat Market: Female Flesh under Capitalism* (Winchester, UK: Zero Books, 2011), 4, 36; Laurie Penny, *Fleischmarkt: Weibliche Körper im Kapitalismus*, trans. Susanne von Somm (Hamburg: Edition Nautilus, 2012).

44 Aapola, Gonick, and Harris, *Young Femininity*, 7.

45 Marnina Gonick, "Between 'Girl Power' and 'Reviving Ophelia': Constituting the Neoliberal Girl Subject," *NWSA Journal* 18, no. 2 (Summer 2006): 1–23.

46 Alison Phipps, *The Politics of the Body: Gender in a Neoliberal and Neoconservative Age* (Cambridge: Polity Press, 2014), 12.

47 Christina Scharff, *Repudiating Feminism: Young Women in a Neoliberal World* (Farnham, UK: Ashgate, 2012), 1.

48 Ibid., 11. See also Foster, *Lean Out*, 62: "The problem with feminism is that the demand for radical and collective action and structural change will never sit well with capitalism."

49 Eva-Maria Schnurr, "Typisch Mädchen, typisch Junge," in *Das F-Wort: Feminismus ist sexy*, ed. Mirja Stöcker (Königstein/Taunus: Ulrike Helmer Verlag, 2007), 16.

[50] Smith-Prei and Stehle, *Awkward Politics*, 23. I will come back to the term "intersectionality" later in this introduction and in subsequent chapters.

[51] Sara Ahmed, *Living a Feminist Life* (Durham, NC: Duke University Press, 2017), 5.

[52] References are to Scharff, Smith-Prei, and Stehle, "Digital Feminisms"; Smith-Prei and Stehle, *Awkward Politics*; Ahmed, *Living a Feminist Life*. Angela McRobbie influentially outlined the simultaneous taken-for-grantedness and dismissal of feminism in postfeminism in *The Aftermath of Feminism: Gender, Culture and Social Change* (London: SAGE, 2009).

[53] Hester Baer, "Redoing Feminism: Digital Activism, Body Politics, and Neoliberalism," *Feminist Media Studies* 16, no. 1 (2016): 20; Scharff, Smith-Prei, and Stehle, "Digital Feminisms," 2.

[54] Ahmed, *Living a Feminist Life*, 6.

[55] Smith-Prei and Stehle, *Awkward Politics*, 114.

[56] Scharff, Smith-Prei, and Stehle, "Digital Feminisms," 8.

[57] Cf. Baer, "Redoing Feminism," 21. See also Hester Baer, "Precarious Sexualities, Neoliberalism, and the Pop-Feminist Novel: Charlotte Roche's *Feuchtgebiete* and Helene Hegemann's *Axolotl Roadkill* as Transnational Texts," in Herrmann, Smith-Prei, and Taberner, *Transnationalism in Contemporary German-Language Literature*, 163.

[58] Aapola, Gonick, and Harris, *Young Femininity*, 6; the authors use "girl" and "woman" interchangeably. Harris, *All about the Girl*, xx.

[59] Harris, *All about the Girl*, xx.

[60] Walkerdine, "Girlhood through the Looking Glass," 21.

[61] The series has also raised questions about white privilege: see here *HBO's "Girls" and the Awkward Politics of Gender, Race, and Privilege*, ed. Elwood Watson, Jennifer Mitchell, and Marc Edward Shaw (Lanham, MD: Lexington Books, 2015).

[62] Meredith Haaf, Susanne Klingner, and Barbara Streidl, *Wir Alpha-Mädchen: Warum Feminismus das Leben schöner macht* (Munich: Blanvalet, 2009), 7.

[63] Ibid., 224, 229.

[64] Emily Spiers, "The Long March through the Institutions: From Alice Schwarzer to Pop Feminism and the New German Girls," *Oxford German Studies* 43, no. 1 (March 2014): 70. See here Jana Hensel and Elisabeth Raether, *Neue deutsche Mädchen* (Reinbek: Rowohlt, 2008).

[65] Spiers, "Long March," 70n2.

[66] The Modern Girl around the World Research Group (Tani E. Barlow, Madeleine Yue Dong, Uta G. Poiger, Priti Ramamurthy, Lynn M. Thomas, and Alys Eve Weinbaum), *The Modern Girl Around the World: Consumption, Modernity, and Globalization* (Durham, NC: Duke University Press, 2008), 9.

[67] Smith-Prei and Stehle, *Awkward Politics*, 150.

[68] Gonick, *Between Femininities*, 6. Subsequent references provided parenthetically in text.

69 Vincent Duindam, "The Concept of 'Socialization': Criticisms and Alternatives," in de Ras and Lunenberg, *Girls, Girlhood and Girls' Studies*, 25.

70 Walkerdine, "Girlhood through the Looking Glass," 23.

71 Natasha Walter, *Living Dolls: The Return of Sexism* (London: Virago, 2010), 73.

72 Cf. Catherine Redfern and Kristin Aune, *Reclaiming the F-Word: Feminism Today* (London: Zed Books, 2013), xvii.

73 See, for example, Beauvoir, *Second Sex*, 584.

74 Ahmed, *Living a Feminist Life*, 49.

75 Beauvoir, *Second Sex*, 14. Subsequent references provided parenthetically in text, preceded by *SS*.

76 Germaine Greer, *The Whole Woman* (London: Doubleday, 1999), 2. Subsequent references provided parenthetically in text.

77 Ahmed observes comparably: "how restricted *girl* can be as a category of emergent personhood" (*Living a Feminist Life*, 53).

78 Ahmed asserts: "The happy stories for girls remain based on fairy-tale formulas: life, marriage, and reproduction, or death (of one kind or another) and misery" (ibid., 49).

79 See here Stacy Alaimo and Susan Hekman, "Introduction: Emerging Models of Materiality in Feminist Theory," in *Material Feminisms*, ed. Stacy Alaimo and Susan Hekman (Bloomington: Indiana University Press, 2008), 1.

80 Judith Butler, *Gender Trouble: Feminism and the Subversion of Identity* (New York: Routledge, 2002), 12.

81 Ahmed sees in transfeminism an important site of challenge and renewal (*Living a Feminist Life*, 227).

82 Braidotti, *Metamorphoses*, 17. Subsequent references provided parenthetically in text, preceded by *M*.

83 Rosi Braidotti, *Nomadic Subjects: Embodiment and Sexual Difference in Contemporary Feminist Theory* (New York: Columbia University Press, 1994).

84 Grosz, *Becoming Undone*, 92.

85 Puar, "Homonationalism as Assemblage," 41.

86 Jasbir K. Puar, *Terrorist Assemblages: Homonationalism in Queer Times* (Durham, NC: Duke University Press, 2007), 212.

87 For example, Ahmed's willfulness is important in and to Smith-Prei and Stehle, *Awkward Politics* (94–99), and is also referenced in Scharff, Smith-Prei, and Stehle, "Digital Feminisms," 12.

88 Ahmed, *Willful Subjects*, 1. Subsequent references provided parenthetically in text, preceded by *WS*. Ahmed cites a translation of the story in which the child is female; the original German title and text do not reveal the gender of the child ("das Kind" is a neuter noun).

89 As they are to Smith-Prei and Stehle's *Awkward Politics*. Smith-Prei and Stehle draw on Ahmed's willfulness to develop their understanding of "awkwardness," which, however, implies "a less directed will" (99).

90 Puar similarly argues for the acknowledgment of complicity as potentially enabling (*Terrorist Assemblages*, 24), and Smith-Prei and Stehle suggest the inevitably circular or complicitous nature of activisms in the contemporary context (*Awkward Politics*, 114).

91 See here Foster, *Lean Out*, a riposte to Sandberg, *Lean In*.

92 Ahmed, *Living a Feminist Life*, 84.

93 Gill and Scharff, *New Femininities*, 7.

94 Ahmed, *Living a Feminist Life*, 21. See also Smith-Prei and Stehle, *Awkward Politics*, 141: "affect . . . goes to the core of how politics might be better conceived for the present day." See also Sara Ahmed, *The Cultural Politics of Emotion* (London: Routlege, 2004); Scharff, Smith-Prei, and Stehle, "Digital Feminisms," 11.

95 See here Baer, "Precarious Sexualities," 168.

96 Puar, *Terrorist Assemblages*, 215.

97 Baer, "Precarious Sexualities," 168.

98 Ahmed, *Living a Feminist Life*, 49, 57.

99 Katie Jones, *Representing Repulsion: The Aesthetics of Disgust in Contemporary Women's Writing in French and German* (Oxford: Peter Lang, 2013), 5.

100 See here Berlant, *Cruel Optimism*: "A relation of cruel optimism exists when something you desire is actually an obstacle to your flourishing" (1). See also Smith-Prei and Stehle's description of "reading for awkwardness": it means "uncovering disruptions of the cruel optimisms of neoliberalism, discovering new avenues for connection and relatability, and searching for new spaces for feminist community and joy" (*Awkard Politics*, 81).

101 Juli Zeh, *Spieltrieb* (Frankfurt am Main: Schöfling & Co., 2004), 423–24:

> Ich küsste ihn und sein Mund war weich wie aus Schamlippen zusammengesetzt. Eine quer gelegte Vagina mit beweglicher Zunge in der Mitte. Ich weiß, wie Vaginen sich anfühlen, wenn man sie küsst. Als Studentin hatte ich immer nur Frauen. Ich glaubte, dass das die einzig verbliebene Art von Liebe sei. Alles andere war abgedroschen, an den unwürdigsten Orten unzählige Male besprochen und verhandelt. Bausparwebung, Kleinwagen, Loveparade, Kita-Platz, von der *Bravo* bis ins *Brigitte*-Dossier, Levi's, Atemfrische, der ganze heterosexuelle Kitsch. Ich konnte nicht mehr. Ich hielt es nicht aus, diese Scheiße zu reproduzieren. . . . ich sehnte mich nach dem islamischen Bilderverbot . . . Gleichzeitig wollte ich ein "Wir" sein. Ich ertrug Sätze nicht mehr, die mit "Ich" anfingen. "Ich" war eine psychologische, literarische oder ökonomische Fiktion, ein handliches Türschild an den Laboratorien der Selbsterschaffung . . . Gebt mir eine Uniform, damit ich ein "wir" sein kann! Aber es gab keine Uniformen mehr . . . Ach, die neunziger Jahre.

Das zwanzigste Jahrhundert! . . . Ist doch vorbei. Ich will nur nicht durch den Mund eines Mannes daran erinnert werden.

[I kissed him and his mouth was soft, as if composed of labia. A slanting vagina with a moving tongue in the middle. I know what vaginas feel like when kissed. As a student, I only had women. I thought that was the only kind of love left. Everything else was shop-worn, discussed and negotiated in the most unworthy of places, x times. Building-society ads, family cars, love parade, nursery place, from *Bravo* [magazine] to the *Brigitte*-magazine special issue, Levi's, fresh breath, all that hetero *kitsch*. I couldn't do it any more. I couldn't stand to reproduce all that shit . . . I longed for the Islamic prohibition on images . . . At the same time, I wanted to be a "We." I couldn't stand sentences that started with "I" any more. "I" was a psychological, literary, or economic fiction, a handy sign on the laboratories of self-creation . . . Give me a uniform so I can be a "we"! But there were no uniforms any more . . . Oh, the nineties. The twentieth century! . . . It's over. I just don't want to be reminded of it by the mouth of a man.] (My translation.)

This fictional post-millennial narrator is post-queer, having dispensed with her 1990s rejection of heterosexuality. This satire on first-person female narration anticipates, in particular, Baum and Hegemann, with their queer rejections of coupledom and of standard imagery, and their simultaneous citation and subversion of cultural products. This narrator questions individuality, and yet the narrative is intensely solipsistic, a feature of certain—but by no means all—of the novels I investigate here. (At the same time, to investigate a single subjectivity is not to deny relationality; the very fact of a text being published and consumed makes it interrelational.)

[102] This is certainly the case with Hegemann and Roche in the German context (see here Smith-Prei and Stehle, *Awkward Politics*, 152), and Moran in the English-speaking one.

[103] Saussy, "Exquisite Cadavers," 17.

Chapter One

[1] Mika, *Feigheit der Frauen*, 77.

[2] Kat Banyard, *The Equality Illusion: The Truth about Women and Men Today* (London: Faber & Faber, 2010), 1. See also Thea Dorn, *Die neue F-Klasse: Wie die Zukunft von Frauen gemacht wird* (Munich: Piper, 2006), 9; Scharff, *Repudiating Feminism*, 10.

[3] Phipps, *Politics of the Body*, 3.

[4] Mika, *Feigheit der Frauen*, 79.

[5] Gill and Scharff, *New Femininities*, 4.

[6] Scharff, *Repudiating Feminism*, 1; McRobbie, *Aftermath of Feminism*. On the influence of McRobbie, see also Gill and Scharff, *New Femininities*, 4.

[7] Smith-Prei and Stehle, *Awkward Politics*, 18.

8 Cf. Scharff, Smith-Prei, and Stehle, "Digital Feminisms," 2.

9 Ahmed, *Living a Feminist Life*, 4.

10 Scharff, "Passages to Feminism," 117.

11 Christina Scharff, "The New German Feminisms: Of Wetlands and Alpha-Girls," in Gill and Scharff, *New Femininities*, 265. See also Hester Baer and Alexandra Merley Hill, "Introduction: German Women's Writing beyond the Gender Binary," in *German Women's Writing in the Twenty-First Century*, ed. Hester Baer and Alexandra Merley Hill (Rochester, NY: Camden House, 2015), 3; Baer, "Redoing Feminism," 22; Scharff, Smith-Prei, and Stehle, "Digital Feminisms," 4.

12 Scharff, "Passages to Feminism," 117.

13 Scharff, *Repudiating Feminism*, 17. In Germany, the prominent figure of Alice Schwarzer is often evoked when feminism is at issue, and feminists are imagined as wearing purple and having hairy armpits. In the United Kingdom, Germaine Greer, suffragettes, and Margaret Thatcher spring to mind, as does the burning of bras.

14 Scharff, "Passages to Feminism," 118.

15 In Germany, the recent spate of relevant publications includes: Dorn, *Die F-Klasse*; Haaf, Klingner, and Streidl, *Wir Alpha-Mädchen*; Sonja Eismann, ed., *Hot Topic: Popfeminismus heute* (Mainz: Ventil Verlag, 2007); Hensel and Raether, *Neue deutsche Mädchen*; Mika, *Feigheit der Frauen*; Stöcker, *Das F-Wort*. In the United Kingdom and the United States, they include: Banyard, *Equality Illusion*; Benn, *What Should We Tell Our Daughters?: The Pleasures and Pressures of Growing Up Female* (London: Hodder, 2014); Moran, *How to Be A Woman* (London: Ebury Press, 2011); Penny, *Meat Market*; Nina Power, *One-Dimensional Woman* (Winchester: Zero Books, 2009); Jessica Valenti, *Full-Frontal Feminism: A Young Woman's Guide to Why Feminism Matters* (Berkeley: Seal Press, 2013); Walter, *Living Dolls*. This is by no means a comprehensive list.

16 This problematic, provocative description represents my attempt to capture both contemporaneity ("new") and the commonality of concerns relating to gender and power that I am arguing can strategically be traced in the diverse writings under discussion ("feminist"). It sits uneasily alongside my already pained use of the term "postfeminist," where this unease is instructive, at least, pointing as it does to the simultaneous (perceived) "pastness" of feminism and its ongoing, necessary existence.

17 Power, *One-Dimensional Woman*, 8. She observes that the term can signal "behaving like a man," being pro-choice, being pro-life, or even, in the context of US politics, being pro-war.

18 Power, *One-Dimensional Woman*, 35; Valenti, *Full-Frontal Feminism*, 14.

19 Penny, *Meat Market*, 36; cf. Roxane Gay, *Bad Feminist: Essays* (London: Corsair, 2014), xi. See also Benn, *What Should We Tell Our Daughters*, 255, and Moran, *How to Be a Woman*, 81. Moran observes that if one were not aware of the aims of feminism and were trying to discern its nature, one could easily presume it were "some spectacularly unappealing combination of misandry, misery

and hypocrisy, which stood for ugly clothes, constant anger and, let's face it, no fucking."

[20] Haaf, Klingner, and Streidl, *Wir Alpha-Mädchen*, 15. Compare the description of feminism as "übel, abgestanden, unappetitlich, peinlich" (bad, stale, unappetizing, embarrassing) in Katja Kullmann, *Generation Ally: Warum es heute so kompliziert ist, eine Frau zu sein* (Frankfurt am Main: Eichborn, 2002), 12.

[21] Moran, *How to Be a Woman*, 85, 80.

[22] Haaf, Klingner, and Streidl, *Wir Alpha-Mädchen*, 18, 20–21.

[23] Dorn, *Die F-Klasse*, 36.

[24] However, one figure prominent in the United Kingdom is Germaine Greer, the Australian-born writer and academic. Moran, whose humorous memoir documents her teenage admiration of Greer's classic *The Female Eunuch*, also recounts her increasingly critical attitude toward the object of her "fandom": "In later years, of course, I would grow Greer-ish enough to disagree with Greer on things she said," mentioning, in this context, Greer's dismissive attitude toward transgender people (Moran, *How to Be a Woman*, 79). See also Penny, *Meat Market*, which critiques Greer's transphobia (38). In the United States, Valenti enjoins those older feminists associated with the National Organization for Women (NOW) with a relatively mild: "Time to pass the torch, ladies!" (Valenti, *Full-Frontal Feminism*, 172). Scharff contrasts the differing attitudes of German and UK feminist texts to earlier feminist figures and movements, finding that unlike the former, the latter "do not forcefully reject 1970s feminism" (*Repudiating Feminism*, 19). See for example Redfern and Aune, *Reclaiming the F-Word*, which explicitly criticizes dismissals of early feminisms (xi).

[25] Spiers, "Long March," 69: "during this time [the late 1960s and the 1970s] . . . Alice Schwarzer came to occupy the position of West German feminism's figurehead and continues to embody the feminist movement in the public imagination of post-reunification Germany."

[26] Haaf, Klingner, and Streidl, *Wir Alpha-Mädchen*, 16–17.

[27] Spiers, "Long March," 77.

[28] Hensel and Raether, *Neue deutsche Mädchen*, 14; see here Spiers, "Long March," 78.

[29] See her account of an encounter with Schwarzer in Dorn, *Die F-Klasse*, 140. Roche's antagonism finds expression in the novel *Schoßgebete*, in which the protagonist engages in imaginary dialogue with the older feminist to challenge the latter's anti-sex views as voiced in *Der kleine Unterschied*, which explored heterosexual sex as a site of oppression. Charlotte Roche, *Schoßgebete* (Munich: Piper, 2011), 17; Charlotte Roche, *Wrecked*, trans. Tim Mohr (London: Fourth Estate, 2013), 12–13. See here Alice Schwarzer, *Der kleine Unterschied und seine großen Folgen: Frauen über sich—Beginn einer Befreiung* (Frankfurt am Main: Fischer, 2002). Schwarzer wrote an open letter to Roche following the publication of the latter's novel; see here Spiers, "Long March," 82.

[30] See Spiers, "Long March," 82.

[31] Miriam Gebhardt, *Alice im Niemandsland: Wie die deutsche Frauenbewegung die Frauen verlor* (Munich: Deutsche Verlags-Anstalt, 2012).

32 Spiers, "Long March," 80. Spiers contrasts this approach with that of Eismann, editor of *Hot Topic*, who according to Spiers shows a willingness to "build bridges between the second wave and contemporary forms of feminism" (85). Spiers here uses the term "New German Girls" as a label for the authors of the texts she explores, differentiating them from "Neufeminismus," or "what the Anglo-American tradition calls second-wave feminism" (71).

33 Spiers, "Long March," 80.

34 Scharff, "New German Feminisms," 266–67.

35 Foster, *Lean Out*: a riposte to Sandberg, *Lean In*.

36 Kira Cochrane, *All the Rebel Women: The Rise of the Fourth Wave of Feminism* (Guardian: Short Books Kindle Edition, 2013). This book is not available in hard copy; references will be given parenthetically in the text in the form of percentages, as displayed on the screen of a Kindle e-reader.

37 Moran, *How to Be a Woman*, 14.

38 Smith-Prei and Stehle, *Awkward Politics*, 15.

39 See here Hester Baer's useful discusson of the phenomenon in "Introduction: Resignifications of Feminism in Contemporary Germany," *Contemporary Women's Writing and the Return of Feminism in Germany*, special issue of *Studies in 20th and 21st Century Literature* 35, no. 1 (2011): 8–11.

40 Eismann, "Einleitung," *Hot Topic*, 11–12, 10.

41 Spiers, "Long March," 70, 71.

42 Carrie Smith-Prei, "'Knaller-Sex für alle': Popfeminist Body Politics in Lady Bitch Ray, Charlotte Roche, und Sarah Kuttner," in Baer, *Contemporary Women's Writing*, 21.

43 See here Emily Spiers, "'Killing Ourselves Is Not Subversive': Riot Grrrl from Zine to Screen and the Commodication of Female Transgression," *Women: A Cultural Review* 26, nos. 1/2 (2015): 1–21.

44 For example, Haaf, Klingner, and Streidl, *Wir Alpha-Mädchen*, 191; Karin Harrasser, "Wunsch, Feministin zu werden: Nahräume politischen Handelns," in Eismann, *Hot Topic*, 235: "Butler sowieso" (Butler, of course); Mika, *Feigheit der Frauen*, 157; Cordelia Thyn, "I'm here, I'm queer, und jetzt?: Homophobie ist eine Strategie," in Eismann, *Hot Topic*, 37; Jenny Warnecke, "Das ist nur zu extrem!: Eine Generationen-Studie," in Stöcker, *Das F-Wort*, 25.

45 Thyn, "I'm here, I'm queer, und jetzt?," 37; Sonja Eismann, "Einleitung," in Eismann, *Hot Topic*, 11.

46 Caitlin Moran, *How to be a Woman: Wie ich lernte, eine Frau zu sein*, trans. Susanne Reinker (Berlin: Ullstein, 2013); Laurie Penny, *Fleischmarkt*; Nina Power, *Die eindimensionale Frau*, trans. Anna Sophie Springer (Berlin: Merve, 2011); Natasha Walter, *Living Dolls: Warum junge Frauen heute lieber schön als schlau sein wollen*, trans. Gabriele Herbst (Frankfurt am Main: Krüger, 2011).

47 Eismann, "Einleitung," 11.

48 Haaf, Klingner, and Streidl, *Wir Alpha-Mädchen*, 43–44.

49 Moran, *How to Be a Woman*, 247.

50 See Banyard, *Equality Illusion*, for example. See also Laura Bates, *Everyday Sexism* (London: Simon & Schuster, 2014), 27; Power, *One-Dimensional Woman*, 8–9.

51 Kullmann, *Generation Ally*.

52 Rebecca Solnit, "Men Explain Things to Me," in *'Men Explain Things to Me' and Other Essays* (London: Granta, 2014), 16.

53 Penny, *Meat Market*, 1.

54 Benn, *What Should We Tell Our Daughters*, 46; cf. Penny, *Meat Market*, 25.

55 Benn, *What Should We Tell Our Daughters*, 47–48. Orbach's book *Bodies* (London: Profile, 2010) has been translated into German: *Bodies: Schlachtfelder der Schönheit*, trans. Cornelia Holfelder-von der Tann (Hamburg: Arche Verlag, 2012). See also Gay, *Bad Feminist*: "I don't think I know any woman who doesn't hate herself and her body at least a little bit" (113).

56 Banyard, *Equality Illusion*, 17.

57 Ibid., 22–23, 31.

58 Bates, *Everyday Sexism*, 95.

59 Valenti, *Full-Frontal Feminism*, 47.

60 Banyard, *Equality Illusion*, 20.

61 Power, *One-Dimensional Woman*, 25.

62 Penny, *Meat Market*, 22, 32.

63 Benn, *What Should We Tell Our Daughters*, 49.

64 Ibid., 17.

65 Power, *One-Dimensional Woman*, 24.

66 Penny, *Meat Market*, 2, 1.

67 Naomi Wolf, *The Beauty Myth: How Images of Beauty are Used Against Women* (London: Vintage, 1991; 1990), 17.

68 Holly Baxter and Rhiannon Lucy Cosslett, *The Vagenda: A Zero Tolerance Guide to the Media* (London: Square Peg, 2014), 5.

69 Elizabeth Day, "Mary Beard: 'I Almost Didn't Feel Such Generic, Violent Misogyny Was about Me," *Guardian*, January 26, 2013. See also Bates, *Everyday Sexism*, 28; Benn, *What Should We Tell Our Daughters*, 2.

70 Mary Beard, "The Public Voice of Women," *London Review of Books* 36, no. 6 (March 20, 2014).

71 Valenti, *Full-Frontal Feminism*, 206.

72 Walter, *Living Dolls*, 124.

73 Penny, *Meat Market*, 23.

74 Bates, *Everyday Sexism*, 41.

75 Banyard, *Equality Illusion*, 41; see also Moran, *How to Be a Woman*, 49.

76 Moran, *How to Be a Woman*, 47, 111, 106.

77 Ibid., 292–93, 295.

78 Moran, *How to Be a Woman*, 198; Valenti, *Full-Frontal Feminism*, 180.

79 Haaf, Klingner, and Streidl, *Wir Alpha-Mädchen*, 54.

80 Mika, *Feigheit der Frauen*, 70.

81 Haaf, Klingner, and Streidl, *Wir Alpha-Mädchen*, 49–51.

82 Li Gerhalter, "Wie Angora: Körperbehaarung ist out—und krause Politik," in Eismann, *Hot Topic*; Sarah Diehl, "Pro-Ana Websites: Selbsbestimmung in der anorektischen Selbstaufgabe," in Eismann, *Hot Topic*.

83 Elke Buhr, "Hauptsache 'natürlich'," in Stöcker, *Das F-Wort*, 123.

84 Haaf, Klingner, and Streidl, *Wir Alpha-Mädchen*, 237.

85 Gay, *Bad Feminist*, 47. Gay advises female readers who proudly declare they have no female friends: "soul-search a little" (48).

86 Cochrane, *All the Rebel Women*, 80%.

87 Valenti, *Full-Frontal Feminism*, 234.

88 Hester Baer, "German Feminism in the Age of Neoliberalism: Jana Hensel and Elisabeth Raether's *Neue deutsche Mädchen*," *German Studies Review* 35, no. 2 (May 2012): 370. See also Scharff, Smith-Prei, and Stehle, "Digital Feminisms," 8. Ina Kerner points to the belated introduction of the term intersectionality to feminist theory in Germany, in "Questions of Intersectionality: Reflections on the Current Debate in German Gender Studies," *European Journal of Women's Studies* 19, no. 2 (2012): 204.

89 Cochrane, *All the Rebel Women*, 5%.

90 Dorn, *Die neue F-Klasse*, 23–24. See here Iris Radisch, "Das Kopftuch ist keine Mode," *Die Zeit*, September 16, 2010, http://www.zeit.de/2010/38/L-Schwarzer.

91 Haaf, Klingner, and Streidl, *Wir Alpha-Mädchen*, 15.

92 Mika, *Feigheit der Frauen*, 8.

93 Ahmed, *Living a Feminist Life*, 234. See also Penny, *Meat Market*, 38. Valenti's 2013 introduction to the reissue of her 2007 book acknowledges the increasing visibility of trans issues and identities as an important development (*Full-Frontal Feminism*, 2–3).

94 See, for example, "Transgender: Weder Mann noch Frau," *Emma* (January/February 2016), http://www.emma.de/artikel/transgender-weder-mann-noch-frau-331433.

95 Moran, *How to Be a Woman*, 139; Benn, *What Should We Tell Our Daughters*, 212; Walter, *Living Dolls*, 15; Valenti, *Full-Frontal Feminism*, 41, 233–34.

96 Haaf, Klingner, and Streidl, *Wir Alpha-Mädchen*, 19.

97 Spiers, "Long March," 81, 79. *Wir Alpha-Mädchen* mentions the existence of women who "gern auf Männer verzichten können" (are happy to do without men)—but the authors assert they have decided to focus on issues affecting "einen Großteil der jungen Frauen, die heute in Deutschland leben" (the majority of young women living in Germany today) (Haaf, Klingner, and Streidl, *Wir Alpha-Mädchen*, 8–9). Mika, in contrast, offers a biting critique of the ideology of heterosexual romance as all-consuming and all-important. Asserting that "we"

(women) are "klar" (of course) interested in men, she nonetheless laments the female obsession with romance over all else (*Feigheit der Frauen*, 36).

98 Stöcker, "Die Sache mit dem F-Wort," in Stöcker, *Das F-Wort*, 12.

99 Mika, *Feigheit der Frauen*, 18.

100 Benn, *What Should We Tell Our Daughters*, 8.

101 Haaf, Klingner, and Streidl, *Wir Alpha-Mädchen*, 191; cf. Moran, *How to Be a Woman*, 77; Valenti, *Full-Frontal Feminism*, 171–82.

102 Ibid., 27.

103 See Benn, *What Should We Tell Our Daughters*, 66.

104 Penny, *Meat Market*, 14–15; Walter, *Living Dolls*, 72.

105 Penny, *Meat Market*, 16.

106 Walter, *Living Dolls*, 79: "The confusion between sexual liberation and the sexual objectification of young girls means that there is a danger that young girls might not be seen as in need of protection from unwanted attention and even assaults."

107 Haaf, Klingner, and Streidl, *Wir Alpha-Mädchen*, 63–64. Subsequent references provided parenthetically in text.

108 Valenti, *Full-Frontal Feminism*, 69–71, for example.

109 Banyard, *Equality Illusion*, 127, 131.

110 Gay, *Bad Feminist*, 129; see also Valenti, *Full-Frontal Feminism*, 73.

111 Banyard, *Equality Illusion*, 107, 116, 111.

112 Sexual violence and rape are also concerns of Elena Stöhr's contribution to *Hot Topic*, in which she cites the statistics relating to these crimes in the United States and Germany, and of the *Alpha-Mädchen*, who also address rape and in particular suggest German legal definitions need clarifying (Stöhr, "I Felt Like I Had Shattered into a Million Pieces: Grrrl Zines und sexualisierte Gewalt," in Eismann, *Hot Topic*; Haaf, Klingner, and Streidl, *Wir Alpha-Mädchen*, 89.

113 Haaf, Klingner, and Streidl, *Wir Alpha-Mädchen*, 98; Banyard, *Equality Illusion*, 41.

114 Ariel Levy, *Female Chauvinist Pigs: Women and the Rise of Raunch Culture* (New York: Free Press, 2006).

115 Walter, *Living Dolls*, 109.

116 Haaf, Klingner, and Streidl, *Wir Alpha-Mädchen*, 98.

117 Bates, *Everyday Sexism*, 108–9; Walter, *Living Dolls*, 108.

118 Mika, *Feigheit der Frauen*, 70.

119 Banyard, *Equality Illusion*, 12, 148–49.

120 Valenti, *Full-Frontal Feminism*, 98.

121 Banyard, *Equality Illusion*, 181; Moran, *How to Be a Woman*, 277, 273. See also Redfern and Aune, *Reclaiming the F-Word*, xv–xvi.

122 For example, Julia Roth, "Frauenkörper—Männersache?: Ein feministischer Blick auf Verhütungspraktiken," in Eismann, *Hot Topic*.

123 See here Benn, *What Should We Tell Our Daughters*, 147; Haaf, Klingner, and Streidl, *Wir Alpha-Mädchen*, 8.

124 Banyard, *Equality Illusion*, 77–81; Benn, *What Should We Tell Our Daughters*, 13; Mika cites statistics relating to housework that demonstrate that the vast majority of such unpaid work is performed by women (*Feigheit der Frauen*, 109).

125 Bates, *Everyday Sexism*, 71; Cochrane, *All the Rebel Women*, 93%.

126 Valenti, *Full-Frontal Feminism*, 249.

127 Haaf, Klingner, and Streidl, *Wir Alpha-Mädchen*, 221, 155; Mika, *Feigheit der Frauen*, 165. See Eva Herman, *Das Eva-Prinzip: Für eine neue Weiblichkeit* (Munich: Goldmann, 2007), and, on this text, Haaf, Klingner, and Streidl, *Wir Alpha-Mädchen*, 154–55. See also Mika's critique of German motherhood in *Feigheit der Frauen*, 153: Mika claims the state provides too little daycare and places the responsibility on the citizens; employers burden employees; employees, in the form of husbands and fathers, put the responsibility on the wife and mother, and the problem becomes one of an individual woman within the four walls of her home.

128 Smith-Prei and Stehle, *Awkward Politics*, 67.

129 Walter, *Living Dolls*, 121; Bates, *Everyday Sexism*, 53.

130 Bates, *Everyday Sexism*, 42; cf. Moran, *How to Be a Woman*, 130.

131 Benn, *What Should We Tell Our Daughters*, 287.

132 Haaf, Klingner, and Streidl, *Wir Alpha-Mädchen*, 133.

133 Benn, *What Should We Tell Our Daughters*, 13.

134 Moran, *How to Be a Woman*, 128.

135 Benn, *What Should We Tell Our Daughters*, 137.

136 Dorn, *Die F-Klasse*, 9, 29; Haaf, Klingner, and Streidl, *Wir Alpha-Mädchen*, 211; Kathrin Hartmann and Kerstin Kullmann, "Wutlos glücklich," in Stöcker, *Das F-Wort*, 148.

137 Benn declares, "how well rehearsed are the statistics on unequal pay!" before citing these and other "depressing" facts (*What Should We Tell Our Daughters*, 14–15). Power notes "the surprisingly resilient pay differential for the same jobs, and the predominance of women in part-time and badly-paid work" (*One-Dimensional Woman*, 20). "Guess what? The pay gap still exists!" writes Valenti (*Full-Frontal Feminism*, 115).

138 Banyard, *Equality Illusion*, 83; Dorn, *Die F-Klasse*, 26; Haaf, Klingner, and Streidl, *Wir Alpha-Mädchen*, 216.

139 Haaf, Klingner, and Streidl, *Wir Alpha-Mädchen*, 216, 218–9.

140 Mika suggests: "Die Strukturen von Staat und Wirtschaft fördern die traditionellen Muster" (*Feigheit der Frauen*, 25; The structures of state and economy promote traditional models). She also provides her own analysis of the barriers preventing equality in the workplace: "Die gläsernen Decken . . . Die old-boy networks . . . Das männlich geprägte Arbeitsumfeld . . . die fehlenden Quoten und und und" (Ibid., 194; The glass ceilings . . . The old-boy networks . . . The

NOTES TO PP. 30–33 ◆ 165

male-dominated working environment . . . the absence of quotas and so on and so on).

141 See Pinkstinks website, http://www.pinkstinks.co.uk/ and Let Toys Be Toys website, http://www.lettoysbetoys.org.uk/.

142 Walter, *Living Dolls*, 157; Haaf, Klingner, and Streidl, *Wir Alpha-Mädchen*, 29–30, 33–34.

143 She further suggests: "the New German Girls' subscription to the neoliberal rhetoric of individualism discourages both politicisation and collective action; paradoxically, they succumb to the postfeminist patriarchal norm even while proclaiming the need for a new type of feminism" (Spiers, "Long March," 88).

144 Schnurr, "Typisch Mädchen, typisch Junge," 22.

145 Mika, *Feigheit der Frauen*, 15, 58.

146 Walter, *Living Dolls*, 33, 73, 120. Subsequent references provided parenthetically in text.

147 Penny, *Meat Market*, 16.

148 Valenti, *Full-Frontal Feminism*, 143.

149 Moran, *How to Be a Woman*, 307.

150 Banyard, *Equality Illusion*, 25, 208.

151 Haaf, Klingner, and Streidl, *Wir Alpha-Mädchen*, 232–34.

152 Banyard, *Equality Illusion*; Bates, *Everyday Sexism*; Moran, *How to Be a Woman*; Eismann, "Einleitung," 12; Haaf, Klingner, and Streidl, *Wir Alpha-Mädchen*, 191.

153 Hensel and Raether, *Neue deutsche Mädchen*, 26. My translation.

154 But see here Spiers, who argues the authors "uncouple sex and politics and the private becomes private once more" ("Long March," 81). Hensel and Raether, *Neue deutsche Mädchen*, 26, 22. See also Baer's useful discussion of this text: "German Feminism in the Age of Neoliberalism." See also Margaret McCarthy, "Feminism and Generational Conflicts in Alex Henning von Lange's *Relax*, Elke Naters's *Lügen*, and Charlotte Roche's *Feuchtgebiete*," in Baer, *Contemporary Women's Writing*, 59.

155 Benn, *What Should We Tell Our Daughters*, 21.

156 Penny, *Meat Market*, 65.

157 Power, *One-Dimensional Woman*, 27, 35.

158 Valenti, *Full-Frontal Feminism*, 7, 9, 17, 65, 121. Cf. Valenti, *Full-Frontal Feminism*: "Yeah, I'm a downer"; "I know it sounds bleak" (67, 113).

159 Haaf, Klingner, and Streidl, *Wir Alpha-Mädchen*, 66–67; Stöcker, *Das F-Wort*; Valenti, *Full-Frontal Feminism*, 218; Moran, *How to Be a Woman*, 100.

160 Though they do not equate this sentiment with happiness (*Awkward Politics*, 17, 43).

161 See here Hartmann and Kullmann, "Wutlos glücklich." Pointing to the gulf between the expectations of young German women and the reality of what awaits them, Hartmann and Kullmann explain: "Frauen spielen mit ihrer Weiblichkeit

. . . Warum nicht. Doch die Widersprüche zwischen dem, was junge Frauen sich wünschen, und dem, was davon im Laufe ihres Lebens wahr werden kann, sind groß. Und gar nicht sexy" (149; Women play with their femininity . . . Why not. But the contradictions between what young women want, and what will actually come about in the course of their lives, are stark. And not at all sexy).

[162] Ahmed, *Living a Feminist Life*, 57.

Chapter Two

[1] Braidotti, *Metamorphoses*, 7. Subsequent references provided parenthetically in text, preceded by *M*.

[2] Emily Jeremiah, *Nomadic Ethics in Contemporary Women's Writing in German: Strange Subjects* (Rochester, NY: Camden House, 2012).

[3] Grosz, *Becoming Undone*, 37. Subsequent references provided parenthetically in text, preceded by *BU*.

[4] "Becoming is the operation of self-differentiation, the elaboration of difference within a thing, a quality, or a system that emerges or actualizes only in duration" (*BU*, 43).

[5] Jasbir K. Puar, "Prognosis Time: Towards a Geopolitics of Affect, Debility and Capacity," *Women and Performance: A Journal of Feminist Theory* 19, no. 2 (2009): 168.

[6] She suggests: "Feminist theory needs to place the problematic of sexual difference, the most fundamental concern of feminist thought at its most general, in the context of both animal becomings and the becomings microscopic and imperceptible that regulate matter itself" (*BU*, 86).

[7] For Judith Butler, "performativity" is "the reiterative and citational practice by which discourse produces the effects that it names." *Bodies that Matter: On the Discursive Limits of "Sex"* (New York: Routledge, 2011), xii.

[8] Ahmed, *Willful Subjects*, 19. Subsequent references provided parenthetically in text, preceded by *WS*.

[9] Ahmed, *Living a Feminist Life*, 84.

[10] Gay, *Bad Feminist*, 314.

[11] Lee Edelman, *No Future: Queer Theory and the Death Drive* (Durham, NC: Duke University Press, 2004), 17.

[12] J. Halberstam, *The Queer Art of Failure* (Durham, NC: Duke University Press, 2011), 3, 2–3.

[13] Phipps, *Politics of the Body*, 13.

[14] Foster, *Lean Out*, 78: "Few people ever get anything radical accomplished by continuing to play the game," Foster notes, and she points to working-class and grassroot feminist movements as important examples of failure to "play the game." Cf. also Maggie Nelson, *The Argonauts* (London: Melville House, 2016): "Reproductive futurism needs no more disciples. But basking in the punk allure of 'no future' won't suffice, either, as if all that's left for us to do is sit back and

watch while the gratuitously wealthy and greedy shred our economy and our climate and our planet. . . . Fuck *them*, I say" (95).

[15] Elizabeth A. Wilson, *Gut Feminism* (Durham, NC: Duke University Press, 2015), 1. Subsequent references provided parenthetically in text, preceded by *GF*.

[16] Cf. Chimamanda Ngozi Adichie, *We Should All Be Feminists* (London: Fourth Estate, 2014): "We should all be angry" (21). See also Ahmed, *Living a Feminist Life*: "Our guts become our feminist friends the more we are sickened" (255).

[17] Ahmed, *Living a Feminist Life*, 243.

[18] Ibid., 257.

[19] Walkerdine, "Girlhood through the Looking Glass," 20.

[20] Antonia Baum, *vollkommen leblos, bestenfalls tot* (Hamburg: Hoffmann & Campe, 2011), 7. Subsequent references provided parenthetically in text, preceded by *vl*. All translations are my own.

[21] See here Berlant, *Cruel Optimism*, 1. See also Baer, "German Feminism in the Age of Neoliberalism," on the effects of neoliberalism on women in Germany (359).

[22] All translations from the novel are my own.

[23] Berlant, *Cruel Optimism*, 11.

[24] J. Halberstam, *In a Queer Time and Place: Transgender Bodies, Subcultural Lives* (New York: New York University Press, 2005), 4.

[25] Ibid.

[26] See, for example, Claire Colebrook, "On Not Becoming Man: The Materialist Politics of Unactualized Potential," in Alaimo and Hekman, *Material Feminisms*.

[27] See references to Beauvoir in the introduction; see also Ahmed, *Living a Feminist Life*, 53.

[28] See here Smith-Prei and Stehle, *Awkward Politics*, 100.

[29] But cf. Scharff, Smith-Prei, and Stehle, "Digital Feminisms."

[30] Ahmed, *Living a Feminist Life*, 49.

[31] See here Inga Bones, *Jenseits von Gut und Böse?: Die Philosophie Friedrich Nietzsches in "Spieltrieb" von Juli Zeh* (Munich: GRIN Verlag, 2013).

[32] Stephen Brockmann, "Juli Zeh, *Spieltrieb*: Contemporary Nihilism," in *Emerging German-Language Novelists of the Twenty-First Century*, ed. Lyn Marven and Stuart Taberner (Rochester, NY: Camden House, 2011), 63, 64.

[33] Juli Zeh, *Spieltrieb* (Frankfurt am Main: Schöffling & Co, 2004). References to the novel provided parenthetically in text, preceded by *S*. All translations are my own.

[34] Cf. Brockmann, "Juli Zeh, *Spieltrieb*," 70.

[35] Berlant, *Cruel Optimism*, 11.

[36] Cf. Brockmann, "Juli Zeh, *Spieltrieb*," 73.

[37] Carrie Smith-Prei and Lars Richter, "Politicising Desire in Juli Zeh's *Spieltrieb*," in *Transitions: Emerging Women Writers in German-Language Literature* (*German Monitor* 76, 2013), ed. Valerie Heffernan and Gillian Pye, 203.

[38] Ibid.

[39] "Wenn ich herausfinden sollte, dass Sie von einem Fall ausgehen, in dem ein von der Scheidungssache Mama gegen Papa korrumpiertes Mädchen unter Ausnutzung seiner Schwäche von bösen Männern missbraucht wurde, ziehe ich meine gesamte Aussage zurück" (S, 545; If I were to find out that you are assuming a case where a girl, corrupted by Mummy versus Daddy's divorce case, was exploited in her weakness by bad men, I will withdraw my entire statement).

[40] "Wir alle sind nicht mehr als leise Stimmen im kakaphonen Chor, gelegentlich ein vorwitziges Solo spielend, nie mehr als wenige Sekunden, wenige Zeilen lange" (S, 566; We are all nothing more than soft voices in the cacophonous choir, occasionally singing an impertinent solo, never more than a few seconds, a few lines in length).

[41] Adichie, *We Should All Be Feminists*, 23–24; Gay, *Bad Feminist*, 88.

[42] Zoë Jenny, *Das Blütenstaubzimmer* (Munich: btb, 1999). References provided parenthetically in text, preceded by B. English quotations from Zoë Jenny, *The Pollen Room*, trans. Elizabeth Gaffney (New York: Simon & Schuster, 1999) provided parenthetically in text, preceded by PR.

[43] Ingrid Löwer, *Die 68er im Spiegel ihrer Kinder: Eine vergleichende Untersuchung zu familienkritischen Prosatexten der jüngeren Autorengeneration* (Bremen: edition lumière, 2011), 67.

[44] Hostility or distance characterize mother-daughter relations in almost all of the works I examine here, a fact with implications for the questions of sisterhood and identification explored further in chapter 4.

[45] From the back cover of Zoë Jenny, *Das Blütenstaubzimmer* (Munich: btb, 1999); quote attributed to "FACTS."

[46] Löwer, *Die 68er im Spiegel ihrer Kinder*, 69. Subsequent references provided parenthetically in text.

[47] As she puts it: "die egozentrische Vulgarisierung einer tragenden Idee der 68er-Bewegung und der sie fortführenden Frauenbewegung. . . . Selbstfindung and Selbstbestimmung des Subjekts" (Löwer, *Die 68er im Spiegel ihrer Kinder*, 76; the selfish vulgarization of a crucial idea of the 68-movement and the women's movement that carried it further . . . finding and defining one's self).

[48] The published translation departs from the German original here: "in den Tod" (to their deaths).

[49] "In Gedanken sehe ich meinen toten Körper im Autopsieraum auf einer hohen Bahre liegen. Der Raum ist sehr sauber . . . Ein Mann in einem grünen Kittel bewegt meinen Körper so, daß er auf der Mitte der Bahre zu liegen kommt" (B, 108; I imagine my dead body lying in the morgue on a high autopsy table. The room is very clean . . . A man in green scrubs positions my body at the center of the table, B, 127).

[50] Helene Hegemann, *Axolotl Roadkill* (Berlin: Ullstein, 2010), 74; Helene Hegemann, *Axolotl Roadkill*, trans. Katy Derbyshire (London: Corsair, 2012), 69. Subsequent references to German original provided parenthetically in text, preceded by AR; references to English translation provided in parentheses alone.

[51] Ursula März, "Literarischer Kugelblitz," *Zeit Online*, January 21, 2010, http://www.zeit.de/2010/04/L-B-Hegemann.

[52] Emily Jeremiah, "The Case of Helene Hegemann: Queerness, Failure, and the German Girl," *Seminar: A Journal of Germanic Studies* 49, no. 4 (2013).

[53] Iris Radisch, "Die alten Männer und das junge Mädchen," *Zeit Online*, February 10, 2010. http://www.zeit.de/2010/08/Helene-Hegemann-Medien.

[54] It features "found" texts, including—notably and notoriously—short extracts of a blog by a writer known as Airen, which brought about accusations of plagiarism and are now acknowledged in an appendix.

[55] Carrie Smith-Prei and Maria Stehle, "The Awkward Politics of Popfeminist Literary Events: Helene Hegemann, Charlotte Roche, and Lady Bitch Ray," in Baer and Merley Hill, *German Women's Writing*, 136. See also Smith-Prei and Stehle, *Awkward Politics*, 157.

[56] Jochen Strobel attempts a diagnosis of Mifti in light of theories relating to borderline personality disorder: "'Untermieter im eigenen Kopf'": Helene Hegemanns Roman *Axolotl Roadkill* und 'Borderline Poetics'," *Euphorion* 108, no. 1 (2014): 25–56.

[57] Helene Hegemann, "Interview mit Helene Hegemann zu ihrem Debüt 'Axolotl Roadkill'," *tip berlin*, December 20, 2011, http://www.tip-berlin.de/kultur-und-freizeit-lesungen-und-buecher/interview-mit-helene-hegemann-zum-debut-axolotl-roadkill.

[58] Cited in Jeremiah, "The Case of Helene Hegemann," 407.

[59] Smith-Prei and Stehle, *Awkward Politics*, 156.

[60] See here ibid., 158.

[61] Ahmed, *Living a Feminist Life*, 55.

[62] Smith-Prei and Stehle, *Awkward Politics*, 160.

[63] Baer, "Precarious Sexualities," 175.

[64] Emma Jane Unsworth, *Animals* (Edinburgh: Canongate, 2014), 24. Subsequent references provided parenthetically in text, preceded by *A*.

[65] This reference to burlesque is interesting in light of a recent revival of that form, defended by Caitlin Moran and satirized by Zoe Pilger in *Eat My Heart Out*, a novel I discuss in chapters 4 and 5.

[66] See the description of squalor here, for example: *A*, 7–8. Also: "Tyler was a dreadful cook, not that she gave a shit" (*A*, 12); "The kitchen was in its usual state of neglect" (*A*, 25); "I ruined everything I cooked" (*A*, 41).

[67] Alice O'Keeffe, "Girls Interrupted," review of *Animals*, *New Statesman*, June 5, 2014, http://www.newstatesman.com/culture/2014/06/nine-year-bender-animals-emma-jane-unsworth.

[68] Cf. *A*, 174: "If we're going to have a baby you should start respecting your body."

[69] "I wasn't judgemental where other people's relationships were concerned . . . Swinging was fine if you both swung . . . But if you had an agreement to be

monogamous . . . then there was a line, and once you crossed that line it was all over" (*A*, 186).

[70] Ahmed, *Living a Feminist Life*, 193.

[71] "A warm domestic scene. People smiling, eating, drinking, happy in each other's company. I thought of my parents' living room, of Jim's bed, and I thought Yes, Okay. All right. I'll have some of that" (*A*, 116–17).

[72] Quoted on the front cover of *Animals*.

[73] Caitlin Moran, *How to Build a Girl* (London: Ebury Press, 2014). References provided parenthetically in text, preceded by *HBG*. Like her protagonist, Moran also became a music journalist while still in her teens, and moved to London in that connection.

[74] She also describes gigs as "the boardroom meetings of young people, where we establish our vibe" (*HBG*, 133).

[75] "All my life, I've thought that if I couldn't say anything boys found interesting, I might as well shut up. But now I realise there was that whole other, invisible half of the world—girls—that I could speak to, instead" (*HBG*, 105).

[76] She is later intimidated by graduates and the possibility they will "turn the conversation to the clever things I have not yet read in the library" (*HBG*, 289).

[77] The British texts this chapter examines are thus more affirmative than the German texts, but the novels by Bathurst, Pilger, and Walsh discussed in subsequent chapters counter a potential argument relating to British writing or culture as more "positive" than German writing or culture. It is interesting to note the role class—a perhaps peculiarly "British" concern—plays in both Moran and Unsworth, and also the fact of the working-class background of both protagonists giving rise to both challenge and pride.

[78] Smith-Prei and Stehle, *Awkward Politics*, 114.

Chapter Three

[1] J. Brooks Bouson, *Embodied Shame: Uncovering Female Shame in Contemporary Women's Writings* (New York: State University of New York Press, 2009), 1.

[2] Ahmed, *Willful Subjects*, 226n29. Subsequent references provided parenthetically in text, preceded by *WS*.

[3] Phipps, *Politics of the Body*, 11.

[4] Dorn, *Die F-Klasse*, 37.

[5] Namely, "langweilige, messbare Symmetrie von Gesichtszügen, Durchschnittlichkeit oder Maße, an denen wir uns orientieren können und sollen" (boring, measurable symmetry of facial features, averageness, or measurements we are supposed to be able to orient ourselves toward). Haaf, Klingner, and Streidl, *Wir Alpha-Mädchen*, 47.

[6] Spiers, "Long March," 83–84.

[7] Jane Jacobs Brumberg, *The Body Project: An Intimate History of American Girls* (New York: Random House, 1997).

[8] Michelle M. Lazar, "The Right to be Beautiful: Postfeminist Identity and Consumer Beauty Advertising," in Gill and Scharff, *New Femininities*, 38.

[9] Charles, *Elite Girls' Schooling*, 33: "A distinct feature of post-feminist media culture, and of the presentation of heterosexually desirable/desiring women, is that the work that must be performed on the self to maintain desirability to men is now couched in terms of individual choice and empowerment, rather than obligation from outside."

[10] Charles, *Elite Girls' Schooling*, 41. See also the description of young women in contemporary popular culture as most often "young, thin, sexually attractive, blond and scantily dressed," in Savigny and Warner, "Introduction," 2.

[11] Susan Bordo, *Unbearable Weight: Feminism, Western Culture, and the Body* (Berkeley: University of California Press, 2003), 166. Bordo alludes here to Foucault's notion of the "docile body": a body marked by power relations.

[12] Baer, "Redoing Feminism," 24.

[13] Penny, *Meat Market*, 29, 66.

[14] Haaf, Klingner, and Streidl, 50.

[15] Buhr, "Hauptsache 'natürlich'," 129.

[16] Unsworth, *Animals*, 39.

[17] "a zoological entity, a genetic data-bank [and] a bio-social entity, that is to say a slab of codified, personalized memories" (Braidotti, *Metamorphoses*, 21). Subsequent references provided parenthetically in text, preceded by *M*.

[18] Grosz, *Becoming Undone*, 28.

[19] See here Butler, *Bodies that Matter*, ix.

[20] Compare: "literature, despite its obvious textuality, gives an odd and paradoxical kind of presence to female bodies by invoking the world of feelings . . . as it tells stories about the embodied self" (Brooks Bouson, *Embodied Shame*, 14). See also Smith-Prei and Stehle, *Awkward Politics*, 171.

[21] Charlotte Roche, *Feuchtgebiete* (Cologne: Dumont, 2008); Charlotte Roche, *Wetlands*, trans. Tim Mohr (London: Fourth Estate, 2009). Subsequent references provided parenthetically in text, preceded by *F* and *W*, respectively.

[22] Yanbing Er, "In Search of Self: The Dysfunctional Feminism of Charlotte Roche's *Wetlands*," *Women: A Cultural Review* 26, no. 4 (2015): 444.

[23] Carrie Smith-Prei, "Knaller-Sex für alle," 28.

[24] Heike Bartel, "Porn or PorNo: Approaches to Pornography in Elfriede Jelinek's *Lust* and Charlotte Roche's *Feuchtgebiete*," in *German Text Crimes: Writers Accused, from the 1950s to the 1970s*, ed. Tom Cheesman (*German Monitor* 77) (Amsterdam: Rodopi, 2013), 113. Subsequent references provided parenthetically in text.

[25] Smith-Prei, "Knaller-Sex für alle," 29.

[26] Ibid., 30. Smith-Prei also discusses here a novel by Sarah Kuttner (b. 1979), which "shares this straightforward approach to the injured, sick, or traumatized female body" (30). Kuttner's text also involves ideas of failure, as its title suggests: *Mängelexemplar* (Defective Copy) (Frankfurt am Main: Fischer, 2009).

27 Smith-Prei and Stehle, *Awkward Politics*, 164.

28 See here Baer, "Precarious Sexualities," 171: Baer draws on Christa Binswanger and Kathy Davis, "Sexy Stories and Postfeminist Empowerment: From *Häutungen* to *Wetlands*," *Feminist Theory* 13, no. 3 (2012): 245–63. For an example of such 1970s reclaiming and renaming, see Verena Stefan, *Häutungen* (Munich: Frauenoffensive, 1975).

29 McCarthy, "Feminism and Generational Conflicts," 61.

30 Compare Laura in Unsworth's *Animals*: "I liked the various smells of myself . . . I liked the raw smells of other people, too." Perfume and aftershave, with their "keen social purpose," are off-putting to her (38).

31 "Meine Mutter hat auf meine Muschihygiene immer großen Wert gelegt, auf die Penishygiene meines Bruders aber gar nicht" (*F*, 18; My mother placed great importance on the hygiene of my pussy but none at all on that of my brother's penis, *W*, 12).

32 Er, "In Search of Self," 445.

33 Smith-Prei and Stehle, "The Awkward Politics of Popfeminist Literary Events," 143. See also Smith-Prei and Stehle, *Awkward Politics*, 35, 164.

34 Helen Hester, "Rethinking Transgression: Disgust, Affect, and Sexuality in Charlotte Roche's *Wetlands*," in *Journal of Lesbian Studies* 17, nos. 13/14 (2013): 251–52.

35 Jones, *Representing Repulsion*, 241. Subsequent references provided parenthetically in text.

36 Noting that "Helen's project of spreading her bacteria and bodily secretions to other people is mirrored by Roche's authorial project of provoking disgust in her readers," she also highlights the ways in which the body is described in the novel in culinary terms (Jones, *Representing Repulsion*, 255).

37 Er, "In Search of Self," 460.

38 Zeh, *Spieltrieb*, 11. Subsequent references provided parenthetically in text, preceded by *S*. All translations are my own.

39 "Die Momente, in denen Ada das eigene Aussehen erträglich fand, waren selten, streng rationiert, und mussten für ein langes Leben reichen" (*S*, 359–60; The moments when Ada found her own appearance bearable were few, strictly rationed, and would have to suffice for a long life).

40 Smith-Prei and Richter, "Politicising Desire in Juli Zeh's *Spieltrieb*," 195.

41 Kerstin Grether, *Zuckerbabys* (Frankfurt am Main: Suhrkamp, 2006), 215. Subsequent references provided parenthetically in text, preceded by *Z*. All translations are my own.

42 Andrew Wright Hurley, *Into the Groove: Popular Music and Contemporary German Fiction* (Rochester, NY: Camden House, 2015), 216.

43 Cf. Zeynep Zeren Atayurt, *Excess and Embodiment in Contemporary Women's Writing* (Stuttgart: ibidem-Verlag, 2011), 1.

44 She reflects:

Allita ist die einzige naturschlanke Frau, die ich kenne. . . . Alle anderen müssen wohl hungern oder sonst etwas tun, wie zum Beispiel viel Sport treiben. Manche Mädchen tun dabei so, als könnten sie essen, was sie wollen, ohne zuzunehmen—nur probiert haben sie es noch nicht. Im Gegensatz zu Jungs, die oft beides können, Schokolade & Alkohol, weil die Jungsnatur wohl zum Schlaksigen tendiert. (*Z*, 40–41)

[Allita is the only naturally thin woman I know. . . . All the others must just starve or do something else, like a lot of exercise. Some girls make out they can eat what they want without putting on weight—only, they've never tried it. In contrast to boys, who can often have both, chocolate & alcohol, because boys naturally tend toward lankiness.]

[45] In Roche's *Feuchtgebiete*, the mother apparently cuts Helen's eyelashes out of envy.

[46] Hurley, *Into the Groove*, 214.

[47] See the following passage:

Immer auf dem Nachhauseweg, immer in der U-bahn, bemerkt Melissa wieder, wie hübsch sie doch ist. Die schnellen Blicke der anderen Frauen, ein unbeteiligtes Mustern, bewunderndes Festhaken, kurzes Ahh, dann wieder die abgestumpften Augen, die "Was geht es mich an"-Haltung. Sofort sitzen die Frauen nämlich wieder in steifer Würde da, als bedauerten sie, nichts zum Verbessern gefunden zu haben. . . . Wie sonderbar ihr diese schmutzigen Leute überhaupt vorkommen. Sollen das etwa die normalen Menschen sein? Diese Leute hier mit ihrer fahlen Haut, mit Falten, Furchen und undefinierbaren Körperfetten überall, sogar am Kinn. Oder sie waren alle auf dem Weg zur nächsten RTL-Talkshow "Hilfe, ich bin so hässlich!" (*Z*, 35)

[Always on the way home, always on the underground, Melissa notices how pretty she is. The swift glances other women give her, an indifferent summing-up, admiring lingering, brief 'oh', and then, again, the dull eyes, the "What's-it-to-me?"-attitude. The women sit there, all stiff dignity, as if regretting finding nothing to reproach. . . . How strange these dirty people seem to her. Are these supposed to be normal people? These people with their dull skin, with wrinkles and furrows and amorphous masses of fat everywhere, even on their chin. Or maybe they were all on their way to the latest TV talkshow, "Help, I'm so ugly!"]

[48] Hurley, *Into the Groove*, 219.

[49] Emily Jeremiah, "Sibylle Berg, *Die Fahrt*: Literature, Germanness, and Globalization," in *New German Writers of the Twentieth-First Century*, ed. Lyn Marven and Stuart Taberner (Rochester, NY: Camden House, 2011), 135–36, 138–40.

[50] Sibylle Berg, *Ein paar Leute suchen das Glück und lachen sich tot* (Stuttgart: Reclam, 1997), 7. Subsequent references provided parenthetically in text, preceded by *EpL*. All translations are my own.

51 "Nora ist beschissen jung und hat noch nicht viel Übung darin, sich nach Schmerz zu schütteln und weiterzuleben" (*EpL*, 138; Nora is bloody young and hasn't had much practice in shaking off pain and getting on with life).

52 Sarai Walker, *Dietland* (London: Atlantic Books, 2015). Subsequent references provided parenthetically in text, preceded by *D*.

53 But see also Walker's critique of UK attitudes in Arwa Mahdawi, "*Dietland* Author Sarai Walker: London is the Most Fat-Shaming Place I've Been," *Guardian*, April 27, 2016.

54 See Atayurt, *Excess and Embodiment*, 21–22.

55 See also Sarai Walker, "Yes, I'm Fat. It's OK. I Said It," *New York Times*, February 6, 2016.

56 See Mahdawi, "London."

57 "The only way I could survive my life was to exist in a fog of denial. Acknowledging what happened around me was almost unimaginable . . . If I ignored it, then it wasn't real" (*D*, 123).

58 Moran, *How to Build a Girl*, 56. Subsequent reference provided parenthetically in text.

59 See here Baer, "Redoing Feminism": "Digital platforms . . . occupy a double function as sites of empowerment and identity formation, on the one hand, and of surveillance and self-monitoring, on the other, particularly for women . . . Like neoliberalism more generally, digital platforms specifically present a paradoxical and contradictory horizon of expectation surrounding the precarious body" (24).

Chapter Four

1 See chapter 1 of this volume, as well as references to worldwide activism in Cochrane, *All the Rebel Women*, 15%. The *Alpha-Mädchen* also attempt a global perspective: Haaf, Klingner, and Streidl, 237–47.

2 Walter, *Living Dolls*, 207.

3 Note the isolation of Hegemann's, Baum's, Berg's, Jenny's, and Roche's characters, and in particular their distance from mother figures.

4 Alison Winch, *Girlfriends and Postfeminist Sisterhood* (Houndmills, UK: Palgrave Macmillan, 2013). Subsequent references provided parenthetically in text.

5 Ahmed, *Living a Feminist Life*, 2.

6 Smith-Prei and Stehle, *Awkward Politics*, 202.

7 Grosz, *Becoming Undone*, 95.

8 Ibid., 3. Subsequent references provided parenthetically in text.

9 Puar, *Terrorist Assemblages*, 212.

10 Cf. Butler, *Bodies that Matter*, xiii.

11 Braidotti, *Metamorphoses*, 40.

12 Ahmed, *Willful Subjects*, 26. Subsequent references provided parenthetically in text, preceded by *WS*.

[13] Elke Naters, *Königinnen* (Cologne: Kiepenhauer & Witsch, 1998), 9. Subsequent references provided parenthetically in text, preceded by *K*. All translations are my own.

[14] See here McCarthy, "Feminism and Generational Conflicts," 57.

[15] She reflects:

> Das kenne ich schon von Marie, daß man nichts mehr von ihr hört, wenn sie einen Mann kennengelernt hat. Erst wenn es wieder vorbei ist, dann muss ich mir das Geheule anhören und trösten und Tränen wischen und neue Männer vorstellen. Ich meine, ich habe auch einen Mann und ein Kind noch dazu, und trotzdem kümmere ich mich um meine Freundinnen. Das heißt, die sind auch weniger geworden die Freundinnen, seitdem. Eigentlich ist nur Marie übriggeblieben. Und jetzt ist die auch wieder weg. (*K*, 90)
>
> [That's so like Marie—you don't hear from her when she's met a man. Only when it's over—then I have to listen to her sobbing and comfort her and wipe her eyes and introduce her to new men. I mean, I do have a husband and a child, and still I take care of my friends. Not that there are many of them these days. There's only Marie, actually. And now she's gone away, too.]

[16] McCarthy, "Feminism and Generational Conflicts," 69.

[17] Elke Naters, *Lügen* (Cologne: Kiepenhauer & Witsch, 1999), 70. Subsequent references provided parenthetically in text, preceded by *L*. All translations are my own.

[18] McCarthy, "Feminism and Generational Conflicts," 70.

[19] Cf. ibid., 71.

[20] Ibid., 71, 72. In McCarthy's view, "*Lügen* ultimately heals seemingly irreparable splits in a manner that bridges the gap between old- and new-style feminists in forward-thinking, or perhaps utopian ways" (70).

[21] Bella Bathurst, *Special* (London: Pan Macmillan, 2002), 28. Subsequent references provided parenthetically in text, preceded by *S*.

[22] Berthold Schoene, "The Wounded Woman and the Parrot: Post-Feminist Girlhood in Alan Warner's *The Sopranos* and Bella Bathurst's *Special*," *Journal of Gender Studies* 15, no. 2 (July 2006): 134. Subsequent references provided parenthetically in text.

[23] Grether, *Zuckerbabys*, 21: "Wenn ich so fein raus wäre wie Allita, so frei und Frau . . . dann wäre unsere kleine Freundschaft ziemlich für die Katz" (If I were as well out of it as Allita, so free and my own woman . . . then our little friendship would be for the chop). Subsequent references provided parenthetically in text, preceded by *Z*. All translations are my own. Sonja also reflects, ironically: "Wer seiner besten Freundin zu sehr ähnelt, kann sich auch gleich mit sich selber anfreunden. Und das will ich mir nun wirklich für später aufheben" (*Z*, 22; If you're too similar to your best friend, you might as well make friends with yourself. And I want to leave that for later). This is ambiguous, implying at once the welcome nature of difference and the need for self-acceptance and love, which appear to be at odds with each other.

24 "Streng genommen sehen sie sich nicht ähnlich, aber ähnlich sehen sie sich doch. Locker machen sie ihr unterschiedliches Aussehen—Kicky blond, Ricky Schwarz . . .—wieder wett" (*Z*, 27; Strictly speaking, they don't look alike, but they do look alike, still. They compete, in a laid-back way, with their different appearances—Kicky blonde, Ricky black-haired).

25 Hurley, *Into the Groove*, 217.

26 Unsworth, *Animals*, 12; cf.: "I loved her. I did. Sometimes" (*A*, 114). Subsequent references provided parenthetically in text, preceded by *A*.

27 Zoe Pilger, *Eat My Heart Out* (London: Serpent's Tail, 2014), 3. Subsequent references provided parenthetically in text, preceded by *EMHO*. Cf.: "Cambridge made me mental" (*EMHO*, 16).

28 Zoe Pilger, "*The Second Sex* by Simone de Beauvoir: Book of a Lifetime," *The Independent*, January 24, 2014. Pilger describes her novel here as "about a young woman, Ann-Marie, in thrall to the myths of post-feminist culture: hyper-sexuality and romantic love as the ultimate goal of life. She meets a second wave feminist, Stephanie Haight, who is equally flawed, but who tries to wean Ann-Marie off slavish romanticism in favour of independence."

29 Ibid.

30 As when Haight tells Ann-Marie, "Gabriella is immensely influenced by Žižek but I just can't get on with his interpretation of Lacan through a Hegelian lens" (*EMHO*, 137).

31 Pilger's thesis is on the concept of romantic subjection in the work of French artist Sophie Calle. See reference to untitled PhD dissertation, Goldsmiths, University of London, http://www.zoepilger.co.uk/phd.

32 In an interview for a magazine, Haight is also quoted as using the term "*false consciousness*," adding "*a retro term these days. There are scant terms now for the forces that make women blind to their own condition, but I'm still fighting*" (*EMHO*, 82; italics in original). Referring to Lacan, and the notion that one internalizes oppression, Haight claims: "Women obey without knowing they are obeying. The choice is always already made" (*EMHO*, 18).

33 Haight invokes this stereotype: "Now feminism is a dirty word, a synonym for hairy lesbian" (*EMHO*, 189).

34 Having lived and worked in the United States, Haight has an "Anglo-American" accent (*EMHO*, 83). She thereby represents, arguably, "Anglo-American" feminism, while other aspects of her biography raise issues of class mobility and the questions of populism v. elitism/academia.

35 Her personal situation does not appear happy. While she lives contentedly without a husband, she waits in vain for her son to come home (*EMHO*, 138). She appears to live with Marge and the latter's daughter—it emerges that she earlier had an affair with Greg, Marge's ex (*EMHO*, 158, 165, 242).

36 See also the deflationary sentence that follows: "We ate dinner under a portrait of an Iranian woman wearing a purdah, aiming a Kalashnikov" (*EMHO*, 12).

37 Back cover of Rachel B. Glaser, *Paulina and Fran* (London: Granta, 2015). Subsequent references provided parenthetically in text, preceded by *PF*.

[38] But her security blanket, a small piece of material she uses to comfort herself, suggests a hidden vulnerability (*PF*, 35, 80).

[39] Her lesbian past emerges later when she recalls her time at Smith: "That had all started with Sally in the yoga shack by the lake. But Paulina couldn't avoid her feelings for Audrey, who gazed at Paulina unabashedly in the dining hall, forcing Paulina to eat in a rugged, macho way to impress her. Then, in a steamy room at the Smith botanical gardens, she felt up Susan Bradley, a girl preoccupied with sustainable living" (*PF*, 40–41).

[40] Paulina laters realizes that she "missed Fran, and the feeling was unique, as Paulina made it a rule to miss no one" (*PF*, 53). She is also accused of being "in love" with Fran (*PF*, 62). When Paulina discovers Fran is seeing her own ex, she "imagined Fran naked"—"too easily" (*PF*, 82).

[41] "Why was Fran imprinted over all her thoughts? It was her face. And that lightness. Fran wasn't attached to the ground—a wind carried her. No. Fran was just a lonely child the woods had taken pity on" (*PF*, 103).

[42] The kiss is diagnosed as follows: "Paulina could not leave beauty alone . . . Fran was unable to resist anyone who wanted her" (*PF*, 125).

[43] Contrasting Paulina with Gretchen, another student, Fran reflects: "Gretchen was the kind of girlfriend she would be offered again and again by the adult world, the real world, but Paulina was someone truly original, someone who existed only once" (*PF*, 76). And for Paulina, "Befriending Fran had been like finding a jewel—a girl whose powerful naiveté was wholly her own" (*PF*, 187). She later realizes: "no other person would do" (*PF*, 237).

[44] Puar, *Terrorist Assemblages*, 23.

[45] Ahmed notes: "A lesbian withdraws from a system that requires that she make herself available to men" (*Living a Feminist Life*, 225).

Chapter Five

[1] Compare Ahmed, *Willful Subjects*, 174, 191–92. Subsequent references provided parenthetically in text, preceded by *WS*.

[2] Bates, *Everyday Sexism*, 18–19.

[3] Valerie Walkerdine, *Daddy's Girl: Young Girls and Popular Culture* (Houndmills, UK: Macmillan, 1997), 81.

[4] Walkerdine, "Girlhood Through the Looking Glass," 18.

[5] Walkerdine, *Daddy's Girl*, 3.

[6] Walter, *Living Dolls*, 73, 95.

[7] Levy, *Female Chauvinist Pigs*.

[8] Grether, *Zuckerbabys*, 65. My translation.

[9] Braidotti, *Metamorphoses*, 99.

[10] See here Rosi Braidotti, *Transpositions: On Nomadic Ethics* (Cambridge: Polity Press, 2006).

[11] Ahmed, *Living a Feminist Life*, 225.

[12] Puar, *Terrorist Assemblages*, 205.

[13] Grosz, *Becoming Undone*, 141. Subsequent references provided parenthetically in text.

[14] Moran, *How to Build a Girl*, 3, 11; cf. *HBG*, 39. Subsequent references provided parenthetically in text, preceded by *HBG*.

[15] She claims: "I am at my best when I am taking my clothes off with a boy. I can make no mistakes, or offend anyone, here. Here, I am a force for the good—making boys who need to come, come" (*HBG*, 276).

[16] Cf. *HBG*, 278–79: "I . . . concentrate on how much *he* is enjoying it."

[17] For Moran, "The idea that pornography is intrinsically exploitative and sexist is bizarre." Moran differentiates between pornography itself and the porn industry, which is exploitative, and argues that a variety of porn should be available—not least because "in the 21st century, children and teenagers get the majority of their sex education from the internet" (Moran, *How to Be a Woman*, 35).

[18] "a large factor in my not-coming is because some of them have been absolutely hopeless" (*HBG*, 239).

[19] For Roche, for example, there is *Macht* (power) in pop videos featuring provocative dancing, as she reveals in an interview in Thea Dorn's *Die neue F-Klasse*. She also jokily discusses her plans to set up a brothel for women. Dorn, *Die neue F-Klasse*, 141, 151.

[20] Roche, *Feuchtgebiete*, 30. English translations of subsequent quotations from Roche, *Wetlands*. Subsequent references provided parenthetically in text, preceded by *F* and *W*, respectively.

[21] In the German original, the last sentence introduces the idea of a male subject potentially keen to approach the women described ("keiner"), where the English translation suggests a kind of (prohibitive) agency on the part of the women themselves ("would never let themselves").

[22] The literal, and in my view more appropriate, translation of the German here: "even as a little girl."

[23] Jones, *Representing Repulsion*, 249. Subsequent references provided parenthetically in text.

[24] See here Baer, "Precarious Sexualities," 168–69. Baer notes the changing attitudes in Germany to body hair over the last twenty years.

[25] Cited on the back cover of Helen Walsh, *Brass* (Edinburgh: Canongate, 2005). Subsequent references provided parenthetically in text, preceded by *B*.

[26] Reactions to the book when it was published in 2004 in some ways recall responses to Hegemann and Roche; the book was widely reviewed and its young author photographed lavishly. See the author's website for examples of reviews from the British press.

[27] Afterward, however, Millie experiences ambivalence: "Half of me wants to take her in my arms, the other, despises her" (*B*, 4).

28 For example, "My cunt is throbbing" (*B*, 59; cf. *B*, 72); "Our bodies make contact, jolting my cunt to life" (*B*, 81); "My cunt somersaults" (*B*, 84); "My cunt is throbbing so hard it hurts" (*B*, 98).

29 She describes her older male lecturer as "terminally fuckable." His arms are "beautiful . . . slim and striated with sinewy muscle"; "I had a wank over them in the library toilets last year" (*B*, 44). Such segmentation and objectification are characteristic of the male or mainstream gaze directed at female bodies.

30 Millie observes a young waitress who has "a pretty face and a delicate physique," but down on her arms and jawline: "A real friend would tell her—that's just ugly, that is. You don't want to be looking at something like that" (*B*, 20). Compare other of Millie's judgments: she notes a blonde "wearing a tiny yellow jumper so tight it makes her breasts look deformed" (*B*, 35); "visually offensive" students, one male, one female (*B*, 77); eyes "scummy with cheap blue mascara" (*B*, 92). Of one woman, she reflects: "She just looks like a very average nineteen-year-old who's [*sic*] tits have skipped puberty" (*B*, 203). Her view of her female lecturer is cruel: "She dresses as to discourage contemplation of her body, and yet somewhere underneath those baggy slacks and blanket blouses there must be tits and a cunt" (*B*, 39); later, there is a reference to her "crude spinster's perfume" (*B*, 113). Millie observes a scantily clad woman in a magazine critically: "Kelly Brook's on the front cover in a lime bikini . . . She looks wide" (*B*, 74). On a night out, she finds "not much to look at in terms of fanny . . . a party of busty middle-aged women, a couple of bottle blonde stripper types and a clutch of nine-to-fivers seeking refuge from the rain" (*B*, 81). She stares at a women's "*huge*" breasts and "commit[s] them to memory" (*B*, 81). Encountering a girl no more than fourteen years of age, she registers her "plain" face, adding: "But the tits, the tits are humongous" (*B*, 182–83).

31 See here Kat Banyard's recent *Pimp State: Sex, Money and the Future of Equality* (London: Faber & Faber, 2016).

32 "When I see a mother and toddler in the street the first thought that flips through my head is how much easier my fist will slide in now that she's been stretched by child birth" (*B*, 23). Later, though, she refers to the partner of a friend as bringing to mind "sucking babies, pendulous breasts and home-cooked dinners": she is "kissable not fuckable. She hasn't let motherhood pull her down though. She's looked after her figure" (*B*, 174). Cf.: "His wife was a casualty of marriage—fat and dowdy and consumed by motherhood" (*B*, 197).

33 Like Hegemann's Mifti, Millie has been brought up by her father since the loss of her mother; in this case, her mother left the family: "It was the shock of my life," Millie reports (*B*, 63). The feminine thus disappears from her life: "Into the boxes and crates went all the feminine, the womanly, the motherly trappings. The touch and the soul" (*B*, 66). And yet her mother is "everywhere," and evoked in almost fetishistic terms through references to "perfume," "mahogany locks," and "alabaster skin" (*B*, 67). Millie remembers a time of familial togetherness, when "everything was safe and happy and forever" (*B*, 159). She reflects of her mother: "That's what she was best at Mum [*sic*]. Being a Mum and a wife" (*B*, 250). The end of the novel, which sees Millie poised to be reunited with her mother, suggests a potential resolution built on the mother-daughter connection.

34 "I *never* saw myself as an object though. I neither identified with the women I objectified or the men that objectified them. I saw myself as something entirely different, as some sex-crazed genderless freak" (*B*, 201). Millie could be described as genderqueer. Ambivalence relating to femininity is hinted at in her reflection that she has never felt comfortable in dresses—"they render me feminine and vulnerable"—but in donning a dress, and applying make-up, she also appears to enjoy the appreciative male responses, and be confident in her attractiveness (*B*, 178). The association of femininity with vulnerability is notable, given Millie's masculine gaze and behaviors. Millie's friend Jamie describes her as being "a jeans and no make-up type of girl. Nails bitten to stumps and soap-scorched hair"—but notes that recently "she's started making an effort and that" (*B*, 193). Millie's relationship with the older Jamie is a key feature of the narrative, and when Jamie tells his fiancée Anne Marie of his plans to include Millie in his stag night, Millie's awkwardness and her failure to belong to (gendered) categories becomes clear:

> "You can't invite Millie to a stag do!"
> "Why not?"
> "You just can't. She's a girl."
> "So?"
> ". . . How the fuck d'you think that makes me look, hey?!"
> . . .
> "Hadn't really thought about it that way, to be fair. She's just another one of my mates and that, Millie. Maybe she could go down to London with the girls then."
> "I don't think so." (*B*, 55)

35 But this is followed by further escapades, for example, an episode in a toilet cubicle which involves self-justification ("She's part of this—she's letting me"), but then, subsequently, the recognition that "that was wrong" (*B*, 217, 234).

36 Bathurst, *Special*, 18, 32, 35. Subsequent references provided parenthetically in text, preceded by *S*.

37 "She'd been here, in a gym, thinking about Caz, all twisted with desire and hate, and her innards had suddenly exploded . . . She was a lesbian . . . It was the worst thing that could possibly happen" (*S*, 123).

38 Cf. Grether's *Zuckerbabys*, discussed in chapter 3.

39 Pilger, *Eat My Heart Out*, 23–25. Subsequent references provided parenthetically in text, preceded by *EMHO*.

40 Pilger, "*The Second Sex* by Simone de Beauvoir."

41 The question of female dependence or emancipation is furthered here:

> "This isn't our first date, Vic. We met in a past life. I was your faithful concubine. But now I'm an empowered women." I corrected myself: "I'm a woman in the process of becoming empowered." I laughed. "If you'll only let me."
> Vic lay down again.
> I rolled another cigarette.
> "No," he said, and tossed it somewhere. "You're desperate."

I laughed. "No, Vic. That's the trouble. I think I'm desperate, I even want to be desperate, but I'm not. The sad truth is that I'm not. Maybe if I was, then you'd love me"

. . .

"You're all the same," he mumbled (*EMHO*, 9).

[42] A reference to Catherine Hakim, *Honey Money: The Power of Erotic Capital* (London: Penguin, 2012).

[43] Hegemann, *Axolotl Roadkill*, 11; Hegemann, *Axolotl Roadkill*, trans. Katy Derbyshire, 5. Subsequent references provided parenthetically in text, preceded by *AR*.

[44] Mifti records later: "Dann knutschen wir [Ophelia and Mifti] aus lauter Langeweile" (Then we snog out of pure boredom). One of them, presumably Ophelia, makes the observation: "Wir sind ja beide so geschlechterverwirrt, Schatz'" (*AR*, 43; We're both so gender-confused, honey, 38).

[45] Translation modified to reflect German original: *Körpern* (bodies), as opposed to published English translation "heads" (*Köpfen*).

[46] But note the English translation takes a different reading of the text at this point (40–41, my italics): "And then you tell her you recognize your dead mother in her. Something *must have got going* inside her . . . scruples or whatever" (Und dann erzählst du ihr, dass du in ihr deine tote Mutter wiedererkennst. Also irgendwie *müsste* sich da was in ihr regen . . . Skrupel oder so; *AR*, 45, my italics).

[47] Baer, "Precarious Sexualities," 175.

[48] She then abruptly asks the man, "Hast du Lust auf Oralsex?" (*AR*, 24; Are you up for oral sex?, 18), an offer he does not take up, to her sadness.

[49] Ahmed, *Living a Feminist Life*, 49.

[50] Novels by Joanna Briscoe and Charlotte Mendelson would be worth exploring in this connection: Joanna Briscoe, *Mothers and Other Lovers* (London: Phoenix House, 1994)—published too early to be included here—and Charlotte Mendelson's *Love in Idleness* (London: Picador, 2001), interesting for its depiction of a (rather timid) queer *Bildung*.

Conclusion

[1] Kate Zambreno, *Green Girl* (New York: Harper Collins, 2014), 109: "This self, this self not yet formed." Subsequent references provided parenthetically in text, preceded by *GG*.

[2] "The agony of becoming. This is what she experiences. The young girl. She would like to be someone, anyone else. She wants, vaguely, to be something more than she is. But she does not know what that is, or how one goes about doing such a thing" (*GG*, 74).

[3] A similar reflection on voyeurism occurs when the narrator muses on celebrities: "They exist to draw attention. Aware of the whole world watching. They are green girls too. We give birth to them. Then we destroy them with our insatiable desire to have entrance into their private lives. This is them unmasked without

makeup, waiting in a queue at the grocery store, blinking from a sex tape . . . we watch and watch" (*GG*, 15).

4 The current popularity of the term (used in this sense) is signalled by the 2015 film *Trainwreck*, starring comedian Amy Schumer.

5 William Shakespeare, *Hamlet* (London: Penguin, 1980), 84.

6 See here Berlant, *Cruel Optimism*.

7 Compare: "She stumbles around, outside of herself, looking at them looking at her" (*GG*, 27); "She is being swept along. She is a pale ghost" (*GG*, 27); "She is not the author of the Book of Ruth" (*GG*, 107).

8 "She would like to run down the street naked and screaming, but she can't. It would be terribly impolite and improper" (*GG*, 81).

9 "To want. To lack. To have a hole," the narrator muses: the perpetual nature of desire (in capitalism) thus comes to the fore (*GG*, 33; cf. *GG*, 166).

10 "She sees herself as a beautiful girl smelling the beautiful flowers. She savors in this image. The girl in front of the perfect roses dotted with raindrops. Shiny eyes. Shiny lips. A perfected surface. A cosmetics ad" (*GG*, 29).

11 Ironically, the same magazine tells Ruth: "It is again the season for a woman with a strong identity," stirring up worry in the reader (*GG*, 61).

12 John Berger, *Ways of Seeing* (London: Penguin, 2008), 41.

13 Laura Mulvey, "Visual Pleasure and Narrative Cinema," in *Feminisms: An Anthology of Literary Theory and Criticism*, ed. Robyn R. Warhol and Diane Price Herndl (Houndmills, UK: Macmillan, 1997), 447.

14 Compare Zambreno's account of her own "terrible digestive problems," in *Heroines* (Los Angeles: Semiotext(e), 2012), 23.

15 As noted, Johanna in Moran's novel at one point gets diarrhoea and finds her period has started (*How to Build a Girl*, 117). In Pilger, there are frequent references to shit, as mentioned. Unsworth's *Animals* also features diarrhoea (54, 89).

16 Agnes "look[s] at Ruth looking at herself in the mirror" (*GG*, 63), and: "They compete with each other. Each one wonders whether the other holds more allure in the mirror. They are tremendously vain" (*GG*, 64). Ruth watches two shopgirls who comparably act as "each other's mirrors. They trade in compliments . . . the false currency for the green girl" (*GG*, 31).

17 Agnes's abortion points to the potential consequences of unprotected heterosexual sex (*GG*, 240–43). It is the experience of pregnancy, rather than the abortion itself, that Agnes finds disturbing: "Imagine—my body becoming some public domain . . . I don't want that" (*GG*, 244).

18 There is an epigraph from Isherwood's *Goodbye to Berlin*, in which the author famously compares himself to a camera (*GG*, 72). Christopher Isherwood, *Goodbye to Berlin* (London: Vintage, [1939] 1989).

19 Cf. "To be a writer she would have to take herself back as a character" (*GG*, 249).

20 See also: "If she had to point at a map she would probably put Bangladesh between India and Pakistan. (It isn't.)" (*GG*, 241).

21 Cf. "A close-up on Ruth, my Hitchcock blonde. Who is the girl behind the counter? I wish to know her. I want to say to her: It must be terrible to be stuck here. I want to look deep into her eyes and say: I see you" (*GG*, 139). See also *GG*, 161: "I am the harsh director."

22 Zambreno, *Heroines*, 252, 297.

23 Compare this critic's view, quoted in the front pages of the book: "I can't recall the last time I read a book whose heroine infuriated and seduced me as completely as Kate Zambreno's *Green Girl* . . . [She is] all-too-recognizable" (Elissa Schappell, *Vanity Fair*).

24 Grosz, *Becoming Undone*, 89.

25 Lindy West, "Fat and Free," *Guardian G2*, May 9, 2016, 8.

26 Ahmed, *Living a Feminist Life*, 15.

27 See Braidotti, *Metamorphoses*, 115–16.

28 Braidotti calls for "a broadening of the traditional feminist political agenda": it should include, "as well as the issue of women's social rights, a larger spectrum of options, which range from cultural concerns related to writing and creativity, to issues which at first sight seem to have nothing to do specifically with women" (*Metamorphoses*, 83).

29 Grosz, *Becoming Undone*, 135.

30 Braidotti, *Nomadic Subjects*. Braidotti draws on Deleuze to conceptualize nomadism.

31 The subject of important work by Scharff, Smith-Prei, and Stehle ("Digital Feminisms").

32 Valenti, *Full-Frontal Feminism*, 3.

33 Baer, "Redoing Feminism," 18.

34 Cochrane, *All the Rebel Women*, 78%; Moran, *How to Be a Woman*, 12.

35 Valenti, *Full-Frontal Feminism*, 182.

36 Angela McRobbie, introduction to *Feminism and Youth Culture: From "Jackie" to "Just Seventeen"* (Houndmills, UK: Macmillan, 1991), xviii.

37 Ahmed recently resigned from her post at Goldsmiths, University of London, citing the institution's failure to address the problem of sexual harassment as her reason for doing so. See "Resignation."

38 Smith-Prei and Stehle, *Awkward Politics*, 194.

39 Denis Campbell and Haroon Siddique, "Mental Illness Soars among Young Women in England—Survey," *Guardian*, September 29, 2016.

40 Cochrane, *All the Rebel Women*, 70%. But she also appeals to comedienne Bridget Christie's view of humor as exposing and skewering the absurdity of misogyny (75%). As we have seen, Caitlin Moran, notably, uses humor in both her memoir and her novel.

41 Sady Doyle, *Trainwreck: The Women We Love to Hate, Mock, and Fear . . . and Why* (Brooklyn, UK: Melville House, 2016), xix. Subsequent references provided parenthetically in text.

Bibliography

Aapola, Sinikka, Marnina Gonick, and Anita Harris. *Young Femininity: Girl-hood, Power and Social Change.* Houndmills, UK: Palgrave Macmillan, 2005.

Adichie, Chimamanda Ngozi. *We Should All Be Feminists.* London: Fourth Estate, 2014.

Ahmed, Sara. *The Cultural Politics of Emotion.* London: Routlege, 2004.

———. *feministkilljoys: killing joy as a world-making project* (blog). https:// feministkilljoys.com/.

———. *Living a Feminist Life.* Durham, NC: Duke University Press, 2017.

———. *Willful Subjects.* Durham, NC: Duke University Press, 2014.

Alaimo, Stacy, and Susan Hekman. "Introduction: Emerging Models of Materiality in Feminist Theory." In Alaimo and Hekman, *Material Feminisms,* 1–19.

———, eds. *Material Feminisms.* Bloomington: Indiana University Press, 2008.

Atayurt, Zeynep Zeren. *Excess and Embodiment in Contemporary Women's Writing.* Stuttgart: ibidem-Verlag, 2011.

Baer, Hester. ed. *Contemporary Women's Writing and the Return of Feminism in Germany,* special issue of *Studies in 20th and 21st Century Literature* 35, no. 1 (2011).

———. "German Feminism in the Age of Neoliberalism: Jana Hensel and Elisabeth Raether's *Neue deutsche Mädchen.*" *German Studies Review* 35, no. 2 (May 2012): 355–74.

———. "Introduction: Resignifications of Feminism in Contemporary Germany." In Baer, *Contemporary Women's Writing,* 8–17.

———. "Precarious Sexualities, Neoliberalism, and the Pop-Feminist Novel: Charlotte Roche's *Feuchtgebiete* and Helene Hegemann's *Axolotl Roadkill* as Transnational Texts." In Herrmann, Smith-Prei, and Taberner, *Transnationalism in Contemporary German-Language Literature,* 162–86.

———. "Redoing Feminism: Digital Activism, Body Politics, and Neoliberalism." *Feminist Media Studies* 16, no. 1 (2016): 17–34.

Baer, Hester, and Alexandra Merley Hill. "Introduction: German Women's Writing beyond the Gender Binary." In *German Women's Writing in the Twenty-First Century,* edited by Hester Baer and Alexandra Merley Hill, 1–17. Rochester, NY: Camden House, 2015.

Banyard, Kat. *The Equality Illusion: The Truth about Women and Men Today.* London: Faber & Faber, 2010.

————. *Pimp State: Sex, Money and the Future of Equality*. London: Faber & Faber, 2016.

Bartel, Heike. "Porn or PorNo: Approaches to Pornography in Elfriede Jelinek's *Lust* and Charlotte Roche's *Feuchtgebiete*." In *German Text Crimes: Writers Accused, from the 1950s to the 1970s*, edited by Tom Cheesman (*German Monitor 77*), 99–124. Amsterdam: Rodopi, 2013.

Bathurst, Bella. *Special*. London: Pan Macmillan, 2002.

Baum, Antonia. *vollkommen leblos, bestenfalls tot*. Hamburg: Hoffmann & Campe, 2011.

Baxter, Holly, and Rhiannon Lucy Cosslett. *The Vagenda: A Zero Tolerance Guide to the Media*. London: Square Peg, 2014.

Beard, Mary. "The Public Voice of Women." *London Review of Books* 36, no. 6 (March 20, 2014): 11–14.

Beauvoir, Simone de. *The Second Sex*. Translated by H. M. Parshley. London: Vintage, [1949] 1997.

Benn, Melissa. *What Should We Tell Our Daughters?: The Pleasures and Pressures of Growing Up Female*. London: Hodder, 2014.

Berg, Sibylle. *Ein paar Leute suchen das Glück und lachen sich tot*. Stuttgart: Reclam, 1997.

Berger, John. *Ways of Seeing*. London: Penguin, 2008.

Berlant, Lauren. *Cruel Optimism*. Durham, NC: Duke University Press, 2011.

Binswanger, Christa, and Kathy Davis, "Sexy Stories and Postfeminist Empowerment: From *Häutungen* to *Wetlands*." *Feminist Theory* 13, no. 3 (2012): 245–63.

Bones, Inga. *Jenseits von Gut und Böse? Die Philosophie Friedrich Nietzsches in "Spieltrieb" von Juli Zeh*. Munich: GRIN Verlag, 2013.

Bordo, Susan. *Unbearable Weight: Feminism, Western Culture, and the Body*. Berkeley: University of California Press, 2003.

Bouson, J. Brooks. *Embodied Shame: Uncovering Female Shame in Contemporary Women's Writings*. Albany: State University of New York Press, 2009.

Braidotti, Rosi. *Metamorphoses: Towards a Materialist Theory of Becoming*. Cambridge: Polity Press, 2002.

————. *Nomadic Subjects: Embodiment and Sexual Difference in Contemporary Feminist Theory*. New York: Columbia University Press, 1994.

————. *Transpositions: On Nomadic Ethics*. Cambridge: Polity Press, 2006.

Briscoe, Joanna. *Mothers and Other Lovers*. London: Phoenix House, 1994.

Brockmann, Stephen. "Juli Zeh, *Spieltrieb*: Contemporary Nihilism." In *Emerging German-Language Novelists of the Twenty-First Century*, edited by Lyn Marven and Stuart Taberner, 62–74. Rochester, NY: Camden House, 2011.

Brumberg, Jane Jacobs. *The Body Project: An Intimate History of American Girls*. New York: Random House, 1997.

Buhr, Elke. "Hauptsache 'natürlich'." In Stöcker, *Das F-Wort*, 119–30.

Butler, Judith. *Bodies that Matter: On the Discursive Limits of "Sex."* New York: Routledge, 2011.
———. *Gender Trouble: Feminism and the Subversion of Identity.* New York: Routledge, 2002.
Campbell, Denis, and Haroon Siddique. "Mental Illness Soars among Young Women in England—Survey." *Guardian*, September 29, 2016.
Charles, Claire. *Elite Girls' Schooling, Social Class and Sexualised Popular Culture.* London: Routledge, 2014.
Cochrane, Kira. *All the Rebel Women: The Rise of the Fourth Wave of Feminism.* Guardian: Short Books Kindle Edition, 2013.
Colebrook, Claire. "On Not Becoming Man: The Materialist Politics of Unactualized Potential." In Alaimo and Hekman, *Material Feminisms*, 52–84.
Connell, R. W. *Gender.* Cambridge: Polity Press, 2002.
Davis, Kathy, and Mary Evans. "Introduction—Transatlantic Conversations: Feminism as Travelling Theory." In Davis and Evans, *Transatlantic Conversations*, 1–11.
———, eds. *Transatlantic Conversations: Feminism as Travelling Theory.* Farnham: Ashgate, 2011.
Day, Elizabeth. "Mary Beard: 'I Almost Didn't Feel Such Generic, Violent Misogyny Was about Me." *Guardian*, January 26, 2013.
Diehl, Sarah. "Pro-Ana Websites: Selbstbestimmung in der anorektischen Selbstaufgabe." In Eismann, *Hot Topic*, 100–105.
Dorn, Thea. *Die neue F-Klasse: Wie die Zukunft von Frauen gemacht wird.* Munich: Piper, 2006.
Doyle, Sady. *Trainwreck: The Women We Love to Hate, Mock, and Fear . . . and Why.* Brooklyn, NY: Melville House, 2016.
Driscoll, Catherine. *Girls: Feminine Adolescence in Popular Culture and Cultural Theory.* New York: Columbia University Press, 2002.
Duindam, Vincent. 'The Concept of "Socialization": Criticisms and Alternatives." In de Ras and Lunenberg, *Girls, Girlhood and Girls' Studies in Transition*, 25–37.
Edelman, Lee. *No Future: Queer Theory and the Death Drive.* Durham, NC: Duke University Press, 2004.
Eismann, Sonja, "Einleitung." In Eismann, *Hot Topic*, 9–12.
———, ed. *Hot Topic: Popfeminismus heute.* Mainz: Ventil Verlag, 2007.
Emma, "Transgender: Weder Mann noch Frau." *Emma* (January/February 2016). http://www.emma.de/artikel/transgender-weder-mann-noch-frau-331433.
Er, Yanbing. "In Search of Self: The Dysfunctional Feminism of Charlotte Roche's *Wetlands*." *Women: A Cultural Review* 26, no. 4 (2015): 443–61.
Ferree, Myra Marx. *Varieties of Feminism: German Gender Politics in Global Perspective.* Stanford, CA: Stanford University Press, 2012.
Foster, Dawn. *Lean Out.* London: Repeater Books, 2015.
Gay, Roxane. *Bad Feminist: Essays.* London: Corsair, 2014.

Gebhardt, Miriam. *Alice im Niemandsland: Wie die deutsche Frauenbewegung die Frauen verlor.* Munich: Deutsche Verlags-Anstalt, 2012.

Gerhalter, Li. "Wie Angora: Körperbehaarung ist out—und krause Politik." In Eismann, *Hot Topic,* 90–99.

Gill, Rosalind, and Christina Scharff. Introduction to Gill and Scharff, *New Femininities,* 1–17.

———, eds. *New Femininities: Postfeminism, Neoliberalism, and Subjectivity.* Houndmills, UK: Palgrave Macmillan, 2011.

Glaser, Rachel B. *Paulina and Fran.* London: Granta, 2015.

Gonick, Marnina. *Between Femininities: Ambivalence, Identity, and the Education of Girls.* Albany: State University of New York Press, 2003.

———. "Between 'Girl Power' and 'Reviving Ophelia': Constituting the Neoliberal Girl Subject." *NWSA Journal* 18, no. 2 (Summer 2006): 1–23.

Greer, Germaine. *The Whole Woman.* London: Doubleday, 1999.

Grether, Kerstin. *Zuckerbabys.* Frankfurt am Main: Suhrkamp, 2006.

Grosz, Elizabeth. *Becoming Undone: Darwinist Reflections on Life, Politics, and Art.* Durham, NC: Duke University Press, 2011.

Haaf, Meredith, Susanne Klingner, and Barbara Streidl. *Wir Alpha-Mädchen: Warum Feminismus das Leben schöner macht.* Munich: Blanvalet, 2009.

Hakim, Catherine. *Honey Money: The Power of Erotic Capital.* London: Penguin, 2012.

Halberstam, J. *In a Queer Time and Place: Transgender Bodies, Subcultural Lives.* New York: New York University Press, 2005.

———. *The Queer Art of Failure.* Durham, NC: Duke University Press, 2011.

Harrasser, Karin. "Wunsch, Feministin zu werden: Nahräume politischen Handelns." In Eismann, *Hot Topic,* 234–39.

Harris, Anita. Introduction to *All about the Girl: Culture, Power, and Identity,* edited by Anita Harris, xvii–xxv. New York: Routledge, 2004.

Hegemann, Helene. *Axolotl Roadkill.* Berlin: Ullstein, 2010.

———. *Axolotl Roadkill.* Translated by Katy Derbyshire. London: Corsair, 2012.

———. "Interview mit Helene Hegemann zu ihrem Debüt Axolotl Roadkill." *tip berlin,* December 20, 2011. http://www.tip-berlin.de/kultur-und-freizeit-lesungen-und-buecher/interview-mit-helene-hegemann-zum-debut-axolotl-roadkill.

Hensel, Jana, and Elisabeth Raether. *Neue deutsche Mädchen.* Reinbek: Rowohlt, 2008.

Herman, Eva. *Das Eva-Prinzip: Für eine neue Weiblichkeit.* Munich: Goldmann, 2007.

Herrmann, Elisabeth, Carrie Smith-Prei, and Stuart Taberner, eds. *Transnationalism in Contemporary German-Language Literature.* Rochester, NY: Camden House, 2015.

Hester, Helen. "Rethinking Transgression: Disgust, Affect, and Sexuality in Charlotte Roche's *Wetlands.*" *Journal of Lesbian Studies* 17, nos. 13–14 (2013): 240–52.

Hurley, Andrew Wright. *Into the Groove: Popular Music and Contemporary German Fiction*. Rochester, NY: Camden House, 2015.

Inness, Sherrie A. Introduction to *Millennium Girls: Today's Girls around the World*, ed. Sherrie A. Inness, 1–12. Lanham: Rowman and Littlefield, 1998.

Isherwood, Christopher. *Goodbye to Berlin*. London: Vintage, [1939] 1989.

Jay, Paul. *Global Matters: The Transnational Turn in Literary Studies*. Ithaca, NY: Cornell University Press, 2010.

Jenny, Zoë. *Das Blütenstaubzimmer*. Munich: btb, 1999.

———. *The Pollen Room*. Translated by Elizabeth Gaffney. New York: Simon & Schuster, 1999.

Jeremiah, Emily. "The Case of Helene Hegemann: Queerness, Failure, and the German Girl." *Seminar: A Journal of Germanic Studies* 49, no. 4 (2013): 400–413.

———. *Nomadic Ethics in Contemporary Women's Writing in German: Strange Subjects*. Rochester, NY: Camden House, 2012.

———. "Sibylle Berg, *Die Fahrt*: Literature, Germanness, and Globalization." In *Emerging German-Language Novelists of the Twentieth-First Century*, edited by Lyn Marven and Stuart Taberner, 133–49. Rochester, NY: Camden House, 2011.

Jones, Katie. *Representing Repulsion: The Aesthetics of Disgust in Contemporary Women's Writing in French and German*. Oxford: Peter Lang, 2013.

Kerner, Ina. "Questions of Intersectionality: Reflections on the Current Debate in German Gender Studies." *European Journal of Women's Studies* 19, no. 2 (2012): 203–18.

Kullmann, Katja. *Generation Ally: Warum es heute so kompliziert ist, eine Frau zu sein*. Frankfurt am Main: Eichborn, 2002.

Kuttner, Sarah. *Mängelexemplar*. Frankfurt am Main: Fischer, 2009.

Lazar, Michelle M. "The Right to be Beautiful: Postfeminist Identity and Consumer Beauty Advertising." In Gill and Scharff, *New Femininities*, 37–51.

Levy, Ariel. *Female Chauvinist Pigs: Women and the Rise of Raunch Culture*. New York: Free Press, 2006.

Löwer, Ingrid. *Die 68er im Spiegel ihrer Kinder: Eine vergleichende Untersuchung zu familienkritischen Prosatexten der jüngeren Autorengeneration*. Bremen: edition lumière, 2011.

Mahdawi, Arwa. "*Dietland* Author Sarai Walker: London is the Most Fat-Shaming Place I've Been." *Guardian*, April 27, 2016.

März, Ursula. "Literarischer Kugelblitz." *Zeit Online*, January 21, 2010. http://www.zeit.de/2010/04/L-B-Hegemann.

McCarthy, Margaret. "Feminism and Generational Conflicts in Alex Henning von Lange's *Relax*, Elke Naters's *Lügen*, and Charlotte Roche's *Feuchtgebiete*." In Baer, *Contemporary Women's Writing*, 56–73.

McRobbie, Angela. *The Aftermath of Feminism: Gender, Culture and Social Change* (London: SAGE, 2009).

————. Introduction to *Feminism and Youth Culture: From "Jackie" to "Just Seventeen,"* ix–xx. Houndmills, UK: Macmillan, 1991.

Mendelson, Charlotte. *Love in Idleness.* London: Picador, 2001.

Mika, Bascha. *Die Feigheit der Frauen: Rollenfallen und Geiselmentalität: Eine Streitschrift wider den Selbstbetrug.* Munich: Goldmann, 2012.

The Modern Girl around the World Research Group (Tani E. Barlow, Madeleine Yue Dong, Uta G. Poiger, Priti Ramamurthy, Lynn M. Thomas, and Alys Eve Weinbaum). *The Modern Girl around the World: Consumption, Modernity, and Globalization.* Durham, NC: Duke University Press, 2008.

Monbiot, George. "The Zombie Doctrine." *Guardian Review*, April 16, 2016, 19–20.

Moran, Caitlin. *How to Be a Woman.* London: Ebury Press, 2011.

————. *How to Be a Woman: Wie ich lernte, eine Frau zu sein.* Translated by Susanne Reinker. Berlin: Ullstein, 2013.

————. *How to Build a Girl.* London: Ebury Press, 2014.

Mulvey, Laura. "Visual Pleasure and Narrative Cinema." In *Feminisms: An Anthology of Literary Theory and Criticism*, edited by Robyn R. Warhol and Diane Price Herndl, 438–48. Houndmills, UK: Macmillan, 1997.

Naters, Elke. *Königinnen.* Cologne: Kiepenhauer & Witsch, 1998.

————. *Lügen.* Cologne: Kiepenhauer & Witsch, 1999.

Nelson, Maggie. *The Argonauts.* London: Melville House, 2016.

O'Keeffe, Alice. "Girls Interrupted" (review of Emma Jane Unsworth, *Animals*). *New Statesman* May 30–June 5, 2014, 50.

Orbach, Susie. *Bodies.* London: Profile, 2010.

————. *Bodies: Schlachtfelder der Schönheit.* Translated by Cornelia Holfelder-von der Tann. Hamburg: Arche Verlag, 2012.

Penny, Laurie. *Fleischmarkt: Weibliche Körper im Kapitalismus.* Translated by Susanne von Somm. Hamburg: Edition Nautilus, 2012.

————. *Meat Market: Female Flesh under Capitalism.* Winchester, UK: Zero Books, 2011.

Phipps, Alison. *The Politics of the Body: Gender in a Neoliberal and Neoconservative Age.* Cambridge: Polity Press, 2014.

Pilger, Zoe. *Eat My Heart Out.* London: Serpent's Tail, 2014.

————. Official website. http://www.zoepilger.co.uk/.

————. "*The Second Sex* by Simone de Beauvoir: Book of a Lifetime." *The Independent*, January 24, 2014. http://www.independent.co.uk/arts-entertainment/books/reviews/the-second-sex-by-simone-de-beauvoir-book-of-a-lifetime-9080851.html.

Power, Nina. *Die eindimensionale Frau.* Translated by Anna Sophie Springer. Berlin: Merve, 2011.

————. *One-Dimensional Woman.* Winchester, UK: Zero Books, 2009.

Puar, Jasbir K. "Homonationalism as Assemblage: Viral Travels, Affective Sexualities." *Jindal Global Law Review* 4, no. 2 (2013): 23–43.

———. "Prognosis Time: Towards a Geopolitics of Affect, Debility and Capacity." *Women and Performance: A Journal of Feminist Theory* 19, no. 2 (2009): 161–72.

———. *Terrorist Assemblages: Homonationalism in Queer Times* (Durham, NC: Duke University Press, 2007).

Radisch, Iris. "Die alten Männer und das junge Mädchen." *Zeit Online*, February 10, 2010. http://www.zeit.de/2010/08/Helene-Hegemann-Medien.

———. "Das Kopftuch ist keine Mode." *Die Zeit*, September 16, 2010. http://www.zeit.de/2010/38/L-Schwarzer.

Ras, Marion de, and Mieke Lunenberg, "General Introduction: Alice in Wonderland. Girls, Girlhood and Girls' Studies in Translation." In de Ras and Lunenberg, *Girls, Girlhood and Girls' Studies in Transition*, 1–6.

———, eds. *Girls, Girlhood and Girls' Studies in Transition.* Amsterdam: Het Spinhuis, 1993.

Redfern, Catherine, and Kristin Aune, *Reclaiming the F-Word: Feminism Today.* London: Zed Books, 2013.

Roche, Charlotte. *Feuchtgebiete.* Cologne: Dumont, 2008.

———. *Schoßgebete.* Munich: Piper, 2011.

———. *Wetlands.* Translated by Tim Mohr. London: Fourth Estate, 2009.

———. *Wrecked.* Translated by Tim Mohr. London: Fourth Estate, 2013.

Roth, Julia. "Frauenkörper—Männersache?: Ein feministischer Blick auf Verhütungspraktiken." In Eismann, *Hot Topic*, 41–51.

Sandberg, Sheryl. *Lean In: Women, Work, and the Will to Lead.* New York: Alfred A. Knopf, 2013.

Saussy, Haun. "Exquisite Cadavers Stitched from Fresh Nightmares: Of Memes, Hives, and Selfish Genes." In *Comparative Literature in an Age of Globalization*, edited by Haun Saussy, 3–42. Baltimore: Johns Hopkins University Press, 2006.

Savigny, Heather, and Helen Warner. "Introduction: The Politics of Being a Woman." In *The Politics of Being a Woman: Feminism, Media and 21st Century Popular Culture*, edited by Heather Savigny and Helen Warner, 1–24. Houndmills, UK: Palgrave Macmillan, 2015.

Scharff, Christina. "The New German Feminisms: Of Wetlands and Alpha-Girls." In Gill and Scharff, *New Femininities*, 265–78.

———. "Passages to Feminism: Encounters and Rearticulations." In Davis and Evans, *Transatlantic Conversations*, 115–24.

———. *Repudiating Feminism: Young Women in a Neoliberal World.* Farnham: Ashgate, 2012.

Scharff, Christina, Carrie Smith-Prei, and Maria Stehle, "Digital Feminisms: Transnational Activism in German Protest Cultures." *Digital Feminisms: Transnational Activism in German Protest Cultures*, special issue of *Feminist Media Studies* 16, no. 1 (2016): 1–16.

Schnurr, Eva-Maria. "Typisch Mädchen, typisch Junge." In Stöcker, *Das F-Wort*, 15–22.

Schoene, Berthold. "The Wounded Woman and the Parrot: Post-Feminist Girlhood in Alan Warner's *The Sopranos* and Bella Bathurst's *Special.*" *Journal of Gender Studies* 15, no. 2 (July 2006): 133–44.

Schwarzer, Alice. *Der kleine Unterschied und seine großen Folgen: Frauen über sich—Beginn einer Befreiung.* Frankfurt am Main: Fischer, [1975] 2002.

Seigworth, Gregory J., and Melissa Greg, "An Inventory of Shimmers." In *The Affect Theory Reader*, edited by Melissa Greg and Gregory J. Seigworth, 1–25. Durham, NC: Duke University Press, 2010.

Shakespeare, William. *Hamlet.* London: Penguin, 1980.

Smith-Prei, Carrie. "'Knaller-Sex für alle': Popfeminist Body Politics in Lady Bitch Ray, Charlotte Roche, und Sarah Kuttner." In Baer, *Contemporary Women's Writing*, 18–39.

Smith-Prei, Carrie, and Lars Richter. "Politicising Desire in Juli Zeh's *Spieltrieb.*" In *Transitions: Emerging Women Writers in German-Language Literature*, edited by Valerie Heffernan and Gillian Pye (*German Monitor* 76): 187–207. Amsterdam: Rodopi, 2013.

Smith-Prei, Carrie, and Maria Stehle, "The Awkward Politics of Popfeminist Literary Events: Helene Hegemann, Charlotte Roche, and Lady Bitch Ray." In Baer and Merley Hill, *German Women's Writing*, 152–53.

———. *Awkward Politics: Technologies of Popfeminist Activism.* Montreal: McGill-Queen's University Press, 2016.

Solnit, Rebecca. "Men Explain Things to Me." In *"Men Explain Things to Me" and Other Essays*, 1–16. London: Granta, 2014.

Spiers, Emily. "Killing Ourselves Is Not Subversive": Riot Grrrl from Zine to Screen and the Commodication of Female Transgression." *Women: A Cultural Review* 26, nos. 1–2 (2015): 1–21.

———. "The Long March through the Institutions: From Alice Schwarzer to Pop Feminism and the New German Girls." *Oxford German Studies* 43, no. 1 (March 2014): 69–88.

Stefan, Verena. *Häutungen.* Munich: Frauenoffensive, 1975.

Stöcker, Mirja, ed. *Das F-Wort: Feminismus ist sexy.* Königstein/Taunus: Ulrike Helmer Verlag, 2007.

Stöhr, Elena. "I Felt Like I Had Shattered into a Million Pieces: Grrrl Zines und sexualisierte Gewalt." In Eismann, *Hot Topic*, 67–73.

Strobel, Jochen. "'Untermieter im eigenen Kopf: Helene Hegemanns Roman *Axolotl Roadkill* und 'Borderline Poetics'." *Euphorion* 108, no. 1 (2014): 25–56.

Thyn, Cordelia. "I'm here, I'm queer, und jetzt?: Homophobie ist eine Strategie." In Eismann, *Hot Topic*, 36–40.

Unsworth, Emma Jane. *Animals.* Edinburgh: Canongate, 2014.

Valenti, Jessica. *Full-Frontal Feminism: A Young Woman's Guide to Why Feminism Matters.* Berkeley: Seal Press, 2013.

Walker, Sarai. *Dietland.* London: Atlantic Books, 2015.

———. "Yes, I'm Fat. It's OK. I Said It." *New York Times*, February 6, 2016.

Walkerdine, Valerie. *Daddy's Girl: Young Girls and Popular Culture*. Hound-mills, UK: Macmillan, 1997.

———. "Girlhood through the Looking Glass." In de Ras and Lunenberg, *Girls, Girlhood and Girls' Studies in Transition*, 9–24.

Walsh, Helen. *Brass*. Edinburgh: Canongate, 2005.

———. Official website. http://www.helen-walsh.co.uk/.

Walter, Natasha. *Living Dolls: The Return of Sexism*. London: Virago, 2010.

———. *Living Dolls: Warum junge Frauen heute lieber schön als schlau sein wollen*. Translated by Gabriele Herbst. Frankfurt am Main: Krüger, 2011.

Warnecke, Jenny. "Das ist nur zu extrem!: Eine Generationen-Studie." In Stöcker, *Das F-Wort*, 23–40.

Watson, Elwood, Jennifer Mitchell, and Marc Edward Shaw, eds. *HBO's "Girls" and the Awkward Politics of Gender, Race, and Privilege*. Lanham, MD: Lexington Books, 2015.

West, Lindy. "Fat and Free." *Guardian G2*, May 9, 2016, 6–8.

Wilson, Elizabeth A. *Gut Feminism*. Durham, NC: Duke University Press, 2015.

Winch, Alison. *Girlfriends and Postfeminist Sisterhood*. Houndmills, UK: Palgrave Macmillan, 2013.

Wolf, Naomi. *The Beauty Myth: How Images of Beauty are Used Against Women*. London: Vintage, 1991.

Zambreno, Kate. *Green Girl*. New York: Harper Collins, 2014.

———. *Heroines*. Los Angeles: Semiotext(e), 2012.

Zeh, Juli. *Spieltrieb*. Frankfurt am Main: Schöfling & Co, 2004.

Index

Aapola, Sinikka, 6, 8
abortion, 27–28, 41, 47, 182n17
abuse, 20, 44, 84, 85, 132, 144. *See
also* sexism; violence; women in
public life, abuse of
academia, 41, 57, 106, 108–9, 130,
134, 149
activism, 20, 140, 148–49. *See also*
Everyday Sexism; feminism; Let
Girls Be Girls; Let Toys Be Toys;
Pinkstinks; SlutWalk
adolescence, 9, 38, 39, 42, 51, 59, 97
adulthood, 97, 98, 104, 120. *See also*
maturity
advertising, 21, 85, 123, 143
affect, 1, 2, 15, 16, 34, 67, 68, 92,
114, 115, 140, 141, 142, 146,
147, 148
Afro-German feminism, 24
age, 2, 8, 9, 23, 42, 52, 71, 107
agency, 2, 3, 9, 16, 29–31, 34–64, 67,
73, 74, 76, 79, 81, 83, 100, 104,
105, 116, 120, 130, 141. *See also*
willfulness
aggression, 36, 37, 104
Aguilera, Christina, 75
Ahmed, Sara, 1, 7, 12–14, 15, 16,
17, 25, 33, 36, 37, 39, 41, 43, 45,
46, 47, 50, 51, 52, 56, 57, 60, 65,
72, 73, 83, 84, 87, 88, 89, 91, 92,
93, 105, 116, 117, 118, 125, 128,
139, 140, 147, 148, 149
alcohol, 55, 56–57, 60, 63, 81, 98
Allen, Lily, 21
Ally McBeal, 22
ambivalence, 9, 10, 33, 36, 54, 94,
101, 107, 113, 126, 128, 138,
143, 144, 146
Americanization, 4, 21

Anderson, Pamela, 81
anger, 1, 15, 34, 36
animality, 39, 73, 89, 116
anorexia. *See* eating disorders
appearance, 22–24, 29, 65–90, 91, 94,
98, 110, 116, 119, 129, 142–44
art, 1–2, 140, 148
assemblage, subject as, 12, 35, 118,
147
Augustine, 12, 56
autobiography, 58, 146, 147
awkward politics, 7
awkwardness, 39, 47, 49, 59, 97, 103,
118, 127, 128, 129, 138. *See also*
awkward politics

backlash, 23
"bad feminism," 36
Baer, Hester, 7, 15, 24, 52–53, 66,
138, 148
"banter," 28
Banyard, Kat, 22, 27, 28, 29, 31, 32
Bartel, Heike, 68, 70
Bates, Laura, 22, 23, 28
Bathurst, Bella, 14, 94, 97–101, 103,
114, 118, 129–31, 138, 139, 142,
144
Baum, Antonia, 14, 37, 38–41, 41,
47, 48, 53, 57, 63, 64, 69, 80, 82,
110, 141, 142
Beard, Mary, 23
beauty, 10, 22–24, 65–90, 107, 116,
142–44, 145. *See also* appearance;
beauty myth, the; female body, the
beauty myth, the, 75, 79, 81, 85, 89,
143. *See also* Wolf, Naomi
Beauvoir, Simone de, 1, 10–11, 12,
16, 39, 78, 91, 106, 107, 131–32,
147

becoming, 1, 2, 9, 12, 34–35, 39, 42, 49, 52, 63, 73, 79, 84, 89, 92, 97, 118, 140, 147, 148. *See also* becoming woman
becoming woman, 1, 58, 85, 142
Benjamin, Jessica, 9, 109
Benn, Melissa, 22, 25, 26, 29, 32
Berg, Sibylle, 14, 67, 68, 80–83, 89, 95, 141, 142, 145
Berger, John, 143
Bergson, Henri, 35, 92
Berlant, Lauren, 5, 15, 38, 44, 141
Bersani, Leo, 37
Beyoncé, 108
Bildung, 11, 50, 58, 61, 100, 131, 139
bile, 36, 37, 41, 61, 71, 140, 150
binarism, 30, 109, 118
biologism, 30
body. *See* female body, the
body hair, 24, 66, 68, 123–24
body image, 20, 22–24, 72
body politic, the, 89
"body project," the, 66, 74, 80, 84, 89, 126
Bond, James, 120
Braidotti, Rosi, 2, 12, 16, 34, 35, 55, 66–67, 93, 105, 117, 148
bravado, 60, 70, 77, 78, 89, 98, 130
Brockmann, Stephen, 41, 44
Brumberg, Jane Jacobs. *See* "body project," the
Buhr, Elke, 66
burlesque, 109, 133
Butler, Judith, 4, 9, 12, 21, 36, 67, 75, 85, 93, 141

capitalism, 4, 6, 29, 32, 94, 127
care, 57, 95, 97, 101
catharsis, 68
celebrity, 74, 77, 81, 85, 103, 140, 142; author as, 15
Charles, Claire, 66
childcare, 25, 28
choice, 9–10, 11, 26, 27, 30, 31, 33, 54, 55, 66, 67, 100, 116
cigarettes, 60, 98
cinema, 83

circularity, 7, 16, 148
Cixous, Hélène, 106
class, 24, 57, 58, 61, 91, 92
clothing, 78, 94, 98
Cobain, Kurt, 82
Cochrane, Kira, 20, 23, 24, 27, 149
commercialism, 140
commodification, 6, 17, 26, 78, 94, 103, 109, 120
comparatism, 4–5, 16
comparative literature, 5
conception, 54
conflict, 91, 92, 98, 104, 114
confusion, 69, 118, 120, 129, 131, 145
consent, 132
constructedness, 100
constructivism, 2, 3, 11, 30, 59
consumerism, 6, 29, 52, 78, 94, 100, 103, 140, 141, 142, 144
contemporary, the, 5
context, 5, 9, 16, 18
contraception, 28, 54, 132–33
control, 74–75
cosmetic surgery, 27, 66, 107
cosmetics industry, 24, 65, 75, 85
Criado-Perez, Caroline, 20
critical youth studies, 2
cruel optimism, 15, 38, 39, 44, 81, 94–95, 141
Cusk, Rachel, 32

Darwin, Charles, 73, 92, 118
Davis, Kathy, 4
death, 37, 39, 47, 83, 89, 97, 100, 104, 142
Deleuze, Gilles, 12, 34, 35, 36, 92, 148
dependence, 103, 108
depression, 74, 84
desire, 26, 50, 56, 82, 91, 94, 96, 99, 101, 104, 105, 108, 110, 113, 114, 116–39, 145
Dickinson, Emily, 146
diet, 74, 88
diet industry, the, 77, 78, 80, 83, 84, 86

difference, 11, 24, 25, 26, 34–35, 92, 102, 103, 105, 133
digital, the, 40, 90
digital feminisms, 7, 148
disciplinarity, 5
discrimination, 29
disgust, 10, 15, 32, 70, 84, 85, 89, 98, 101, 110, 118, 122, 125, 129, 138, 140, 143, 145
disorientation, 97
divorce, 44, 72, 110
Dorn, Thea, 19, 20, 24–25, 32, 65
Doyle, Sady, 150
drag, 85
Driscoll, Catherine, 2, 3
drugs, 49, 50, 55, 56, 98. *See also* alcohol; cigarettes
Duindam, Vincent, 9
Dunham, Lena, 8, 145
dystopia, 83

eating disorders, 20, 22, 32, 65, 72, 74, 75–76, 78, 79, 80, 81, 99, 101, 102, 130
Edelman, Lee, 36, 37, 49
education, 22, 29, 38–39, 41, 43, 50, 57, 61, 81, 149
Eismann, Sonja, 21, 32
Eliot, George, 14
elitism, 20, 149
Emma, 32, 162n94
employability, 38, 81
Er, Yanbing, 70, 71
essentialism, 30, 90
ethics, 34, 41, 42, 44, 54, 55, 61, 63, 117, 118, 125, 127
ethnicity, 92
Evans, Mary, 4
Everyday Sexism, 20, 32, 116, 148

failure, 9, 13, 15, 32, 33, 34, 36, 37, 42, 49, 50, 52, 63, 65, 69, 70, 71, 72, 82, 97, 122, 135, 139, 140, 142, 143, 150
family, 38, 57, 58, 63, 68, 103, 104, 127, 135
fantasy, 136, 137, 139, 145

fashion, 78, 94, 141, 142. *See also* glamor
fat, 22, 23, 58, 61, 67, 80, 81, 83–84, 85, 89, 119, 121; activism, 84; studies, 84
female body, the, 6, 16, 22–24, 26, 33, 53, 64, 65–90, 109, 116, 121, 122–25, 126, 130, 139, 142–44, 146
female chauvinism, 124. *See also* Levy, Ariel
femininity, 1, 2, 3, 4, 6, 9–11, 15, 94, 101, 107, 134, 146; as brand or resource, 6, 22; as caring and/ or maternal, 6, 97, 101, 127; as decorative, demure, docile, frivolous, immature, obliging and/ or stupid, 6, 8, 11, 14, 43, 45, 64, 66, 68, 72, 73, 74, 79, 84, 102, 142; as deficiency, 29, 67; as passive, 3, 8, 11, 30, 31, 39, 47, 106, 145; as spectacle, 90, 109, 150
feminism, 2, 7, 14, 15, 16, 17–33, 53, 96, 99, 100, 101, 105, 109, 114, 132, 133; "1970s," 19, 26, 65, 69, 91, 149; as "beyond the waves," 20; definitions of, 18, 32; fourth-wave, 20; in Germany, 7, 17–33; lesbian, 115, 117; as local, 4; materialist, 12, 67; and neoliberalism, 6–7, 17, 20, 91, 108; second-wave, 8, 46, 69, 106, 107, 108, 110, 122; as transnational, 4; in the UK, 7, 17–33; in the US, 17–33. *See also* activism; digital feminisms; feminist life, living a; feminist theory; "gut feminism"; transfeminisms
feminist life, living a, 7
feminist theory, 2, 3, 12, 16, 37, 106, 108–9, 130, 142
Ferree, Myra Marx, 4
FGM, 24, 25
Firestone, Shulamith, 109
flesh, 22, 23, 78, 80, 110
flexible working, 29
Foster, Dawn, 6, 20, 37, 52, 149

Foucault, Michel, 67, 171n11
Fraser, Janet, 66
Frauenbewegung, die, 8
Frauenquote, 29
friendship, 24, 62, 94, 95, 96–97, 101, 103, 105, 109, 121
futurity, 38, 41, 47, 54, 81, 127

Gay, Roxane, 24, 36
Gebhard, Miriam, 20
gender, 1, 7, 11–12, 29, 30, 42, 61, 62, 64, 71, 92, 93, 107, 124, 128, 129, 133
gender studies, 4, 12
generation, 2, 8, 19, 26, 42, 45, 51, 52, 105, 108, 114
German fiction, 15
German Idol, 22
Germany, 4, 7, 8
Germany's Next Top Model, 22
Gill, Rosalind, 6, 14, 15, 17
Gilmore Girls, 22
girlhood, 3, 6, 140. *See also* femininity
girls' studies, 2, 4
glamor, 98, 99, 121, 142. *See also* fashion
Glaser, Rachel B., 14, 94, 103, 110–14, 139, 144
global capitalism, 4
globalization, 4
Gonick, Marnina, 3, 6, 8, 9
green girl, the, 16, 139, 140–47, 150
Greer, Germaine, 10, 26, 122
Grether, Kerstin, 14, 60, 67, 68, 74–80, 81, 85, 89, 91, 94, 101–2, 103, 114, 117, 119, 141, 142, 144
Grimm, Jacob, and Wilhelm Grimm, 12, 89
Grosz, Elizabeth, 1, 12, 16, 34, 35, 39, 47, 67, 73, 92, 118, 147, 148
grotesque, 68, 103, 105, 109, 110, 114, 131, 132, 139
"gut feminism," 36, 53, 102, 143. *See also* Wilson, Elizabeth A.

Halberstam, J., 34, 36, 37, 38–39, 49, 55
"happiness myth," the, 33, 37

harassment, 116. *See also* online harassment
Harris, Anita, 6, 8
hedonism, 58
Hegemann, Helene, 14, 37, 39, 48–53, 57, 63, 64, 69, 81, 82, 110, 115, 118, 125, 127, 134–38, 139, 141, 142
Hensel, Jana, 8, 19, 32
Herman, Eva, 28
Hester, Helen, 70, 125
heteronormativity, 25, 38, 44, 127, 128, 134, 139
heterosexism, 117, 118, 134
heterosexuality, 19, 25, 39, 40, 69, 78, 100, 103, 104, 111, 118, 120, 121, 123–24, 128, 131, 132, 139, 145
Heti, Sheila, 32
Hollywood, 21, 85, 144
homophobia, 129
hostility, 37, 110, 116, 144
housework, 25, 28
humanities, the, 148
humanity, 10, 11, 16, 31, 78, 147, 148
humor, 68, 69, 77, 119, 121, 123, 133, 138, 149
Hurley, Andrew Wright, 74, 79, 102
hygiene, 68, 69, 122
hyperbole, 68, 119

ideals, 22, 23, 24, 27, 29, 39, 41, 44, 63, 73, 78, 79, 83, 84, 85, 89, 90, 118, 150
identification, 9, 16, 24–26, 59, 60, 91–115, 93, 105, 116, 142, 144–45
identity, 9, 12, 15, 38, 92, 114, 117–18, 141, 146, 147; politics, 35, 92; and recognition, 9
illness, 24, 33, 56, 89, 131
imagery, 47, 64, 77, 101
images, 74, 76, 85, 90, 93, 103, 104–5, 126, 130, 142. *See also* imagery
"imposter syndrome," 29
individualism, 6, 7, 30, 34, 45, 59, 65, 66, 93, 104, 144

individuality, 34, 35, 45, 74, 92, 97, 100, 101, 136
inexperience, 120, 138
insanity. *See* madness
intentionality, 13, 14, 35, 60, 70
internalization, 9, 22, 29, 52, 55, 63, 73, 75, 93, 119, 129
internationalism, 91
Internet, the, 4, 20, 27, 40, 41, 57, 65, 106, 120, 148
interpellation, 16, 59, 65, 66, 72, 75, 100, 126, 141. *See also* internalization
intersectionality, 6, 7, 12, 16, 24, 25, 26, 35, 91, 92, 93, 147, 149
intertextuality, 49
intimacy, 94, 107, 110, 111, 113, 115, 127, 144, 146
Irigaray, Luce, 35, 130
irony, 94, 110, 128, 145, 146
Islam, 25, 32

Jeffreys, Sheila, 22
Jenny, Zoë, 14, 37, 45–48, 49, 63, 64, 81, 82, 97, 142, 145
Jewish-German feminism, 24
Jones, Katie, 15, 70, 123, 124
joy, 33, 119, 121

killjoy, the, 41, 149
kinship, 103
Kullmann, Katja, 22

"lads' mags," 20
Ladyfeste, 21
Larkin, Philip, 63
Lazar, Michelle M., 66
lesbian desire and relations, 25, 85, 96, 104, 113, 115, 128, 129, 130, 145. *See also* feminism, lesbian; queer
Let Girls Be Girls, 26
Let Toys Be Toys, 30
Levy, Ariel, 27, 117
likeability, 45
literariness, 15–16, 63, 145–47. *See also* literary texts; literature; willfulness, and literature

literary studies, 148
literary texts, 34
literature, 140, 146
Lohan, Lindsay, 21
"lookism," 78
love, 104, 107, 108, 110, 113, 121, 131
Löwer, Ingrid, 45, 46, 47, 48

Mädchen, 6–7, 39, 79
madness, 100, 105, 139, 149. *See also* PTSD; suicide; trauma
makeovers, 6, 74, 83, 84, 87, 140
makeup, 23, 65, 66, 67, 75, 85, 87, 142
male gaze, the, 63, 78, 88, 121, 123, 127, 128, 143
marriage, 39, 55, 103–4
masculinity, 11, 120. *See also* men
masochism, 100. *See also* S/M
masturbation, 70, 119, 123, 145
materialism, 39, 52, 63
maturity, 38–39, 55, 59, 71, 79, 82, 101
McCarthy, Margaret, 69, 96, 97, 115
McRobbie, Angela, 17, 149
media, the, 4, 12, 19, 24, 30, 40, 72, 77, 80, 87
men, 25, 100. *See also* masculinity
menstruation, 121
mental illness. *See* madness
Merkel, Angela, 29
migrant women's feminism, 24
Mika, Bascha, 3, 17, 23, 25, 27, 28, 30
Millett, Kate, 26
mimicry, 51
Modern Girl around the World Research Group, the, 8
Monbiot, George, 6
money, 17, 29
Moran, Caitlin, 14, 19, 21, 25, 26, 28, 29, 31, 32, 33, 37, 39, 48, 58–63, 64, 89, 91, 118–21, 138, 144, 149
Moss, Kate, 81
mother-baby bond, 120
mother-daughter relations, 91, 173n45, 96, 101, 115, 110, 128, 134, 137, 144. *See also* mothers

motherhood, 28, 41, 53–54, 55, 69
mothers, 45, 49, 68, 71, 78, 97, 122, 123, 144
Mulvey, Laura, 143. *See also* male gaze, the
music business, the, 77

Naters, Elke, 14, 93–94, 94–97, 103, 114, 115, 144
National Socialism, 40
negativity, 10, 11, 32–33, 34, 36, 37, 39, 52, 61, 97, 143, 145
neoconservatism, 6
neoliberalism, 1, 5–7, 15, 30, 34, 35, 36, 37, 38, 39, 40, 54, 59, 61, 63, 65, 66, 67, 72, 74, 77, 83, 94, 97, 101, 109, 114, 115, 117, 139, 140, 141, 144, 147; and postfeminism, 6, 109, 144, 147; and willfulness, 13–14. *See also* feminism, and neoliberalism
neuroreductionism, 30
"new determinism," the, 30
new-feminist texts, 18, 26, 29, 31, 32, 65, 91, 158n16
Nietzsche, Friedrich, 41
nomadism, 12, 34, 55, 117, 148
nonhuman, the, 35, 47
normativity, 73, 88, 101, 107, 109, 116, 130. *See also* norms
norms, 9, 22, 24, 27, 29, 52, 53, 55, 60, 61, 66, 85, 87, 88, 89, 90, 93, 98, 101, 118, 122, 124, 141, 149, 150

objectification, 2, 22, 29, 31, 65, 117, 126, 131, 132
One Billion Rising, 148
online harassment, 29
Orbach, Susie, 22
otherness, 2, 11, 73, 84, 88, 98

parenting, 54, 55
parody, 38, 70
Penny, Laurie, 6, 19, 21, 22, 23, 26, 31, 32, 65, 66, 68, 78, 86, 94, 122, 124

performativity, 36, 67, 85, 89, 100, 141
"personal," the, 32
phallocentrism, 134
phenomenology, 13, 36
Phipps, Alison, 6, 17, 37, 65
Pilger, Zoe, 14, 94, 103, 105–10, 114, 118, 131–34, 138, 139, 144
Pinkstinks, 30, 148
Playboy bunny, the, 26
pleasure, 26, 58, 63, 113, 119, 120, 123, 124, 138
"Popfeminismus," 20–21, 74
Popliteratur, 21, 74, 94–95
popular culture, 21–22, 29, 30, 60, 77, 98, 103
pornification and pornographization, 16, 28, 68, 86, 116, 117, 118, 125, 129, 133, 139, 145. *See also* pornography
pornography, 4, 23, 26, 27, 65, 70, 76, 87, 105, 106, 120, 121, 125–26, 128, 130, 131
postfeminism, 1, 6–7, 15, 16, 17, 19, 39, 52, 74, 83, 91, 97, 100, 105, 106, 108, 109, 110, 115, 132, 133, 139, 140; and willfulness, 14. *See also* neoliberalism, and postfeminism
postmodernism, 41, 80, 81, 95
power, 3, 9, 17, 22, 29, 44, 92, 93, 97, 98, 103, 107, 111, 120, 124, 134
Power, Nina, 18, 21, 22, 23, 32, 68, 78, 86, 122, 124
precarity, 7, 38, 40, 57, 66, 121, 141
pregnancy, 54
present time, the, 5
privacy, 23
promiscuity, 126
prostitution. *See* sex work
psychosis, 49–50
PTSD, 27
Puar, Jasbir K., 12, 15, 35, 92, 93, 115, 117–18, 128, 139
pubic hair, 23, 27

queer, 37, 38, 47, 49, 50, 52, 54, 69, 88, 94, 104, 111, 115, 117–18, 125, 131, 134–35, 139, 144. *See also* queer desire; queer theory
queer desire, 25, 53, 88, 94, 114, 115, 117, 126, 128, 129, 139
queer theory, 37, 42, 128

Rabenmutter, 28
race, 85, 91, 92. *See also* racism; white privilege
racism, 24
Radisch, Iris, 49, 136
Raether, Elisabeth, 8, 19, 32
rape, 26, 27, 83, 100, 130; culture, 27
"raunch culture," 27, 117, 118
refusal, 36, 37, 42, 49, 51, 52, 63, 66, 69, 71, 72, 94, 122, 135, 140, 142, 150
relationality, 57, 93, 97, 110, 111, 114, 135
representation, 91, 101, 143
repression, 113, 117, 131, 139
reproductive futurism, 37, 38, 44, 54, 69, 127, 135
resistance, 13, 77, 115
Richter, Lars, 44, 73
Riot Grrrls, 21, 60
Roche, Charlotte, 14, 19–20, 21, 67, 68–71, 82, 89, 110, 118, 119, 121–25, 138, 144
role models, 46, 60, 62, 63, 76, 77, 91, 97, 101, 107, 120, 144
romance, 40, 44, 62, 69, 82, 113, 131, 145

sadism, 82, 138. *See also* S/M
Sandberg, Sheryl, 6, 20
satire, 41, 44, 52, 55, 63, 83, 84, 86, 94, 97, 105, 106, 109, 110, 111, 114, 122, 146
Saussy, Haun, 5
Scharff, Christina, 4, 6, 7, 14, 15, 17, 18, 19, 20
Schoene, Berthold, 97, 97–98, 100
Schwarzer, Alice, 19, 20, 21, 24, 26, 32, 121–25

segmentation, of female bodies, 16, 23, 80, 86, 124
self-harm, 61, 82, 85
sex, 116–39, 144–45. *See also* sexual activity; sexual desire; sexual relationships; sexuality
sex/gender distinction, 11–12
sex industry, the, 65, 120, 121, 124, 126, 127, 128
sex work, 27, 32, 124, 125, 126, 127
sexism, 7, 17, 24, 26, 27, 29, 65
sexual activity, 82, 96, 113, 135, 137, 145
sexual desire, 16, 26–28, 33, 44, 58, 63, 70, 94, 96, 111, 113
sexual difference, 6, 30
sexual relationships, 103
sexuality, 91, 92, 107, 110, 118, 145. *See also* desire; heterosexuality; queer; romance; sexual activity; sexual desire; sexual relationships
sexualization, 10, 65, 66, 109, 116, 117. *See also* pornification and pornographization
Shakespeare, William, 141
shame, 22, 23, 65, 84, 99, 113, 118, 120, 122, 124, 129, 147
shit, 110, 121, 139, 182n15
sincerity, 114, 145
sisterhood, 16, 24–26, 90–115, 116, 144–45
slut-shaming, 120
SlutWalk, 27, 148
S/M, 120, 133
Smith-Prei, Carrie, 4, 5, 7, 9, 20, 21, 28, 33, 39, 42, 44, 49, 51, 52, 68, 69, 70, 73, 92, 149
socialization, 9, 30, 37, 43
Solnit, Rebecca, 22
Spiers, Emily, 8, 19, 20, 21, 25, 30, 65–66
Stehle, Maria, 4, 5, 7, 9, 20, 28, 33, 39, 42, 49, 51, 52, 69, 70, 92, 149
stereotypes, 91
Stöcker, Mirja, 25
Streep, Meryl, 29
suicide, 41, 82, 83, 107

television, 22, 24, 41
tension, 91, 94, 95, 98, 100, 101,
    111, 114, 131
trainwreck, the, 16, 139, 140, 141,
    149, 150
trans activisms and debates, 12, 25,
    159n24. *See also* transfeminisms
transfeminisms, 92
transgression, 94, 115, 128, 138, 139.
    See also refusal; resistance
translation, 4
transnational turn, the, 5
transnationalism, 4–5
trauma, 27, 45, 48, 49, 63, 68, 69,
    82, 83, 85, 98

Ugly Betty, 22
Unsworth, Emma Jane, 14, 37,
    53–57, 58, 63, 64, 66, 94, 103–5,
    114, 144

Vagenda, The, 23
Valenti, Jessica, 18, 22, 23, 24, 25, 26,
    28, 31, 32, 33, 65, 148, 149
veil, the, 25, 32
victim-blaming, 27
violence, 17, 27
virality, 4, 16, 148
visual, the, 4
vitalism, 39, 48, 51, 58, 59, 63, 141
volition, 13, 16, 29–31, 34–64, 116,
    141
voluntarism, 12, 36, 54, 59, 63

Walker, Sarai, 14, 67, 68, 83–89, 119
Walkerdine, Valerie, 2, 8, 116
Walsh, Helen, 14, 115, 118, 124,
    125–29, 138, 139
Walter, Natasha, 10, 21, 23, 25, 26,
    27, 30, 31, 68, 91, 116–17, 122,
    125
weight, 16, 22–24, 68, 75, 80, 81, 83,
    85, 101, 119, 142
weight-loss industry, the. *See* diet
    industry, the

well-being, lack of, 24, 56
West, Lindy, 147
white privilege, 124, 146
wholeness, 10, 31, 36, 136, 145, 148
will, 3, 13, 15, 16, 35, 41, 42, 45,
    46, 48, 50, 53, 54, 55, 56, 57, 59,
    60, 63, 65, 73, 74, 80, 81, 82, 84,
    88, 89, 103, 104, 111, 116, 125,
    141
willfulness, 9, 12–14, 34, 35, 36, 41,
    43, 45, 46, 48, 50–51, 53, 56, 58,
    61, 63, 68, 69, 70, 72, 74, 87, 88,
    89, 93, 94, 103, 105, 116, 117,
    118, 123, 124, 128, 134, 138,
    139, 140, 143, 148, 149, 150; as
    gendered, 14, 149; and literature,
    14, 15–16, 42, 63. *See also*
    postfeminism, and willfulness
willing submission, 13, 60, 77, 87
willpower, 13, 53, 56, 74, 103
Wilson, Elizabeth A., 34, 36, 37
Winch, Alison, 91, 94, 101, 114
Winehouse, Amy, 21
Wir Alpha-Mädchen, 8, 19, 21, 24,
    25, 26, 27, 29, 30, 31, 32, 33, 65,
    66
Wolf, Naomi, 23, 65, 75
womanhood, 9, 98, 143
women in public life, abuse of, 23,
    28–29
women's studies, 4, 87
women's voices, silencing of, 23, 29
women's writing, 15
work, 28, 29, 38, 39, 40

young people, 3–4, 41–42
young women, 2, 3–4, 6, 18, 24, 25,
    27, 28, 149. *See also* femininity;
    girlhood

Zambreno, Kate, 14, 16, 85, 139,
    140–47, 149
Zeh, Juli, 14, 15, 37, 39, 41–45, 47,
    48, 51, 57, 63, 64, 67, 68, 71–73,
    78, 81, 89, 141